AF330053

PERFORMANCE CONTROL

PERFORMANCE CONTROL

Service and Resource Control
in Complex IBM Computing Centres

Tore A. HØIE

Advisory Systems Specialist
Lyngby
Denmark

1982

NORTH-HOLLAND PUBLISHING COMPANY – AMSTERDAM • NEW YORK • OXFORD

© NORTH-HOLLAND PUBLISHING COMPANY, 1982

All rights reserved. No part of this publication may be reproduced, stored in a retrieval system, or transmitted, in any form or by any means, electronic, mechanical, photocopying, recording or otherwise, without the prior permission of the copyright owner.

ISBN: 0 444 86517 9

Published by:
NORTH-HOLLAND PUBLISHING COMPANY – AMSTERDAM • NEW YORK • OXFORD

Sole distributors for the U.S.A. and Canada:
ELSEVIER SCIENCE PUBLISHING COMPANY, INC.
52 Vanderbilt Avenue
New York, N.Y. 10017

Library of Congress Cataloging in Publication Data

Høie, Tore A., 1942–
    Performance control.

    Bibliography: p.
    Includes index.
    1. Data processing service centers—Management.
I. Title.
HD9696.C62H64   1982   658'.054   82–18805
ISBN 0-444-86517-9 (U.S.)

PRINTED IN THE NETHERLANDS

Disclaimer

The information contained in this document has not been submitted to
any formal test and is presented on an 'AS IS' basis without any war-
ranty either expressed or implied. The programs described work or are
intended to work in an internal IBM environment.

Some programs mentioned herein are not generally available to customers. Other programs may have been changed since this document was
written. Generally this is a presentation of Method, exemplified by a
specific implementation.

Most examples have been derived from work performed at the Information
Systems Centre (ISC), Denmark, with kind permission of IBM Denmark.
The examples have been revised to support the text and can not be used
to reconstruct ISC's internal operations. The **method** outlined in this
book is however close to the method employed for performance control
at ISC, Denmark in 1981.

TABLE OF CONTENTS

CHAPTER 1

INTRODUCTION

'Would you tell me please which way I ought to go from here?'

'That depends a good deal on where you want to get to', said the cat.

'I don't much care where -', said Alice.

'Then it doesn't matter which way you go', said the cat.

Lewis Carroll

1.1 INTRODUCTION

1.1.1 Discussion of contents

A performance control system should ensure that the computing centre delivers the agreed service and will continue to do so with reasonable resource usage.

The purpose and basis of such a control system was sketched in 'Central Systems Architecture' (reference 1).

This book describes the implementation of these ideas in a very complex environment, attempting to use existing (IBM) software products when possible and creating new programs when desirable.

Performance control in this book is mostly concerned with MVS based systems, especially when running major online applications like IMS and VSPC. These applications normally have very high priority, but any component in a complex centre's service pattern needs follow-up and may constitute a problem. In most cases 'a problem' means that a group of people have their productivity impaired, and become unsatisfied.

VM examples are provided when VM performance control systems contain ideas that are relevant to a general environment, and can serve as additions to the MVS concepts presented.

The outlined methods and products enable a small group of people (for example one project leader and a backup) to implement supervision and capacity planning of medium, large or complex centres with little investment in hardware or software. The supervision is more detailed than most centres have established today (1981).

Only IBM products are described. Other products may be used as well. Experience indicates that most of the work necessary in constructing a control system goes into definitions: Selecting who should have what information when, and what should be the action resulting from that information.

Most control products described here have broad organisatorial impact and a wide span of technical facilities. Describing each one in detail would be confusing to most people, needs an enormous amount of paper and is well done in the respective user guides.

The philosophy of 'Central Systems Architecture' is that you select what you need to fulfill your requirements. This means that it is not necessary to implement or even test out all facilities in a product; only what is needed is selected.

Therefore, only components directly relevant to the overall performance control system are discussed in this book. Thus a path is provided in the present jungle of detail. The path is not optimal, and it misses some beautiful scenery. But it gets you to your goal - provided you have one and it is not vastly different from the objectives sketched here.

We face a situation parallel to what R.M. Pirsig describes in 'Zen and the Art of Motorcycle Maintenance': 'There are an infinite number of facts about a motorcycle, and the right ones just do'nt dance up and introduce themselves'.   The world of modern computing is no less complex, and a quest for values no less complicated.

Some products described in this document are not generally available. It is the method that is regarded as important, not the products. The outlined methods and program designs may prove helpful in building your own system.

The main principle followed in the control system is 'management by exception'. When everything works according to set norms, only standard reports are distributed to underline this fact. No action is initiated until some service level is not reached.

The control thus established has little to do with 'tuning'. A better term than 'tuning' is **adjustment**. Adjustments should only be initiated when the control system informs that service is not acceptable or some critical resource is utilized more than expected.   This leaves another critical resource - the systems programmers - unworried and free to do other work as long as the system functions as planned.

Cost is not covered. Still, in order to set a feasible price for a service, that service must be defined and measured. In doing so, the basis for cost control is established.

A relevant question relates to the implementation level described in this document. Why is a perfectly functioning centre not chosen, with all concepts neatly in place?

Experience shows that the described performance control components can be introduced, tested and rendered operative in a one to two year time frame, without major expenditures or operational inconveniences.

This book therefore describes what to do in an environment that corresponds to many centres of today. Most centres have some of the performance control components in place, but few seem to have total control of their services and resources. This book states the requirements for such control, even though all components are not shown fully implemented.

Another reason for publishing this book now was given to the author at the 1981 ECOMA (European COmputer Measurement Association) conference: 'We cannot afford to wait' (for developments in this area). In particular there are surprisingly few textbooks for EDP **production**. One basic axiom of this book is that, as EDP centre service is the responsibility of 'operations', i.e. the production groups, service should also be controlled by these. The book provides guidance as to how performance control is prepared for production, and contains some theory that can help operators/supervisors understand basic control requirements and parameters.

1.1.2 Example environment

Most examples refer to an imaginary computing centre, called the Complex Computing Centre, CCC. The centre runs the following major services:

> IMS for order inventory and control, accounting, budget etc.
> TSO for program development and test
> Batch for administration, test and external customers
> VSPC for internal and external use
> CMS for technical applications, test, text editing etc
> Other subsystems under VM/370 for test and demonstrations
> Network software to control domestic and foreign
>   access and to serve as one interface to all services.

A further description of CCC services is given in Chapter 10 together with an outline of the hardware configuration. Most examples in the book refer to environments that resembles the CCC configuration and load, believed to represent most aspects of performance control requirements.

The users belong to different departments with different budgets. Some are external customers with unknown budgets. Performance control, forecasting and capacity planning therefore center on user group requirements and must be integrated by controllers - or central systems architects.

Chapter 10 contains a report of the above mentioned Complex Computing Centre's service during one year, going from unacceptable or disastrous in the beginning of the year, to a commonly agreed 'good' at year end. This is a fictional report, but corresponds well with experience.

1.1.3 Robustness

Because developments are rapid within all fields of computing, a relevant question is: 'When hardware and software change, will this book still be useful?'

During the time when this book was written, an MVS version featuring 2000 megabytes virtual storage was announced. A much more flexible disk subsystem than the one presented here is possible with the same version. This changes the emphasis in the book: virtual storage surveillance and disk follow-up become less important - at least for a while.

Resulting from the new announcements will be new applications and higher expectations. Soon even the new supercomputers are filled with work and supporting a cloud of terminals. More complex and more vulnerable environments are created; control will be more important than ever.

Another concern is control system components. A new version of the Service Level Reporter is just announced, featuring several functions missing in the components described in this book.

Very few paragraphs were revised for this reason, however, because 'Performance Control' only uses control tool **implementations** as examples. The emphasis is on what to measure and for what purpose, enabling a continuous, automatic control system executed by people directly responsible for user service.

1.2 PERFORMANCE

Performance - as described in reference 1 - is a measure of the degree that a computing centre fulfills its purpose. Hopefully the purpose is stated in **measurable objectives.**

Usually, the objectives will consider several aspects of service, primarily responsiveness and availability. To ensure that the centre fulfills its purpose, objectives need to be established, measured, presented to the users and planned for the future.

A centre running with 'good' performance fulfills all its objectives. There is no direct tradeoff between aspects of performance - if one group experiences excellent response times, this does not necessarily outweigh poor text processing facilities offered to another group.

In this book three levels of performance indicators are identified:

1.   Primary performance indicators

Parameters that are directly reportable in response to performance objectives, such as response times and availability.

2.   Secondary performance indicators

Parameters directly related to primary performance indicators. These parameters generally express **resource expenditures** to produce performance. Examples are: processing time, disk busy time.

3.   Tertiary performance indicators

Resources and parameters indirectly related to primary performance indicators. Examples are: software buffer usage, time to retrieve mass storage volumes, paging overhead etc. etc..

This distinction has been made because many measurement products and methods concentrate on **tertiary performance indicators.** In some cases this approach is necessary simply because nothing else is available. Notably this is the case for the implementations of MSS and partly network control presented here.

A long term objective should be to implement a hierarchial control system that concentrates on primary performance indicators. The present book covers primary performance indicators in chapters three and four (both on service), and goes on to the background information, secondary and sometimes tertiary indicators in chapters 5 through 7. A case study is included to provide a management overview of centre service and resource usage, concentrating on the higher level performance indicators.

Currently those secondary and tertiary indicators must be followed for anomaly identification and as a basis for for capacity planning. As the computing environment in a complex centre becomes more and more stable, a much less rigorous methodology can be followed for the lower order performance indicators, for instance measuring every week or month.

1.3 PRODUCTIVITY

The productivity of a computing centre is closely linked to its performance as sketched on Figure 1.

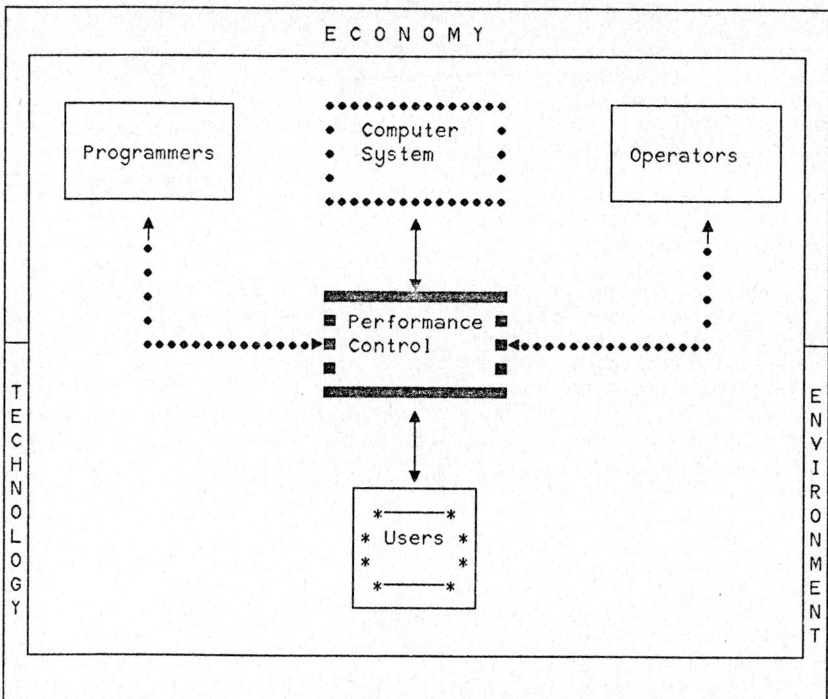

Figure 1.   Productivity - dependent on performance

The productivity of programmers, operators and end users depend on a well
functioning EDP service.   Before expanding on this, productivity should be
defined.

Freely after Websters Dictionary, productivity is the power to produce
'goods that have an exchange value'; i.e. marketable goods; something
somebody will pay for.   Productivity is thus measured by the value of the
goods produced.   According to Figure 1, this has to be done within a
framework of economy (cost), technology (tools, techniques, methods) and
environment - for instance social atmosphere; the ethos.

From Samuelson's Economics we learn that:'Less than half of the increase
in productivity per capita and in real wages can be accounted for by the
increase in capital itself.   Considerably more than half the increase in

productivity seems to be attributable to technical change - to scientific
and engineering advance'.

In the EDP industry it is reasonable to assume that the role of scientific
and engineering advance is more significant.

Productivity is not necessarily synonymous with work effort, for instance
100s of tape mounts or 1000s of assembler lines. Because the result of
the productivity must be marketable, it must be expressed in end user
terms: reliable operation, acceptable response times or easily accessible
functions.

Because the computer system's end users must be productive towards **their**
end users: the company customers or the centre's serviceable community,
computer centre objectives in these terms must be specified. Are holiday
bookings efficient, are tax returns correctly and timely computed, or are
the bank cashier's queues reasonably small?

Combining the aspects of performance control systems (as defined in chapter 2), the various dependant groups can obtain information on how to
improve their own work.

The computer system provides one tool, or a set of tools, that the end
users need for their productivity. Performance control should tell how
good that tool is. As indicated on Figure 1 on page 6, the control system
can feed back analogous information to programmers: how good is the system
as **their** tool, or to the operators: how well are they doing their job?

1.4 ORGANISATION

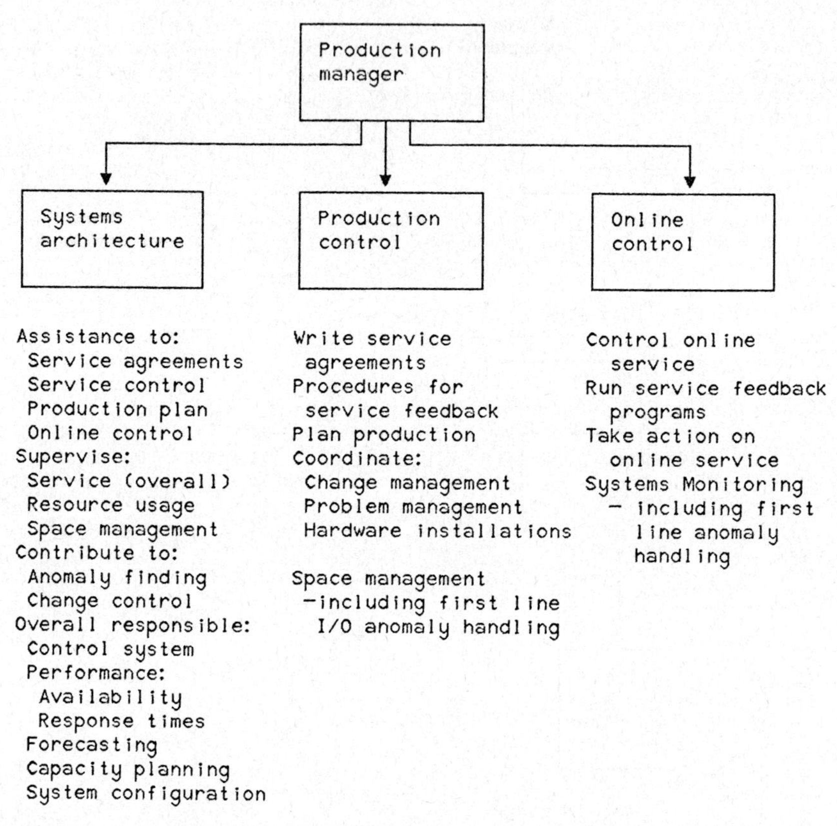

Figure 2.   Performance control system organisation example

Figure 2 shows the most pertinent parts of the organisation elements needed for performance control. Because the performance control system is
built on systems architecture concepts, the system architecture group is
fundamental in the performance control system implementation.

Adjustments and other detail performance work is still the domain of the
systems programmers in this organisation. Detailed investigation of software or hardware requires knowledgeable specialists. The control system
should however ease the burden on these popular individuals.

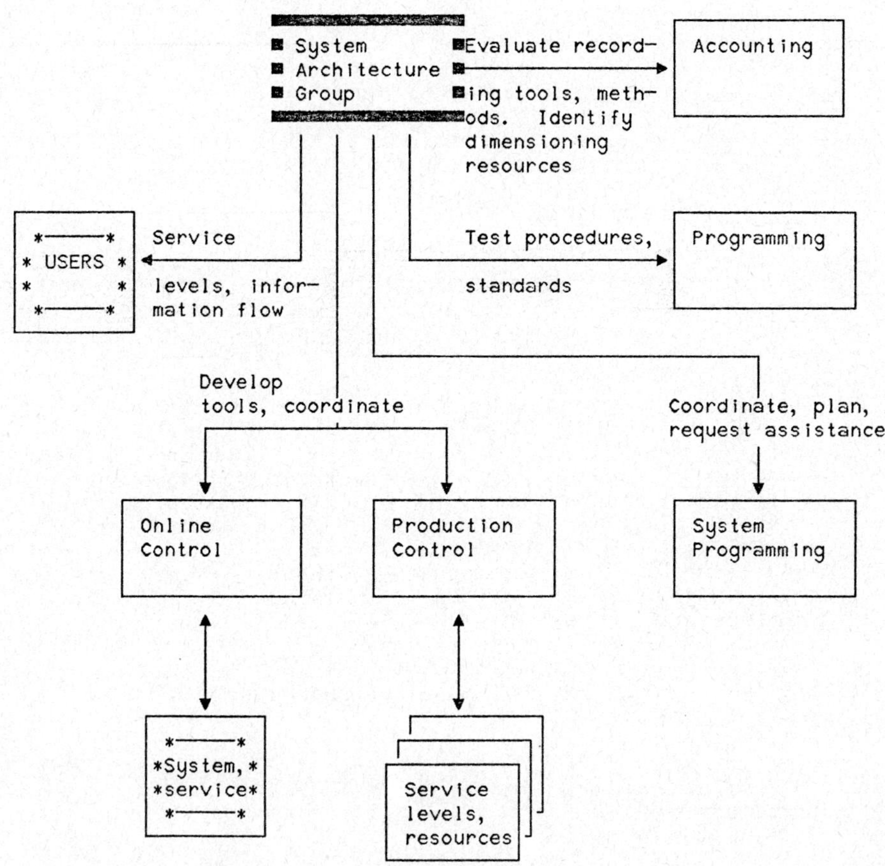

Figure 3.   Performance control related to systems architecture

The idea on Figure 3, is that the Systems Architecture Group develops tools and coordinates the performance control process. The actual execution of the process resides with the people directly responsible for the relevant service. In the depicted organisation, the systems programming group has been relieved of these duties, believed to be somewhat remote from a systems programmer's other tasks. Figure 3 does not state who should send what information to who. In a mature performance control system, the executors of distribution tasks should again be the people responsible for the service, i.e. operators/supervisors and production control. As second line anomaly handlers the system architecture group could serve. This group would still perform capacity planning and probably resource surveillance; they need to be updated on technical matters.

1.5 INTENDED AUDIENCE

Most terms in this book should be understood by a professional with about
one year experience in a relevant IBM based computer centre. Readers with
relevant non-IBM background are referred to the IBM Glossary (reference
11) for an explanation of IBM-specific terminology.

Uncommon acronyms are 'translated' in the index (Appendix II).

The book is meant for:

Category	Purpose
SYSTEMS ARCHITECTS	Reference Ideas Planning information
SYSTEMS PROGRAMMERS	Reference Ideas
MANAGEMENT	General education Ideas Planning information Reference
SENIOR OPERATORS OPERATION PLANNERS	General education Reference Ideas
OTHER CATEGORIES	Some or all of the above

Figure 4.   Intended audience for 'Performance Control'

Experience shows that performance control is a good way of learning the
intricacies of a complex system's hardware and software. Accordingly, the
present book should be useful as an introductory text book for systems
programmers, systems architects and senior operators, and anybody with
work related to these areas.

Students expecting to take on any of these jobs will find this book relevant, perhaps to ease the transition from the university to the often very
different computing centre environment.

Hopefully, production planning and quality control will establish itself
in its own right like for other technical subjects. Perhaps this book
will help.

1.6 ACKNOWLEDGEMENTS

This book has been possible only through the use of resources of the Information Systems Centre in Copenhagen, and due to the helpfulness of the colleagues there.

Direct contributions to the book have been provided by:

Arne Borg   (RMFMON user programs)
Jens Bang   (Availability reports)
Helge Rasmussen   (Availability reports)
Henning Kristoffersen (Availability reports)
Martin Laursen   (Coauthor of DISK and KWU programs)
Leif Schiøler   (MSS, Colour Plots)
Fl. Dreyer   (Colour plots)
Bent Filstrup   (SLR maintenance)
Preben Thomsen   (Text processing procedures)

Proofreading and helpful suggestions have been made by:

Arne Borg
Knud Ove Hamann
Henning Kristoffersen
Knud Koldkjær
Martin Laursen
Peter Olsen
Torben Jørgensen

Special thanks to **H. Pat Artis**, Moreno Associates, **Andreas Børlin**, IBM Switzerland and **Ole Nordhild**, IBM Nordic Field System Centre, for encouragement, proofreading and helpful suggestions.

The book is printed on an IBM 3800 laser printer. It was prepared using SCRIPT and GML (Generalized Markup Language). The black and white figures were either produced from VM virtual reader files or using XEDITG; an internal product made by Mr. G.H. Tuttle, IBM UK. Colour figures were produced using the Graphical Data Display Manager (GDDM), sometimes interfaced from other products (APL Graphpak and the Service Level Reporter described in next chapter).

CHAPTER 2

PERFORMANCE CONTROL SYSTEM FUNDAMENTALS

In Paradise, they tell us, Houris dwell,
And fountains run with wine and oxymal:
  If these be lawful in the world to come,
Surely 'tis right to love them here as well. ...

Heed not the Sunna, nor the law divine:
If to the poor his portion you assign
  And never injure one, nor yet abuse,
I guarantee you heaven, and now some wine! ...

Omar Khayyam

2.1 INTRODUCTION

2.1.1 Chapter contents

This chapter provides definitions used later in the book; what is a performance control system, and how is it used. The purpose of an EDP centre is to render service to users; this service is defined and provides the basis for the rest of the book.

One set of users of the performance control system itself are those same persons that depend on the centre's services as tools for at least part of their work, and should be informed as to how efficient are these tools they are using.

Another performance control system user category is centre management that need to know how well the centre is doing and what resources are spent delivering the services. They also need an assessment of future resources: hardware, software, information or skills needed in the future to continue delivering acceptable service.

The third control system user group consists of the production and system professionals needing to know firstly if the service they have delivered (preferably are delivering) is acceptable, secondly a detailed assessment of resources required. The professionals also need to investigate if there have been problems in the system, perhaps not covered by a problem report. Quite valuable is a feeling of the service pattern: What service runs where and when, and what effect has that on the system and other services.

Preferably reports to the three categories of control system users should be compatible - ideally subsets or supersets of each other - so that communication between the three categories is facilitated.

The components used in the actual implementation of the performance control system described in the later chapters are introduced. These components are here actual program systems; in the general case, the components shown are but examples. However, taken together, and with due appreciation of the limits of current tools, economy and skills, the components provides a total overview of service rendered and resources used in a complex computing centre.

2.2 WHAT IS MEANT BY A PERFORMANCE CONTROL SYSTEM?

2.2.1 The purpose of performance control

The purpose of a computing centre is to provide service to its users.

In order to ensure that this service is acceptable and will be acceptable in the future, controls are needed.

Ideally all aspects of service should be measured continually and in minute detail. In a complex centre this is not feasible, partly because the direct cost of such control would be prohibitive, but more because meaningful data is lost in an avalanche of numbers.

In order to use the term 'performance control system', ideally all components should be defined such that all users of the performance control system receive or can get exactly the data they need - no more, no less.

Today this is only a long term objective.

2.2.2 Performance control system users

Three levels of performance control system users can be identified:

1. Management

requiring trends, graphs, fractions - in general **processed** numbers.

     Examples: Monthly trends
               Percentage unacceptably long responses
               Availability reports
               Total service reports

An example of a set of Management Reports is included in chapter 10.

2. Users and user representatives, support groups

requiring **selected** data pertaining to their environment and processed to address their requirements and level of understanding.

     Examples: Response times per application/transaction
               Hourly load and response for relevant application(s)
               Management type reports for relevant application(s)

3. Systems support and operations

needing **raw** data to determine exactly how the system functions - in addition to the above data.

     Examples: Trend plots

                Detailed system data
                Reports relevant to the other two groups

Preferably all data should be derived from a common database so that the
reports are compatible and consistent, although with differing degree of
detail.

2.2.3 Purpose of a performance control system

There are several reasons for establishing performance control in a formal
system:

   Service:

            Provide basis for service objectives
            Check if service objectives are met
            Provide feed-back on service to users
            Provide input to accounting

   Operations:

            Complement system supervision
            Complement network supervision
            Provide feedback on operator service
            Help identify problem areas in daily operations

   Anomaly management:

            Identify anomalies
            Identify bottlenecks
            Provide background data for problem solving
            Identify heavy users of scarce or expensive resources
            Identify abnormal usage

   Planning:

            Identify future problem areas
            Provide input to forecasting and capacity planning
            Provide background information for daily planning decisions
            Educate personnel

   Improvements:

            Provide basis for service adjustments
            Identify non-optimal methods:
                           management
                           programming
                           operational methods
                           planning
            Identify superior/inferior products (hardware, software,
            applications, methods)
            Establish critical values for monitoring
            Establish a 'robust' environment that delivers agreed service at
            most load combinations
            Evaluate changes

In order to get maximum benefit from measurements, standard procedures should be established and followed. An example of such a procedure is listed below:

* Define objectives
* Select measurements
* Decide timing
* Perform measurements
* Publish results

2.2.4 Service objectives

The basis for a performance control system is service objectives. The objectives should describe:

* What is measured (e.g. response time, availability)
* How is it measured (with what means)
* When is it measured (time of day, week etc.)
* Where and how is the data stored
* How are the users and others informed on service rendered

The list is further discussed below.

Feedback should be in understandable terms, including graphs/tables showing trends.

The principle of Roman law was that all laws should be controllable. This is also applicable when designing service objectives. All objectives should be **controllable** - i.e. in most cases **measurable.** Cost for control should be included in cost/benefit studies.

2.2.5 Selecting measurements

The above considerations strongly impact what measurements should be collected. Other concerns relate to the way of collecting data, and programs to extract and present data.

Collecting data

Performance data is in MVS continually recorded in these datasets (for a further flow see Figure 6 on page 24):

            SMF/RMF
            IMS logtape (if applicable)
            MSS trace (if applicable)

SMF, Systems Measurement Facility and **RMF (Resource Measurement Facility)** recording can be limited to selected systems occurrences, but these performance logging systems are normally in a complex environment enabled to

record most system incidents, such as logons/logoffs, resource usage, paging behaviour, device usage etc. etc. SMF and RMF data are physically
logged on the same dataset(s). The part of the logged data logically
belonging to RMF can be directly extracted by different RMF extract programs mentioned in the next section. SMF also features some extract programs, but the range is not so comprehensive. SMF recording is more
detailled, making it suitable e.g. for accounting.

The IMS logtape records IMS transaction occurrences, for instance when it
arrives in the system, when it starts execution etc. etc. The logtape's
primary purpose is to serve during restart situations as it contains all
that has happened during the active period. For this same reason, the
logtape is an accurate performance recording tool.

The MSS trace similarly records occurrences in the MSS system. Note that
there is no direct bridge between the MSS trace and SMF/RMF. We need to
look at the times and dates to find out what events took place at the same
time, for instance long batch turnarounds and high MSS activity.

Most IBM computing centres store raw monitor data collected by SMF/RMF on
tape or mass storage, enabling any SMF/RMF based report to be recreated.
This is a versatile tool for detail investigations. However, the tools
for historical comparisons in the standard SMF/RMF extract programs are
inferior to SLR. SLR, the **Service Level Reporter** for instance allows you
to compare service for different days, months, years based on the same
table.

GTF (the General Trace Facility) can trace in detail most software occurrences in standard MVS. Such a tool cannot be run continually due to the
cost. Experience shows, however, that in most cases it is possible to
recreate the abnormal situations if the system supervisors react quickly
enough, for instance starting a GTF trace _after_ the occurrence, assuming
that there will still be _some_ references to the data sets causing the
anomaly.

To measure busy time on a disk head of string, or a disk storage control,
a hardware tool is needed. The data is not recorded by IBM software.

Programs to extract and present collected data

Another factor is the availability of measurement tools and their limitations.

For instance the Service Level Reporter, SLR, does not currently (1981)
record VSPC and VM data, and homespun applications are needed to extract
the data from SMF (the Systems Measurement Facility or systems monitor).
Available late in 1982 there is a new version that can process most common
types of monitor data, including VM, VSPC and even network data.

Data for SLR are collected in tables that should be easily accessible by
its users. The tables thus collected contain historical data, perhaps for
more than a year, with totals and subtotals for all selected types of
information. Even with a Mass Storage Subsystem, the amount of stored
measurement data must be limited.

2.2.6 Timing

The following control structure is suggested:

Continual online monitoring of system, using RMF or a similar tool (Appendix I, references 23-24).

Continual daily SMF/RMF recording to tape, enabling investigations far back into history. Week/day tapes are stored. History tapes may be kept longer for accounting purposes.

Note: a lot of the discussion below refer to tapes. This is probably the most common storage medium for historical data. However, experience shows that tape is a poor recording medium for historical SMF/RMF data. Somehow, for mysterious reasons, recording parts disappear and render the whole statistic uncertain. Tape is mostly used when secondary storage, i.e. disk, is too restricted and/or expensive, and is therefore an example of **tertiary storage**. Another form of tertiary storage is Mass Storage, MSS, that removes some of the problems with tape, for example needing to know if there has been overflow to a work tape.

SLR tables are mostly hourly based, and concentrated on service given to major subsystems. The SLR database is updated daily or weekly.

Detail SLR reports are kept 1 - 2 months, overall reports are kept for 13 months.

Weekly updates of any programs designed to supplement SLR.

Traces are started when needed - and possible.

2.2.7 Recording

If possible, historical data should be recorded to a yearly database or to a migration structure imitating a yearly database. It should also be possible to define databases/tables to span years, for example February 1981 to February 1982. There is a need for long term storage of yearly average/maximum data. Perhaps this should be stored in a separate table. The table need not be very big, but should be kept for a long time, perhaps across many different software releases and hardware technologies.

Data for monitoring and continuous resource control are either online or assembled, extracted, analyzed and stored on a week/day basis. A 10 minute resolution is usually required to analyze anomalies. This higher resolution can be obtained for instance by extraction from SMF/RMF tapes, possibly in the tape library or on MSS

Continuous control means that few parameters are selected for comparison against target values. When everything is normal, nothing further need be done. However, if an anomaly is indicated, then a more detailed analysis is required,

2.2.8 Publishing

Some users/departments/support groups will receive paper output on a regular basis.

In a well designed control system, the amount of published data is minimized.   Many reports are prepared for terminal display, like for instance
SLR colour graphs and all the APL display programs described later in this
document.   In this case, the recipient may as well use the terminal to
extract reports.

There are many advantages of a terminal based publishing system. Paper is
saved, the reports are easier to keep updated, and many types of reports
are difficult to mass produce on paper, for instance colour graphs and
fullscreen pictures.   'Help' facilities are much easier to establish if
the recipient is working in an online environment, for instance with APL
fullscreen capabilities.

A **control room** featuring selected reports and monitoring terminals may
prove a good investment, especially if a program like SLR release 2 is
used to produce colour output. The control room could include network and
system supervisors to simulate a 'command bridge' where all control
aspects of a complex system converge.

In addition different user groups should be presented feedback on what
service the centre has given according to the automatic control system.
It will then be possible to obtain critisism on service, on the control
system, or on factors not covered by the control system. Such feedback
can be made part of the control system.

2.3 USE OF THE CONTROL SYSTEM.

The control system should address the following main areas:

* Service definitions and measurement

* Resource control

* Anomaly identification and resolution.

* Capacity planning

2.3.1 Service definitions and feedback

The control system is valuable in establishing the objectives it will later measure, and to suggest changes to the same service objectives.

The service feedback enable users to quantitatively evaluate the service they get, and to suggest changes expressed in terms understandable by systems and production people.

Systems and production people can adjust the system within the established objectives and know when to leave the system unchanged.

2.3.2 Resource control

The usage of any resource in the system should ideally be followed on a continual basis. This is not feasible in very complex system, where a selection of control candidates is advisable. At least the following resources should be followed:

a. Processor time - preferably by major application

b. Real storage - also by major application

c. Virtual storage.

d. Selected disks, for instance the most busy ones, or
    the critical ones for high priority applications.

e. Communication system - for instance the most critical lines

2.3.3 Anomaly identification and resolution.

This involves finding out that the system is not behaving as expected and why.

The first step, and very often the most difficult, is to realize as soon as possible that an anomaly has occurred. Some procedures for spotting anomalies are discussed in chapter 7.

When the anomaly has been found, there ought to be a standard procedure to handle the anomaly. Mostly the procedure is part of Problem Management. The anomaly - now called a problem - is logged and handed over to somebody believed to be able to solve the problem. The Problem Manager follows the problem through all phases, but normally does not attempt to **solve** the problem himself/herself. Problems reported and recorded may be of different origin:

   a. Poor procedures - for instance sending output to the wrong address.

   b. Human errors - for instance cancelling runs that should have been allowed to proceed.

   c. Hardware errors.

   d. Errors in standard software - for instance in MVS, IMS, VSPC etc.

   e. Errors in user developed programs. These errors are not limited to abnormal conditions. Users would experience as errors any condition leading to responses different (longer) than usual, for instance recovery of database deadlocks lasting more than 20 seconds.

Performance anomalies is included in the problem management procedure. Chapter 7 indicates a procedure for following up performance anomalies.

2.3.4 Capacity planning

Controlling resource usage is an absolute requirement for capacity planning. The feedback can be used directly to find out how much of each resource is used now, or indirectly as a feedback to users to inspire feasible forecasts and inform of any desired change in the service pattern.

A sensible control system will as time goes by, gather sensitivity data: 'What happens if...'. A lot of such information is already assembled today, but very often depend on individuals' memories and ability to communicate. The control system is intended to catalog such information in a format accessible by all involved parties.

2.4 COMPONENTS OF THE CONTROL SYSTEM

Software components of the control system described in this book are:

Control system tools:

Program ID	Identification (IBM order)	References (Appendix I)	Purpose
SLR	5740-DC3	20-22	Trends, resources
RMF	5740-XY4	23-24	Resources, bottlenecks
SDSF	5798-DAL	29	Syslog display and search facility
GTFPARS	5798-CQQ	25	Disk references, seeks
MSS trace/SMF correlation aid	5796-PJX	27	MSS usage
NCCF	5735-XX6	36	Network operator control
NPA	5798-CZR/CZT	37	Network load/resources
NSRS	IBM Internal	38	Combines the above two
TRMS	IBM Internal		Network response times
APL extract	IBM Internal		Load, RMF extract
VMAP	5978-CPX	39	VM performance analysis
SMART	5696-PNA	40	VM online monitoring

Related/referenced tools:

Program ID	Identification (IBM order)	References (Appendix I)	Purpose
DC monitor part of IMS	5740-XX2	33	IMS analysis
IMSPARS	5798-CQP	34	IMS analysis
TPNS	5740-XT4	30	Benchmarking
VM Predictor	AIDS-SE-19R	41	VM modelling
ANIMSVS	5798-CHJ	43	IMS program analysis
IMSPARS	5798-CQP	42	IMS performance analysis
NPDA	5735-XX8	44	Network problem ccntrol
VAMP	IBM Internal		Network access control
JDCA	5796-PHN	49	Space management
VM Resource Limiter	IBM Internal	50	VM resource control

Presentation/display tools:

Program ID	Identification (IBM order)	References (Appendix I)	Purpose
GDDM	5748-XXH	31	Colour plot - SLR and general
APL Graphpak part of APL	5748-AP1	32 / 35	Colour plot - APL

Figure 5. Supervision tools

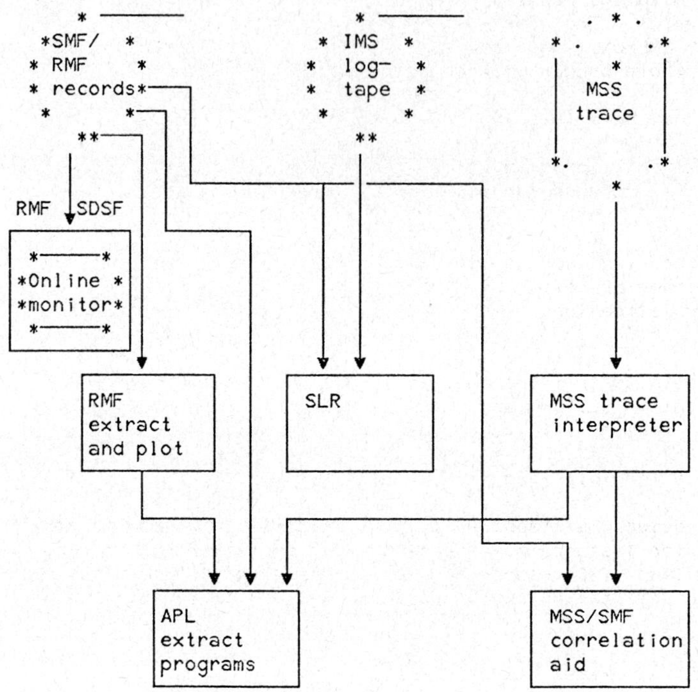

Figure 6.   Performance control data collection (central system)

A flow diagram showing the relationship between the most important of
these programs is shown in Figure 6.

2.4.1 Resource Measurement Facility (RMF) and related programs

The RMF program family consists of the following products:

RMF name	Name used in this book
Monitor I session	RMF extract
Exception report	Exception report
Post processor reports	RMF plot
Monitor II display session	RMFMON
Monitor II background session	RMFMON background

The online monitor, RMFMON, extracts measurement data when the system is running and displays results on a screen. The screen image may be subsequently printed. The facility SDSF is in this book assumed to be integrated with RMFMON, and certain other extension has also been made to RMFMON. The whole bundle will be referred to as RMFMON.

Display data can be printed by the background session programs.

The 'RMF extract' program referred to on the figure consists of tabular reports that can be used for detailed performance analysis/ anomaly tracking.

Output can be limited to selected occurrences, for instance high swap rates or extreme processor utilizations. An **exception report** can be prepared for such situations. This alerts the analyst of any abnormal occurrences.

The prerequisite is that the analyst is well informed on the **normal** status of the computer system, and that the performance control system catches **all** (or at least most) abnormal occurrences. Otherwise it can work against its purpose and give a false sense of security. RMF exception reporting is a feasible long term objective.

RMF plot provides a graphical display of some resource over time. This resource may for instance be processing time or disk response time. Average and maximum TSO users may also be followed in this fashion. This facility is excellent for spotting abnormal situations (anomalies).

2.4.2 The Service Level Reporter (SLR)

SLR collects a large part of the SMF/RMF information and stores this information in tables for instance related to IMS or TSO resource consumption. The great advantage of SLR is its history facilities. As shown later in this book, SLR can provide trends for hourly, daily or monthly usage that are essential for performance work. In addition, SLR's more detailed reports can be used for exception reporting - for instance catching one specific hour of poor IMS response.

As shown on Figure 6 on page 24, SLR collects some of its data from IMS logtapes that contain detailed information on each IMS transaction. More specific information on this will be given in the next chapter.

2.4.3 MSS trace reduction programs

Data from the MSS trace can be extracted by a trace interpreter program provided as standard software. The data need to be converted from original hexadecimal to alphanumeric/decimal. This can be easily done by a small converter program.

Trace data can be further analysed, for instance finding hourly activity, by other programs. The examples included in this book assume these programs to be in APL; this is only to ensure fast programming an easy bridge to colour facilities.

The MSS data interpreter, or officially the 'MSS trace/ SMF correlation aid', can be used to extract performance relevant data from the MSS trace. MSS trace output can be combined with SMF data to present a meaningful picture of how user service is impacted by MSS.

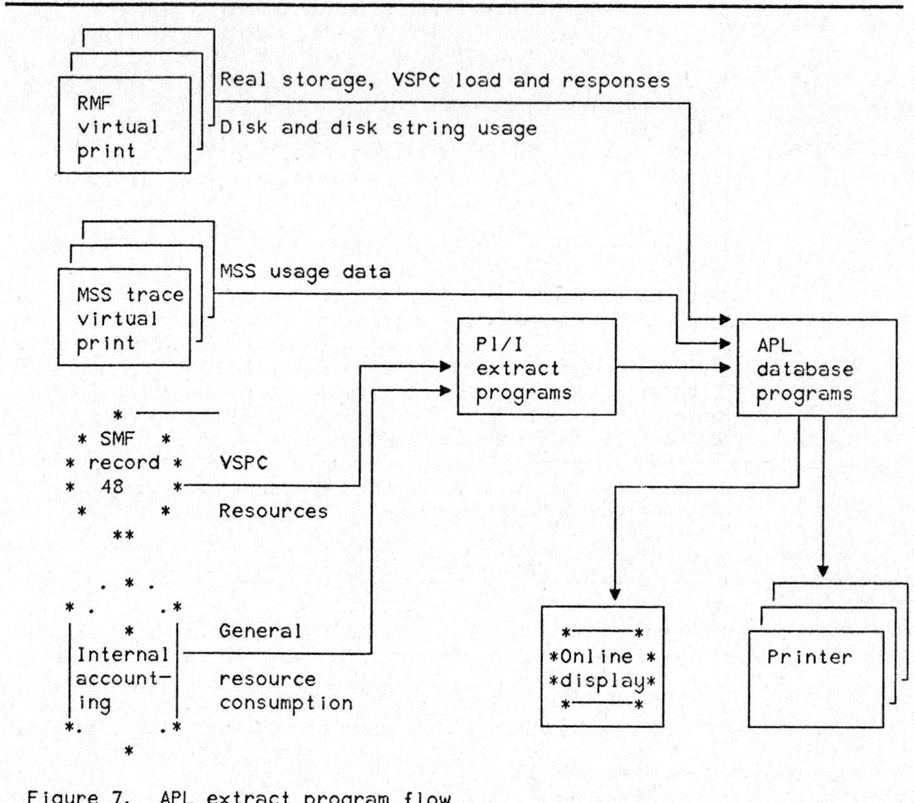

Figure 7.   APL extract program flow

Name	Key variables	Description
TRX	Paging, real storage	Paging and Workload reports are extracted from RMF and sent to VM. The data is read from VM's virtual reader into APL where an extract program updates the database.
DISK	Disk load and response	Disk data are extracted from RMF and assemmbled into an APL database as for TRX. Activity for all (four) processors are added and the 20 most active disks are printed. The result is stored in a file.
VSPCX	VSPC load: processor time user load	A PL/I program extracts data from SMF and presents them to APL under VM as for TRX. (not discussed further in this book)
KWU	Processor time print lines EXCPs	Another PL/I program extracts data from a file created from SMF records 4, 5, 6 etc etc.
VSPCRESP	VSPC trans- actions per hour and response	The values for transaction load and VSPC response is extracted from the RMF workload report and assembled in an APL database
MSSAPL	MSS performance	Miscellaneous MSS performance indicators are extracted from the MSS trace and read into an APL program that stores selected data in a database, enabling for instance historical colour plots.

Figure 8.   APL programs for surveillance data extraction

2.4.4 APL extract programs

Figure 7 on page 26 shows how data is collected in some APL programs developed specifically for performance surveillance. The programs are listed in Figure 8.

Chapter 7 contains a user guide to the DISK program that is typical of the implementation of all the APL extract programs.

The program features a collection mechanism, reducing 10-20000 print records to about 50 pages of report, partly on day basis, partly on week basis.   Weekly data are stored. These data can be used to produce trend reports in colour, online, under APL.

The 50 pages report includes a description of data and what to observe in
the document, including key indicators as shown in Figure 106 on page 171.
The report can be run and acted upon by ordinary production personnel.

This highlights some requirements for a good performance control tool:

1. **It should be based on standard recordings (DISK is based on RMF)**

2. **A legible report should be produced at regular intervals**

3. **Data stored for future use in a database should be minimized**

4. **The stored data should be online accessible**

5. **Data should be presentable on a plot that can be used as a per-
    formance key indicator.**

6. **The control system should be extensible (DISK is based on APL).**

7. **Data should be collected and acted upon by production people.**

2.4.5 Network Communications Control Facility (NCCF)

The communications network serves to deliver data between users and application, and is therefore an important component when considering performance. Note the term 'a component'; even though the network may consist of
1000s of parts, it may be regarded as just another computer system component.

The product NCCF, when added to VTAM networks, enables the operator to
control the network environment using specially designed commands.

The connection between NCCF and other (following) network tools is
sketched on Figure 10 on page 31.

History from the sessions can be saved in a database that can be used for
statistical purposes and integrated with other information as suggested
below.

NCCF, NPDA and NPA are generally available. NSRS and TRMS are for IBM
internal use only.   However, they bring out important aspects of a performance control system, and are included here to show how the total
structure **could** be.

2.4.6 Network Problem Determination Application (NPDA)

As its name indicates, NPDA is primarily used for error tracking.
However, problem management is closely linked with the control system -
and is related for instance to the time required to fix an error that
causes unavailability of a system component.

Errors on some communications equipment (or indeed on any computer component) may not cause a system down. The response times may be prolonged,
however, when error logging and bypass/correction need system resources.

In addition NPDA gives traffic counts for selected lines, and provides indications of busy percentages.

2.4.7 Network Performance Analyzer (NPA)

NPA contains functions for network data collection and reduction.

The NPA log is processible by SLR version 2, and can give information on line loads, communication controller loads etc., using SLR reporting facilities.

2.4.8 VTAM Application Monitor Program (VAMP)

VAMP is a network tool used in internal IBM centres to provide access control to different applications offered.

Figure 9 on page 30 shows application selections for ISC Denmark. Only applications marked ONLINE are running, for instance CPHIMST = IMS test and CICS are not running. VAMP gives access independent of host processor for application.

The highlighted message has occurred because a requested application was not available to my terminal at that time.

There are six TSO options on the screen. Each option relates to a user group. 'Logon' will have no effect in this system, the user has to give the group option relating to his/her user identification. This **VAMP logon exit** has been implemented to prevent users from logging on to a system where they do not belong. The exit can be further used to control the TSO user mix on a vulnerable processor, for instance limiting the access to 1 control terminal, 10 programmers and 10 general users.

Notice that even VM (CPHVM1 on the menu) is available through this interface. VTAM capabilities must then be provided under VM.

2.4.9 Network Statistics Reporting System (NSRS)

NSRS, and internal IBM system, collects statistics into one reporting system as shown on Figure 10 on page 31.

```
IBM COPENHAGEN      INTERNATIONAL NETWORK MONITOR ON MVSA        LU-NAME=FKFS2018

OVERVIEW SCREEN            09:30, MONDAY   , DECEMBER  14, 1981
APPLNAME STATUS           C I APPLNAME STATUS         C I APPLNAME STATUS       C
--------------------------------------------------------------------------------
CCTSO    ONLINE  04:45 I I FIS2   * ONLINE  07:51   I KGVM4  * OFFLINE 04:29
DCTSO    ONLINE  04:45 I I EIS    * ONLINE  07:51   I ORLIMS * OFFLINE 09:08
DPTSO    ONLINE  04:45 I I Y      * ONLINE  07:51   I MZESS  * ONLINE  08:22
ISTSO    ONLINE  07:57 I I N      * ONLINE  07:18   I VOLTS1 * ONLINE  09:20
EUTSOA   ONLINE  04:29 I I VE2IMS * ONLINE  08:42   I WINVM5 * ONLINE  09:21
EUTSOB   ONLINE  07:58 I I HONE   * ONLINE  07:31   I WINVM6 * ONLINE  09:21
CPHIMSP  ONLINE  07:08 I I TSMA   * ONLINE  07:51   I WINSNA * OFFLINE 04:29
CPHIMST  OFFLINE 04:29 I I TSMB   * OFFLINE 04:29   I SEMIS  * ONLINE  09:01
CICS     OFFLINE 04:29   I TSMT   * OFFLINE 04:29   I WV1IMS * ONLINE  07:51
CICST    OFFLINE 04:29   I ETS2   * ONLINE  07:51   I CPHVM1 * ONLINE  02:22
VSPC     ONLINE  08:19   I USA    * ONLINE  07:51   I
VSPCT    OFFLINE 04:29   I ITSAPL * ONLINE  09:20   I
CP2IMT * OFFLINE 04:29 I I KGVM1  * OFFLINE 04:29   I
MTC    * ONLINE  04:29   I KGVM2  * OFFLINE 04:29   I
--------------------------------------------------------------------------------
==> TYPE 'TPNEWS' BEFORE SIGN ON.
==> TYPE APPLNAME AS SHOWN ABOVE FOR CONNECTION
 VAMP064   INPUT NOT RECOGNISED
==>



 *    Application accessible through international network.
 I    Application news display available (column C)
```

   Figure 9.   VAMP application selection screen for ISC Denmark

Load and availability data can be provided **per application.**

NSRS data can be processed by GIS (Generalized Information System). GIS's
great advantage is that reports can easily be designed and implemented,
providing a rather open-ended report system.

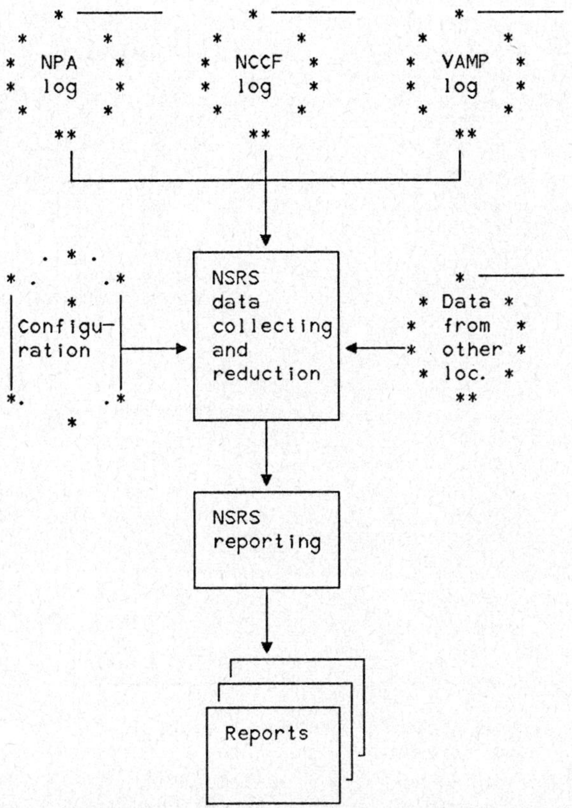

Figure 10.   NSRS data flow

Total response times including network time are not directly obtainable in
the NSRS system.   A Canadian system, TRMS, that is classified as IBM
internal, the Teleprocessing Response Measurement System, uses an IBM
Series 1 minicomputer to gather response statistics.   Response data are
planned to be available both online and historically.   As a result, network response and load data for each single application and each single
transaction can be made available.   This coincides with the requirements
for a performance control system.   Apart from the obvious uses in reporting service and finding resource usage, the measurements can be used to
investigate different applications and their usage of teleprocessing.   It
is for instance not unimportant whether an application sends only updated
screen areas or the full screen when only a comma has been changed.

In the future, network data ought to be reportable along with the central
system data, using a common collecting and reporting system, for instance
SLR.

2.5 CONCLUSION

An EDP centre's primary purpose is to deliver service to its users. Controlling that the service is adequate and that resources to render the service are reasonable is therefore one of the most important tasks in a modern computing centre.

Service and resources should be controlled continually. Instead of ad hoc performance measuring we want an ongoing process designed to feed back service data to implicated parties: Users, management and professionals, and to provide data for planning and adjustment.

As more and more of the performance control system become automatic, the production people: operators and supervisors, take over responsibility for service and service feedback.

The tools described are examples of implementations based on commonly available software, usually with minor or major changes. These changes could implicate a postprocessing program in a high-level language, for instance APL with graphic facilities. No programs described here require extensive changes or specialized skills. By providing the end result and the method, most professionals at the 'central systems architect' level should be able to implement the described procedures quite easily.

CHAPTER 3

SERVICE AGREEMENTS

'Among you, whoever wants to be great must be your servant, and whoever wants to be first among you must be the willing slave of all'.

Matthew 20, 26-27

3.1 INTRODUCTION

3.1.1 Chapter contents

In this chapter the general term 'service' as applicable to computer service centra is defined.   Some general guidelines for writing a service
agreement are given.   The chapter goes on to present examples of the
implementation of service agreements and offers some comments on required
or desired adjustments.

It is important for the understanding of the service agreement procedure,
to note that the service agreement is a result of negotiations between the
user (the 'customer') and the computing centre. Like other negotiated
agreements, a service agreement is therefore often:

*   Non optimal - at least from a measurement point of view

*   Difficult to change

Different major services, like TSO, VSPC or CMS that basically deliver the
same kind of 'goods', should ideally be measured in the same manner,
assuming that the end users of the services are characterised by similar
technical and psychological behaviour. This is difficult to implement in
today's environment, and the result is another step away from the optimal
solution.   A basic requirement for a service agreement is that the parameters described should be **measurable.**

Chapter 4 describes further what can be measured under today's IBM implementation and how to link measurement results with a service level agreement.

3.1.2 The service concept

The philosophy of 'Central Systems Architecture' is based on service.   The
book of the same name introduces service as follows:

The purpose of a computing centre is to give service to its users (reference 1).

Service is comprised of the following:

Facilities: Hardware and software needed to perform the assigned
                   tasks and any associated tasks. This includes access to
                   these facilities, for instance through an appropriate
                   communications network.

Availability: A ratio comparing the time the above facilities are
                   available to the user, to the total time the user may
                   want or is promised these facilities.

                   Connected to this is security. Quantitatively this would
                   be the chance that unauthorized persons got access to
                   above facilities, and the consequences of this. And: the

chance of data or program destruction and its consequences.

Response time: Time from input is delivered (entered at a terminal)
                   till output is received (starts occurring at a terminal).

                   We may also consider response times or turnaround times
                   for batch jobs. This is the time from the job is entered
                   into the system till the output is available. In the
                   current environment, output may be available at the ter-
                   minal, making paper print superfluous or less critical.

Assistance/   Training and assistance needed for the user to benefit
accessability   properly from the facilities offered.

                   Assistance is usually supplied by support groups, to 'get
                   started' or to resolve error situations, but may also be
                   in the form of documentation or 'help' programs.

                   Accessability is also concerned with being able to use
                   any program, preferably at one's own terminal and with
                   that terminal's features.

The service should be defined per major application, and possibly in
greater detail: per department, application, project or whatever.

Some service is given to the centre's own staff, for instance programmers,
but in most cases with the end purpose of providing benefit to persons
outside the computing centre organization.

3.1.3 Service levels

When users of a certain large Danish TSO service were asked what kind of
response times they would want, the consensus could be expressed: 'As now,
perhaps a little bit better'.

Their average response times were then in the order of 8-9 seconds.

In another Danish company, running a CMS service with subsecond average
response times, the same question was asked. The answer was almost identical: '- Perhaps a little bit better'.

This highlights one of the difficulties in setting service levels. There
is little commonly accepted previous experience, and therefore the users
tend to relate response times and availability to what they currently
experience. With the advent of improved technology, service all over the
computer community improve, and this cannot but influence all users to
wish for the same or better response times as their neighbour.

This leads to unquantifiable, changing service levels. Because service
level is a major parameter for system design, adequate system design is
very difficult - if not impossible - in such an environment.

No rules for setting service levels are given in this document, but some
of the considerations are highlighted. The result will probably be a

vague starting point, and firmer service levels as experience accumulates. This enables the systems designer to propose a service level trend and include that in capacity planning.

The same kind of arguments and patterns seem valid for availability service levels and availability related to system design.

The importance of service to the user has been emphasised by Doherty (references 3 and 4), for instance saying:

'If response delays as long as two seconds were standard in our Research Centre, it would cost us a minimum of 36 million seconds of lost time per month. That is 10000 userhours, or 60 people lost full time for the month'.

and

'The value of the person's time for human interactive work is normally more than 20 times greater than the cost of computing'.

and

'Response times must usually be subsecond. This directly affects performance. Response time delays can lead to human delays, irritation, and more mistakes. Subsecond computer response times also opens up broad new areas of applications'.

The latter statement provides a rather difficult objective for an ordinary computer centre. Subsecond response times are expensive in equipment and follow-up. The departure from most centres' current state would be radical. However, it is possible even now to interact with users to find a service pattern that fulfill **their** current requirements, as further described in this and later chapters. But quite clearly, the long term objective has to be the subsecond respond times advocated by Doherty.

The 'new areas of applications' present an interesting dilemma. Service is clearly connected with function, and if users can easily produce flashing colour graphs of a database extract, that is seen as an aspect of good service. On the other hand, such applications require tremendous computing resources, and this should be included in capacity plans - on top of the extra resources required to achieve improved response times and extra availability.

Schneiderman (reference 5) points out the need for **consistent** response, proven by psychological studies. An average response time of 4 seconds may be perceived differently if most response times are close to the average, or if the response times vary from subsecond to minutes. Some observations on user behaviour added later in this chapter underline this concern.

Scneiderman also points out that responses should depend on the amount of work initiated by the command. For instance updating a text screen should be quick - also because the user is then in a highly interactive mode. Copying a large dataset will by most users be accepted as a slow response command. The problem here is that an increasing percentage of users are quite unaware of the effect a certain command has on the data processing environment, as more and more users are not DP professionals.

Doherty and others have pointed out that long response times produce aggressions, digressions, memory losses and daydreaming, meaning that even the people that **have** received their answer are slower to respond. In the response time range most computer centres operate, the delay can be estimated to be equal to the increased response time.

Some assessment on the influence of different response time levels can be done based on actual measurements. If 200 interactive users are waiting to have work done for them by the computer system, then halving the response time will halve the time these 200 users are waiting for an answer. Assuming that these users have more work for the computer when the first piece of work is finished, then the 200 users are twice as productive if average response time is halved.

In addition the author's observations indicate that there is a learning or conditioning process involved when using a terminal and an interactive system. If terminal response is slow, people tend to adjust their work patterns accordingly, and somehow think and react slower, perhaps over and above what is implied in the losses pointed out by Doherty.

Even discarding the aftereffects, there is a tremendous payoff when reducing response times. Halving the response times in the above example would enable the 200 persons to do the work of 400. Assuming this to be productive would make it feasible to invest up to 200 people's salaries in computing equipment. In Denmark one person costs an average computing firm around 40000 US Dollars per year. 200 people's salaries could buy this firm several 3033s, or other equipment meant to improve service.

200 people waiting for the computer at any one instant - how many total employees will that correspond to? The answer depends on the degree of computerisation implemented in the firm. With increased dependence on the computer, a firm employing 2000 - 4000 people may easily have 200 people waiting at any instance for an answer from the computer.

The argumentation is reinforced when considering **availability.** Improving availability can largely be done by the same means that response times are improved by. For instance running major applications on separate computers with separate resources would help both availability and response times. An investigation of the cost of un-availability could be done along the same lines as for response times. The cost is a function of outage. Directly, outage time could be subtracted from uptime and the cost calculated. The difficulty is that the work **could** be done later, but the same inconvenience and productivity loss to users as mentioned for response times apply. For availability there is also the possibility of loosing already performed work, for instance a long-running program that is **nearly** finished, not knowing when the service is again available, and perhaps having restart problems (where exactly was I?).

A further note on availability: Improved availability seems primarily connected with management practices, for instance change and problem management. There is another aspect to availability: Hardware. The hardware itself may be more or less reliable. Besides, system design can provide bypasses and backups to avoid any infected areas. The implementation of this would be too much to cover in this book, and the interested reader is referred to system design manuals or general texts like 'Central Systems Architecture'.

Contradicting these arguments for better service is the reasoning put forward by many people, especially 'old-timers' within computing, who gained,
certainly well deserved, admiration when compiling a 500 statement assembler program correctly first time:

'The increased service leads to less accuracy; the extra computer service
is used to correct people's mistakes rather than increasing their productivity'.

Correct - to a point. But can we afford high salaried professionals
spending days over a program to weed out every feasible mistake, even if
it may be good for their self-images?

My personal experience is parallel to what is encountered in speed
reading: people can do more in shorter time and comprehend - or produce -
more. This phenomenon has been ascribed to a model of the human brain
that instinctively sounds true: people do not think altogether serially,
but tend to queue up 'instructions' about what to do next in their brains
(Doherty again) - just like a computer. Any distraction, for instance
unexpected long response times, disturbs the 'instruction buffers' and
lowers productivity.

3.2 IMPLEMENTATION OF SERVICE AGREEMENTS

Because 'service agreement' is a fairly new concept, few guidelines exist, and most of those pertain to only two aspects of service:

> Availability
> Response times

Here two such agreements are presented. In the actual agreements these are accompanied by long and carefully worded disclaimers, special situations, dates for new negotiations etc. etc.

3.2.1 Components of a service agreement

Every computing centre will have their own ideas and guidelines on what to include in a service agreement. In Figure 11 a rough outline is presented to serve as an initial idea.

The Service

> Hours of working
> Purpose and impact of service
> Expected peaks or particularly important periods
> Relationship to other services - including priorities
> Security handling, including backups
> Volumes - transactions per second, jobs per day etc.

Conditions

> Exclusions - what is not covered in the agreement
> Under what conditions are the agreements valid
> Handling during abnormal periods
> User responsibilities - for instance booking or forecasting

The Computing Centre Environment

> Major software and hardware components offered to the user
> - including for instance network and terminal facilities
> Responsibilities at release changes, major installations etc.
> Assistance available to the user

Service Levels Offered

> Expected availability
> Expected response times
> Method of feedback on services.

Figure 11. General service agreement - one service

In Figure 11, considerations for one service are presented. With all human, legal and technological aspects covered, the service agreement can easily become a very complex document.

It is important to know that a service agreement should be the object of careful planning and implementation. In this book, we are however most interested in the relation between the service agreements and performance control, and will concentrate on the technical aspects and consequences of the service agreement.

3.2.2 Availability service agreement

Availability is perhaps the most important aspect of service. If the service is not available it cannot be used. Availability to the end user means that the requested application or transaction should be available on his/her terminal, no less.

For computing centre people, availability may need to be broken down into components in order to analyse outage causes, and also to investigate the end result of unavailability occurrences.

As an example, please refer to Figure 12.

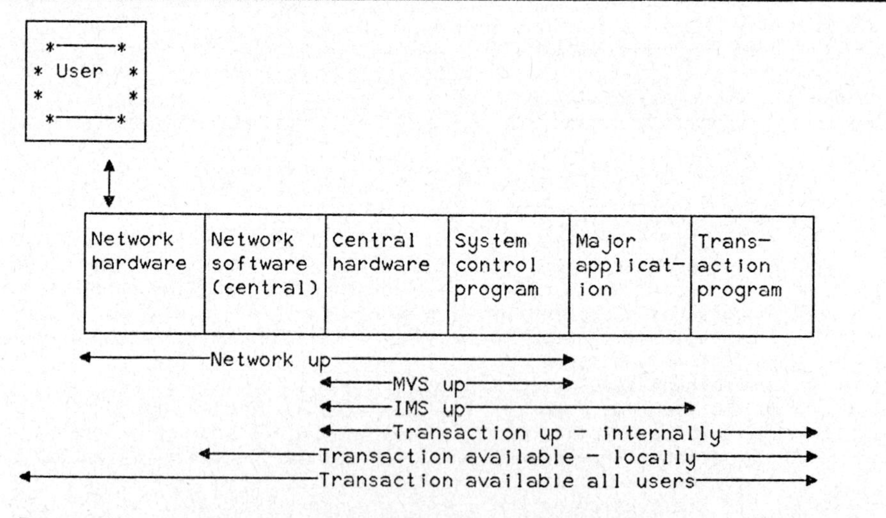

Figure 12.   Availability considerations, IMS example

For the service, a certain IMS transaction, to be available to the user, all logical components shown on Figure 12 must be up. The transaction may be up and running locally even if no network hardware is running. A remotely attached terminal however needs all components. Especially with network, there are special considerations, for instance may a bypass of an hardware error be possible; the network is then still regarded as running. In a distributed net there is also network software in different network components; this level of detail is not shown on Figure 12.

The main point of the figure, is that service to users is only possible
(transaction available) when a number of components are running, and only
seldom (here to locally attached terminals) is limited service possible.

A major problem in availability measurement is that the real, user experienced availability (usually unavailability is more felt) is very difficult
to obtain apart from using some measuring device at the terminal, for
instance a stop watch. This is difficult with several hundred or thousand
terminals online.

Instead, availability components are measured, and hopefully the resulting
experience bears some ressemblance to the system behaviour that the user
perceives.

Un-availability is composed of several logical parts as sketched on
Figure 13.

Notice problem	Report problem	Decide action	Implement action	Restart system	Notify user

←————————————Unavailability, operations view————————————→

Figure 13.   Unavailability components

Figure 13 gives no relative importance to the different components.
Attention should be drawn to the 'notice problem' part. This is usually
done fairly quickly by the **user**. However, the user may think the problem
will pass away, or that somebody else has reported it or may not know how
to react to the problem. 'Notice problem' on the figure is as seen by the
operators/supervisors. To quickly catch a problem, monitoring mechanisms
and user procedures should be established. Even then it may be difficult
to assess unavailability loss to the **user**. The user has additional problems. Even if he/she is notified of the successful restart, it may take
time before other tasks can be cleared away to restart computing. The
user may in the meantime forget where he/she was and loose additional time
in trying the wrong options. Some work may be lost during the restart,
and it is not always clear even to a DP professional exactly how much.

Sometimes the old problem occurs again after restart. Often the stop has
caused a build-up of work, affecting response times after restart. Users
may easily be rendered somewhat pessimistic under such circumstances, and
their view of unavailability may radically deviate from measurable outage
time.

Service type	Target uptime - allowed weekly stops	
	First shift	Other shifts
IMS	97% - 3 stops	n/a
IMS applications	96% - 4 stops	n/a
Test IMS	n/a	n/a
TSO	98% - 2 stops	98% - 1 stop
VSPC	98% - 2 stops	98% - 1 stop
VM/370	98% - 2 stops	98% - 1 stop
Network software	99% - 1 stop	97% - 1 stop
Network hardware	99% - 1 stops	98% - 1 stop

The following IMS applications are measured separately:
Order entry, inventory, maintenance and project control

n/a: Not applicable - either service not run, or no need/possibility
      for measuring available.

The selection of some applications to be measured separately was done
based on the importance of those transactions to the overall service
pattern.

   Figure 14.   Service objectives - Availability

In some cases unavailability is caused by a combination of wrong terminal
handling and non-informative terminal messages. Somebody may be having an
intense conversation with network software, but not be aware of who
they're talking to, and really wanting to use VSPC. This can be overcome
by user education, or by providing a booklet containing the most common
error situations. Another way is to provide more informative software
messages.

All this should be borne in mind when examining the very much simplified
picture in the service agreement, Figure 14.

Some services in the example, like IMS, are not currently run outside
first shift.

Because IMS applications (user perceived transactions) are many - over 200
- a separate record is kept for selected major applications. To the
users, their **application** must be running in order that they should regard
their service as available.

Stops are measured separate from uptime; a high number of small stops can
be more detrimental to user productivity than few, long outages.

What is measured is what is seen, understood and measured by the operations people (or a recording program). Uptime or downtime relate to what
is recorded, and meeting objectives **may** be a sign that the recording mechanism is poor, rather than of excellent performance, if careful management
practices are not followed.

3.2.3 Response time service agreement

Figure 15 shows a tentative service agreement on response times.

Service	Number of responses below:			Average
	2 sec	4 sec	6 sec	resp. sec
IMS applications:				
- group 1	65%	90%	95%	4
- group 2	n/a	60%	80%	6
- group 3	n/a	50%	40%	8
Test IMS	n/a	50%	40%	8
- measured only				
after agreement				
TSO	70%	80%	85%	4
VSPC	90%	95%	99%	1
VM/370	80%	90%	95%	n/a
Network	85%	92%	97%	3
- when measurement				
possible				

Figure 15.   Service objectives - internal response times.

Again, the service objectives concentrate on **internal** measurements, awaiting integrated network data. Response times to the user are made up of
several components, like for availability, Figure 12 on page 40. Some of
these components are difficult to measure, like the network part. Even
when network data are available, they need to be integrated with internal
response time measurements to follow each transaction or application
through its different stages.

Figure 15 states that for instance for IMS group 1 applications - light
and high priority work - 65% of all (primary) transactions should finish
within 2 seconds; 90% should finish within 4 seconds etc. The average
should be below 4 seconds - here an hourly average is meant. If the average was over a longer period, a lower average could be given. Chapter 4
gives a further explanation of terms used and the method of measuring
response times.

The objectives are relatively moderate to enable the centre to meet objectives even after increased loads.

To users, the service agreements shown in Figure 15 may not accurately
reflect their view of their terminal environment. A few 'hang-ups' each
day can destroy their image of the system. In one practical example,
these 'hang-ups' were measured to be in the order of one half minute, but
the user could not know in advance if the system had gone down, if
responses would be repeatedly slow, or what.

Ideally, those 'hang-ups' should be measured for each user. This is possible in IMS by an extension to the Service Level Reporter (references 20
through 22).

However, the computing necessary is rather heavy. An approximation is found by listing responses above 15 seconds for each transaction type.

When these hangups for light IMS transactions are below one percent of the total light transactions, users seem satisfied. Quantifying long response times could be an important addition to service objectives.

All objectives can hardly be met all the time unless the system is heavily overdimensioned for the average load. A 20 percent miss - or 1 day per week - seems reasonable and a statement on the allowable amount of hang-ups ought to be included in service objectives.

The database applications are divided into groups with different response objectives. This has been done based on:

> Resource usage
> Relative importance
> Historical response time

A direct relation between resource usage and response time was not found, and therefore grouping was made partly dependent on what response times had historically been recorded for a certain transaction.

Response times in different application types are sometimes measured differently. In the example on Figure 15 on page 43, IMS and TSO would be measured by SLR, and VM/370 by a 'benchmarking' program. Results from the VM benchmarking program is shown on Figure 44 on page 81. A better form of feedback is by way of the VM predictor program that yields 'real' (internal) response times and loads, see Figure 149 on page 248.

VSPC reports only on 'VSPC service'. This is the real response time when VSPC commands are executed. However, when a system like APL is used, the APL transaction is broken down into constituent VSPC commands. Feedback from a system based on this form of recording is shown on Figure 33 on page 70.

The measurement approach affects the feedback to the users. Of the methods just described, the SLR based recording will provide the most meaningful feedback to the <u>users</u> because it is based on their work and does not involve guesses as to what type of transaction they use at any point in time.

3.2.4 <u>Batch service agreement</u>

Batch service agreements and measurements are difficult to establish. The most <u>efficient</u> way of distributing load, is to let batch absorb what power is left when the interactive systems run adequately.

This may, however, be unacceptable to an impatient programmer submitting a background compile or a budding author waiting for a typed manuscript.

A compromise could be: Let short, high-priority jobs get enough resources to finish within one half hour (input queue + execution time), and give the remaining work specific objectives when <u>necessary.</u>

Consequently: Some batch jobs will have no service objectives and will be executed, if resources are available, during the day or during overnight service - if possible.

Batch objectives could state the percentage of jobs allowed late, or per-centage of days when jobs are allowed to arrive late. Measurements could support this, and also for instance collect information on jobs early. If the number of jobs finished early decreases, it may be a sign that a capacity limit is approached.

A penalty could be introduced for using the system during prime shift. It seems, however, that most users are able to cost justify better turnaround, and the penalty sometimes has no effect unless other actions support moving batch work from first shift. Perhaps more attractive is some sort of positive reward for sending jobs to second or third shift, preferably for unattended execution, with no requirement for operator interference.

3.3 FORECASTING

Service is dependent on load (volume) and resources.   It is an absolute
requirement that load and resource usage should be forecasted accurately.

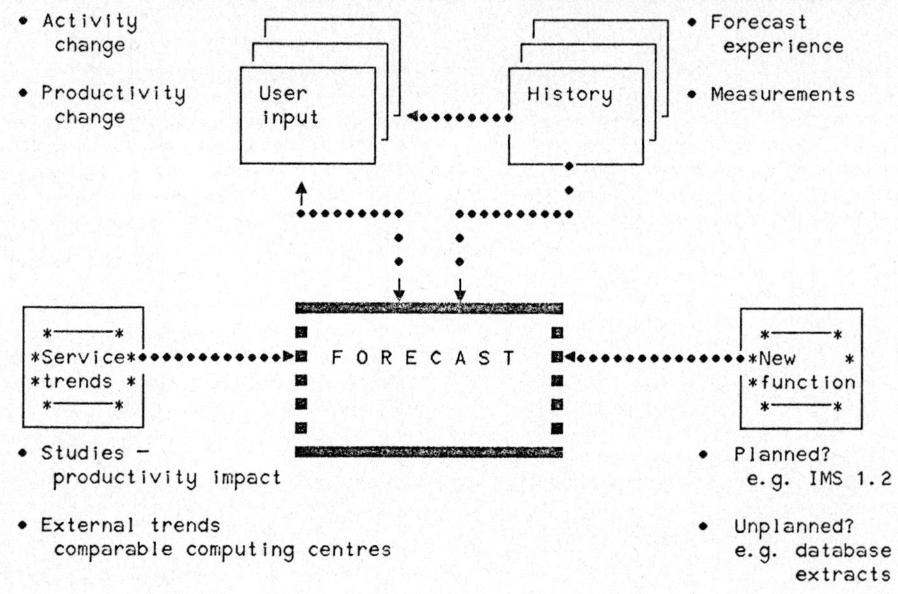

Figure 16.   Forecasting cycle

Figure 16 shows parameters impacting forecasting. Users (should) know
changes in activity level, for instance a forecasted 20% sales volume or
an expansion of the production department by 30 people.   Managers may
push for a productivity increase: certain statements should be finished
before noon; or an inventory status taken every day instead of every week.

The performance control system ought to provide information on past
resource usage and perhaps also experience from earlier planning cycles to
provide a framework for the forecast. Performance controllers may also
overrule the user input if it seems unfeasible and ask for another set of
input data, or provide an alternative.

Both users and forecast coordinators may be aware of new facilities
desired, necessary, or somehow just coming, such as extended colour facilities, access from one terminal to all major applications, database
extracts or whatever.

Both users and forecast coordinators may also be aware of service (usually
improvement) trends that perhaps users will not work without. A productivity impact study may also show that another response time level may be
more optimal for company cost benefit. As both hardware costs and people
salaries change, that 'optimum' also changes, and it may be necessary to

plan with hardware cost and people salaries of serveral years into the future.

To impress the forecasting methodology on people, it is advisable to operate a rigid forecasting structure. This can be reinforced by administrative procedures, for instance sign-offs and specially designed forecast documents. Figure 17 on page 48 and Figure 18 on page 49 show examples of such reporting forms.

Referring to Figure 17 on page 48, monthly average and peak level of resource usage is required, preferably on a **working day** basis.

The peak can be used to plan work that is not yet fixed in time. This work may for instance be shown as peak load for 4 months, when it is only expected to need two months. If a new facility or an extension to a present facility can be described in on-off terms, its resource impact is shown separately on the figure.

If there is a substantial increase in resource usage in a new or an extended facility, a separate form is needed.

Note: the described forecasting forms present the **absolute minimum** requirement. In addition a description of the nature of load changes should be requested. If the experience level of the forecaster is **low, more** data is usually required.

To be adequate in an interactive environment, forecasts should even include IOs, space requirements, real storage and virtual storage.

This suggests a close cooperation between users and the capacity planners for instance using a commonly agreed feedback mechanizm. Figure 51 on page 94 is such a feedback report, that can even provide IOs and lines printed per forecast unit.

Also, the requirements for load in peak periods should be explicit. Are those peak periods daily, weekly, monthly, quarterly or what? Can they be accurately predicted and can other work be removed when they occur? Is the same service as usual necessary?

The current state of computing seems to be such, however, that even processing units are difficult to forecast with reasonable accuracy. A suggested approach is to concentrate on constructing reasonable forecasts in terms of processing units, and estimate other parameters as being proportional.

A first approach for a user would be to forecast the number of **transactions** (IMS, TSO, VSPC) per time unit, for instance month, based on history. This could be converted to processing units based on historical, average CPU usage per transaction (from SLR). That transaction's share of input/output operations can also be found from SLR. The real storage is more difficult to estimate because the transaction uses several components of the IMS system; it would then be reasonable to stipulate that real storage usage by the transaction is proportional to usage of other resources, perhaps letting input/output operations weigh more heavily than processing time.

MVS FORECAST (processing units per average day shift)									
Applic.:	Batch		TSO		IMS		VSPC		GIS
Level:	Ave	Peak	Ave	Peak	Ave	Peak	Ave	Peak	Ave	Peak
Month: Jan										
Feb										
Mar										
Apr										
May										
Jun										
Jul										
Aug										
Sep										
Oct										
Nov										
Dec										
Year:										
New facilit. descr:										
Resource	Ave	Peak	Ave	Peak	Ave	Peak	Ave	Peak	Ave	Peak
Level:										
Extended facilit. descr:										
Resource	Ave	Peak	Ave	Peak	Ave	Peak	Ave	Peak	Ave	Peak
Level:										
Total:										

Figure 17. Forecasting form for MVS data

VM/370 FORECAST (CCU per average day - 24 hrs)									
Usage :	CMS		VS1		DOS		MVS		Other sub.	
Level:	Ave	Peak	Ave	Peak	Ave	Peak	Ave	Peak	Ave	Peak
Month: Jan										
Feb										
Mar										
Apr										
May										
Jun										
Jul										
Aug										
Sep										
Oct										
Nov										
Dec										
Year:										
New facil. describe										
Res.	Ave	Peak	Ave	Peak	Ave	Peak	Ave	Peak	Ave	Peak
Level:										
Extended facil. describe										
Res.	Ave	Peak	Ave	Peak	Ave	Peak	Ave	Peak	Ave	Peak
Level:										
Total:										

Figure 18.   Forecasting form for VM/370 data.

3.4 CONCLUSION

Establishing service objectives is clearly the responsibility of each individual firm, and individual objectives will result.

The brief guidance with examples included here, is only the top of the iceberg of substantial meticulous groundwork, finding objectives that are both:

    Meaningful to the user

    Measurable - and reportable with reasonable expenditure

A common starting point with performance objectives is with users not knowing exactly what they want, a control system that cannot measure what we believe the users want, and cumbersome reporting procedures.

Some of these problems remain in the system described in this book, but most performance control is here automatic, accepted (in the cases referred to) and performed with reasonable expenditure of resources: human and systems.

Work continues in searching for objectives better suited to user requirements, and the effect of improving or reducing services.

Another concern is the quality of user forecasts. In order that service in the future will be acceptable to our users, we first need their assessment of future requirements in terms of service level, facilities and load.

Improved service costs resources, and most corporations are not able to provide excess capacity 'just in case'. The performance control system helps forecasting by providing historical data. Projections from history and knowledge of coming applications have often proved more accurate than user predictions.

In the performance control system described in this book, there is sufficient data to enable the user to specify input in his or her terms, for instance in transactions per month. This can be converted to resource usage by using data from the performance control system. Having then a common basis with the user, it is easier to create an understanding of the importance of subsequent follow-up.

User predictions and history can be combined by providing adequate feedback to users, but skilled user forecasts seem to require a long absorption process. Given time, forecasting can be intergated into the control system, providing more feedback relative to forecasts.

CHAPTER 4

FOLLOW UP ON SERVICE AGREEMENTS

In the evening praise the day
Your wife when she is burned
Your daughter when she is married
Your spear when it has been tried
Ice when you came safely over
Beer when it has been drunk

Hávamál, verse 81
The Older Edda

4.1 INTRODUCTION

4.1.1 Chapter contents

Typical services for a modern, complex computer center are discussed relative to performance, especially response time measurements. To evaluate
response times, load - or volume - of work is necessary. This load can be
expressed in transactions per second, number of active users etc.

The chapter discusses different perceptions of response times and loads,
and how to measure these in common software products.

Experience indicates that to the **user,** response time, availability and
even accessability are not separate concepts, but all aspects on one very
diffuse term: service. This is particularly true for non-EDP trained
users, but even seasoned EDP professionals seem confused as to the direct
source of their frustrations when service is not good.

The chapter shows attempts at merging different aspects of of reports -
availability, response time and help, into one total service report.

4.1.2 Service types

A number of different services can be offered from a complex centre. The
service agreements in Figure 14 on page 42 and Figure 15 on page 43 list
some of them, and in addition, batch can be regarded as a separate flora
of services.

Ideally all (interactive) services in the centre are treated in the same
manner, with batch as a natural extension.

This is difficult to establish. Standard measurement systems are not compatible over the whole range of services, and the users are different in
their demands on the system and hence different in respect to required
feedback.

IMS users may be limited to one or two transaction types - that must run
well for their world to be a happy one. A TSO user may wander over the
total spectrum of interactive offerings, whereas a VSPC user prefers homespun APL programs. To the latter two categories, good average responses
are required, perhaps with emphasis on short tasks.

Because of the rather large differences, it is advisable to create different control systems for each major service or application. These control
systems may be based on the same software and similar methods.

In order to measure the services, the controller should know exactly what
is measured and how that compares with the user's experience of the
system. With current products, intimate systems knowledge is required.
Some of the commonly needed knowledge is outlined in this and the following chapter. In addition, the reader ambitious to establish a performance
control system should supplement with detail studies of both system components and measurement programs (see references).

4.2   THE SERVICE LEVEL REPORTER (SLR)

The name 'Service Level Reporter' indicates SLR's central role in recording and reporting service and following up service agreements.

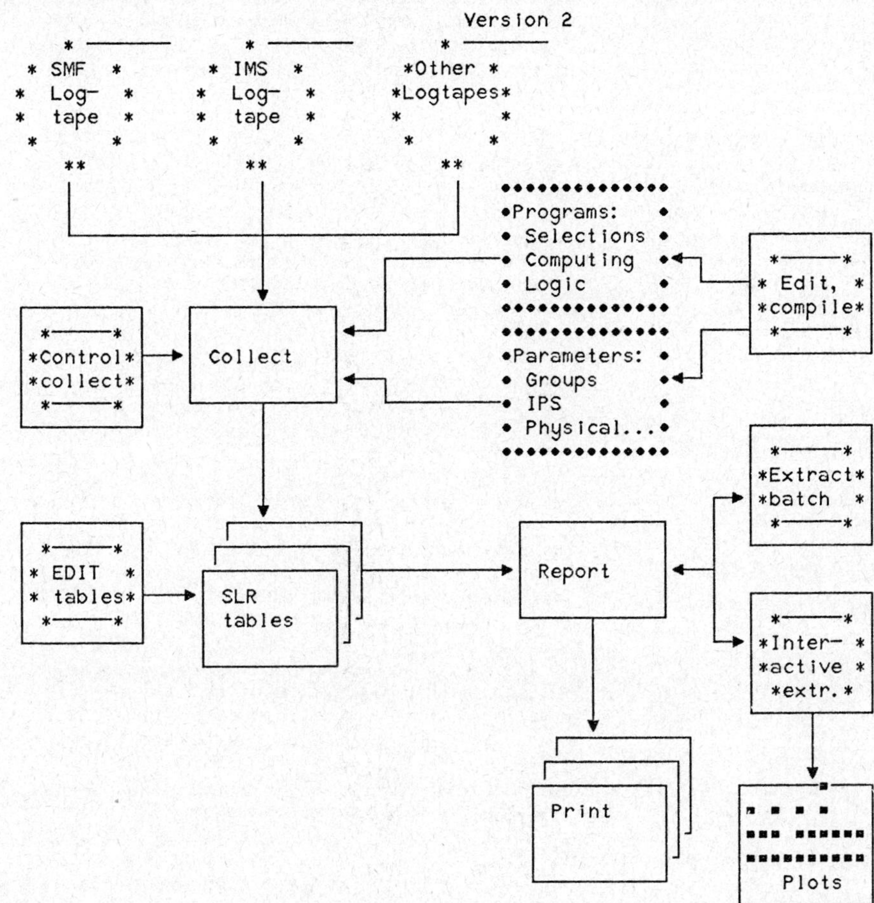

Figure 19.   SLR operational and user interfaces

4.2.1   Operation

As Figure 19 indicates, SLR recording and reporting involves several human
interactions.   Analogous tasks usually have to be planned even when using

other products. The following discussion of SLR can be seen as a general
outline of operation requirements for performance reporting programs.

The main interfaces are shown on Figure 19 on page 53 as terminals:

Start and control collect	The collect jobs are prepared and scheduled. The result is checked for errors. Space is planned (e.g. on MSS). Tables are evaluated for current and future space requirements. Possibly tables are split into short-time and historical databases, giving additional maintenance but faster access for SLR extracts.
Edit and compile Programs and Parameters	The programs describe what data is to be extracted from SMF/IMS, how it is handled and stored in tables. The parameters provide information on the specific computer centre environment, for instance IMS transaction groupings, batch classes (IPS), machine power etc.
Edit tables	The resulting tables may have to be further edited because some recordings are faulty e.g. due to abends. The recording logic may also be changed, and already stored data updated to reflect the new logic.
Extract	This can be done in two major modes: 1: Batch A batch job containing SLR commands is submitted in the usual fashion. 2: Interactive Using the same command syntax, reports can be obtained interactively. Tables can also be displayed as they are stored. A link with GDDM provides colour plot facilities.

In addition, new releases may be introduced, and current releases updated.

4.2.2 Recording

On Figure 20 on page 55, a constructed example of an SLR table is shown.
Like any table, it consists of **columns** and **rows.**

The SLR columns are each reserved for one data item, for instance average
response time. Each row contains one record of the predefined data items.
The **column headings** can be used as a later reference to the data in that
column.

Each row contains one set of recordings for the column items. In
addition, the rows contain totals. Box 1 on Figure 20 on page 55 points
to one such recording.

The columns are divided into **key columns** and **data columns**. They are identical apart from the fact that the key columns can be summed to totals
(the TOT on Figure 20) in addition to straight recorded data. The corresponding total values will naturally be calculated also for data columns.

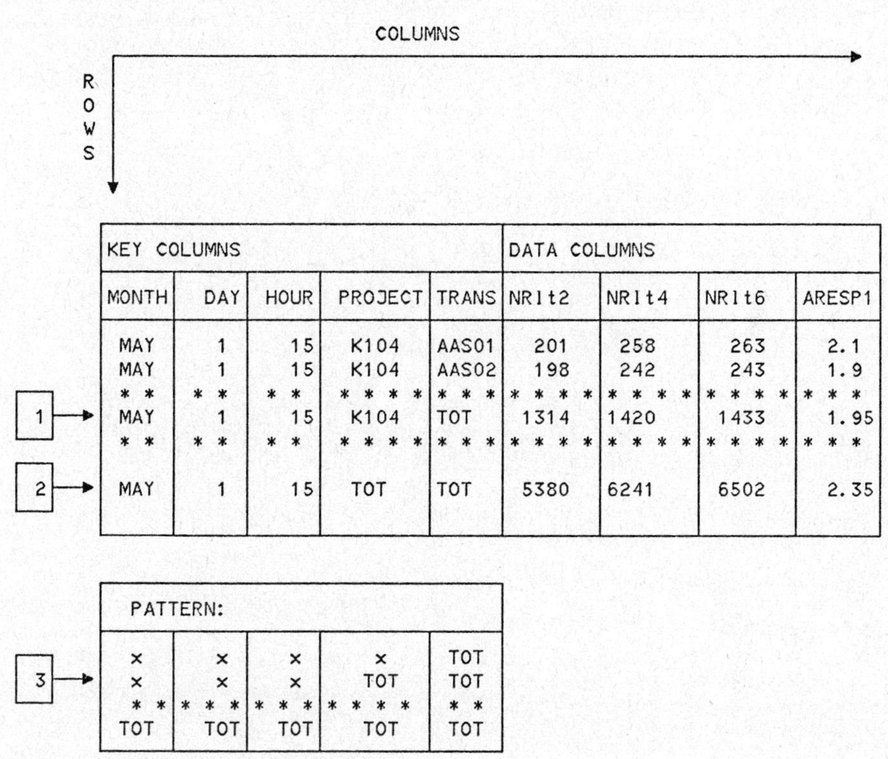

KEY COLUMNS					DATA COLUMNS			
MONTH	DAY	HOUR	PROJECT	TRANS	NRlt2	NRlt4	NRlt6	ARESP1
MAY	1	15	K104	AAS01	201	258	263	2.1
MAY	1	15	K104	AAS02	198	242	243	1.9
* *	* *	* *	* * * *	* * *	* * * *	* * * *	* * * *	* * *
MAY	1	15	K104	TOT	1314	1420	1433	1.95
* *	* *	* *	* * * *	* * *	* * * *	* * * *	* * * *	* * *
MAY	1	15	TOT	TOT	5380	6241	6502	2.35

(Box 1 points to the "MAY 1 15 K104 TOT" row; box 2 points to the "MAY 1 15 TOT TOT" row.)

PATTERN:				
x	x	x	x	TOT
x	x	x	TOT	TOT
* *	* * *	* * *	* * * *	* *
TOT	TOT	TOT	TOT	TOT

(Box 3 points to the PATTERN table.)

PROJECT: The PROJECT responsible for the transaction
TRANS: The TRANSaction measured
NRlt2:   Number of Responses less than 2 seconds
NRlt4:   Number of Responses less than 4 seconds
etc.
ARESP1:   Average RESPonse time 1 (explained later in the chapter)

Figure 20.   SLR table example

The totals can occur for just one key column or for any combination of key
columns.   On Figure 20, box 2 points to an occurrence of totals for the
project K104.   There is also a line for the total of all projects in hour
15 on May 1.

If all combinations of all key data are included, tables may become very
large.

Therefore only some combinations are selected, shown in the PATTERN.   Box
3 shows   that the combination of totals for **all transactions and all projects** is valid.

4.2.3 Command language

Extracts from the SLR tables are requested using the SLR command language.
It is always necessary to specify:

1.   Name of table (e.g. Report IMSR)

2.   Columns selected from that table (e.g. SEL Columns(TRANS ARESP1))

3.   Rows selected for those columns (e.g. SEL Rows(ARESP1>10 and TM)

          This selects for this month (TM) transactions that have longer
          average response than 10 seconds. The lower case characters,
          e.g. ows in Rows, can be omitted.

4.   Output command (e.g. PRINT)

          PRINTs the selected data. They could also be plotted, using for
          example the PRINT CHART command to produce colour output.

Other commands can control print width, print characters, sorting etc.
There is also an EDITing language for tables.

The commands can be included in a batch job. The SLR commands can also be
executed online in a TSO environment. This is necessary if the PRINT
CHART command is to be used. The TSO environment contains a menu that
enables a person possibly unaccustomed to SLR to follow walk-through specifications and thus be introduced to SLR facilities.

See Figure 24 on page 61 and the following for examples.

4.3 RESPONSE TIMES

4.3.1 IMS

A **primary transaction** originates when a user requests a menu screen, when
he or she selects an item from that menu and at exit from the menu. Different menu items are regarded as the same transaction. It is the primary
transaction that the **user** perceives as a transaction.

A transaction may originate another transaction, it may start a batch program or never be finished. These cases are regarded as **secondary transactions.** **Primary and secondary transactions** together add up to the **total
transactions,** that is the **IMS system's** view of the transaction load.

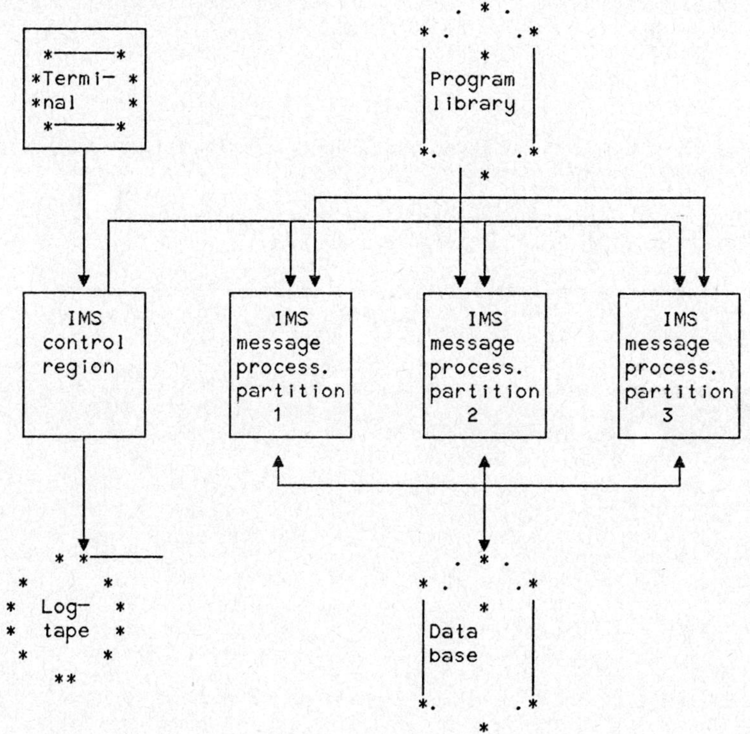

Figure 21.   IMS Transaction Flow

Measuring programs may not differentiate between different types of transactions, and it is therefore important to find out what exactly is
reported. This document is mostly concerned with primary transactions; as
are IMS users.

A transaction originates at a terminal as shown on Figure 21 on page 57
and travels through the communications system to the host computer.
Delays may be incurred in the communications system due to:

     Terminal controller queuing
     Terminal controller handling
     Coding/decoding to line message
     Queuing for lines
     Line delay
     Administration in the communications system
     Handling in the communications controller(s)
     Queuing in the communications controller(s)

In a complex net it may be difficult to establish the exact values for
each of the components, and a simulation or measurement system is therefore important.

Once arrived in the IMS system running in the host computer, the arriving
transaction is (normally) logged on tape or disk to provide restart information.   At the same time, transaction start time is logged. Inquiry
transactions may be specified such that they are not logged because
restart information is not needed. This prevents those transactions from
being analysed by logtape analysis tools, though.

Afterwards, the transaction is queued for a Message Processing Partition
(MPP).

A free MPP selects a transaction or message dependent on which transaction
classes are allowed to run in that region, in which order these classes
are specified, and then priority within each class. The specification of
these parameters is normally done by a systems programmer.

To avoid some hang-ups and to even out queues, each transaction class is
normally defined in at least two regions, and the highest priority transactions are ordered first within the region.

This means that in busy periods, low priority transactions will suffer if
there is not an adequate number of MPPs. Because each MPP costs extra
resources (especially real storage), the tendency is often to limit the
number of MPPs.

The program needed to process the transaction is normally fetched from the
program library that resides on one or more disks. Because some programs
may be quite large, load on the program library is an important parameter
to watch.   See example on Figure 112 on page 186, where the program load
disks (IS1090 and CCBB53) are among the busiest and slowest.

A transaction program can be defined to be always resident in one or more
MPPs.   This is called preloading and offloads the program libraries.
Instead the paging mechanism is more used, because the program's pages can
be stolen between each use.

The balance between preloading and program library residence is difficult
to determine. Low paging load and high program library usage tend to
favour preloading.   However, preloading may be difficult due to virtual
storage restrictions.

The databases usually reside on several disks. The databases are usually
added to and expanded dynamically, and the successful system has to cope
with increasing transaction loads.

Load on database disks is therefore another important parameter to supervise. See example on Figure 112 on page 186.

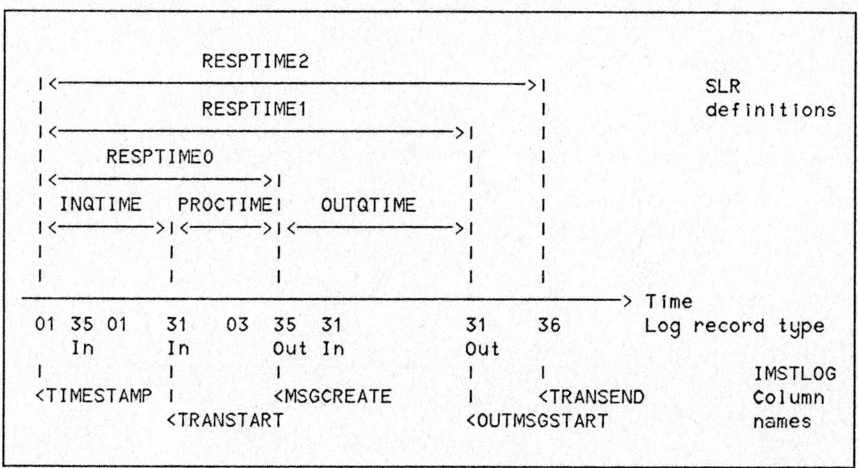

Figure 22.   IMS system events

The start and stop times for different system events are logged and can be
used to analyse the IMS system. Figure 22 shows such records and their
relation to system events as presented by SLR.

To evaluate the meaning of the terms, event definitions are helpful:

Type	Definition
TIMESTAMP	Transaction start time
TRANSTART	Transaction starts in MPP
MSGCREATE	Transaction processing finished
OUTMSGSTART	Output screen sent
TRANSEND	Transaction finished

Note that the output may consist of several screens with manual intervention required.   Therefore RESPTIME2 is a doubtful system measure.
RESPTIME0 provides only IMS internal response times. By subtracting
RESPTIME0 from RESPTIME1 we get some measure of output and networking
delay. The difference between RESPTIME0 and RESPTIME2 is the time to produce and send all screens.

For a one screen message, the three response times should be fairly close.
If they are not, there could be an anomaly in the system.

The 'Log record type' gives the number of the IMS log record created at a
certain event.

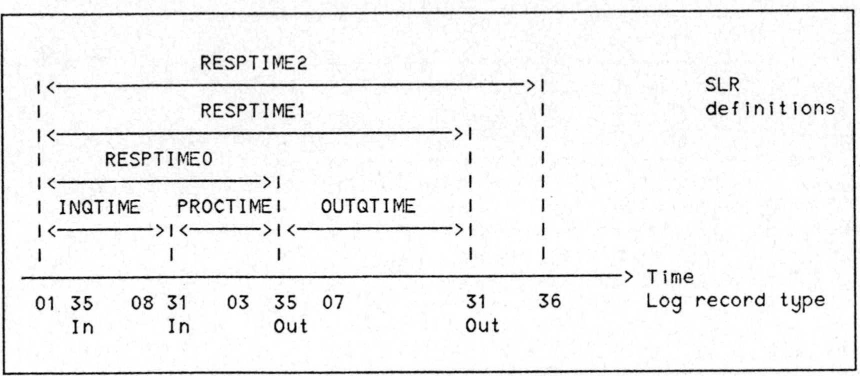

Figure 23.   IMS start and end transaction recording

The record pattern on Figure 23 shows definitions when the transaction is
both the first and the last processed:

Based on these recordings, SLR data are extracted.   However, it is necessary to know exactly what output is obtained.

We may decide that the following are required, related to <u>primary trans-
actions</u> only:

        Average response time
        Number of responses below 2 seconds
        Number of responses below 4 seconds
        Number of responses below 6 seconds
        Number of responses below 15 seconds
        Number of responses above 15 seconds

Figure 24 on page 61 indicates a transaction increase over the year, with
seasonal fluctuations. Tuning activities in April had good effect, but as
nothing further was done over the summer, the system somehow deteriorated.
This is common experience - one likely reason is that there is a subtle
change in workload mixture that loads the ('tuned') system differently.

Note the close connection between total transactions and primary transactions - they increase and decrease in harmony - and between average
response and responses over 15 seconds ('hang-ups').

```
SEL C(MONTH NTRANS PRIM1 PRLT2 PRLT4 PRLT15 PRGT15 ARESP1)
                        NTRANS= Number of transactions
                        PRIM1 = Number of primary transactions
                        PRLT2 = Percent of responses below 2 seconds
                        PRLT4 = Percent of responses below 4 seconds
                        etc.
                        ARESP1= Average RESPTIME1 seconds
SEL R(Y=81 & MONTH¬=TOT) All months in 1981, but not the total
PRINT
```

IMS TRANSACTION STATISTICS

MONTH	NTRANS	PRIM1	PRLT2	PRLT4	PRLT6	PRLT15	PRGT15	ARESP1
	ANTAL	ANTAL	% < 2	% < 4	% < 6	% < 15	% > 15	SEC
JAN	753564	565422	**	**	**	**	**	2.13
FEB	639692	477204	**	**	**	**	**	2.01
MAR	685854	514960	**	**	**	**	**	2.43
APR	726974	595455	54.33	85.11	88.13	95.68	4.32	3.22
MAY	818410	608640	67.02	87.33	89.18	96.67	3.33	2.28
JUN	863425	647948	75.35	90.11	94.44	98.39	1.61	2.34
JUL	809673	601069	76.99	90.88	95.04	98.73	1.27	2.12
AUG	866503	644362	71.22	87.15	92.43	97.94	2.06	2.68
SEP	877966	657908	70.44	87.36	92.75	98.25	1.75	2.52

** Not recorded

Figure 24.   SLR IMS trends

The percentage responses above 15 seconds (the physical number may be 10
or 20 - whatever is regarded as a hang-up), seem directly related to user
satisfaction.   In a complex IMS system hang-ups are difficult to avoid
altogether because the transactions may interfere with each other in various ways. Reducing hang-ups must therefore be carefully planned and needs
careful follow up by for instance SLR.

The asterixes indicate that there may be an experimentation phase till a
generally agreed, programmed and tested implementation of a particular SLR
table is in place.

An example of hang-up recording is shown in Figure 25 on page 62.

Both these reports are tailored for **management** but are interesting even to
other recipients.

Figure 26 on page 63 shows a more **user** oriented report, concentrating on
single applications or transactions, TRANS.

Percentage of responses below the set limits are provided as a direct
feedback on the service agreements (Figure 26 on page 63). The averages
can be recorded over several months to show trends (Figure 27 on page 64).

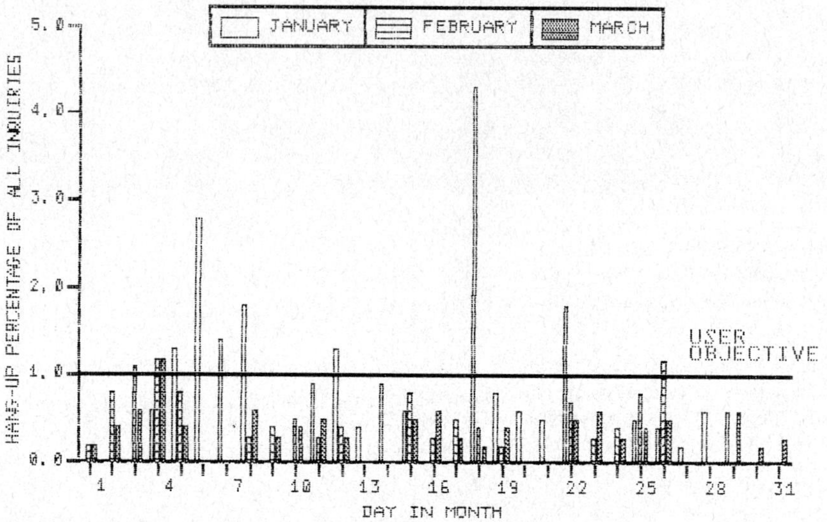

Figure 25.   SLR IMS Responses above 15 seconds.

Recordings from one day or even one week are seldom sufficient proof that
hang-ups are reduced, because they are often highly application dependent
and sensitive to all variations in application load pattern, e.g. month
end peaks.

Trends in the number of primary transactions are shown on Figure 28 on
page 65.   The peaks may be recording errors, that should be edited away.
Investigating July 13 showed that this **was** in fact a highly loaded day -
very interesting to a controller.   Should more resources be allocated, or
should users warn that a peak is imminent? Do users know that such a peak
is likely? In the example, the users knew to a certain extent, and better
communication was established as a result of the report.

Some such peaks will occur whatever the precautions - it is difficult to move time dependent peaks - and capacity planning must consider the extra requirement.

The figure indicates an increase in the number of primary transactions over the first half of 1981. Note that weekends and holidays are not included, and that one particular row in each day column can only contain one letter type - in this case meaning one month. January 1 is a holiday, and the As therefore do not occur in column 1. February 13 is however a Friday, but the Bs do not occur in column 13. February is therefore equal to one of the other months on the 13th, the figure does not say which. A numerical table would give the answer; however we are here interested in **trends,** not any specific day.

```
SEL C(MONTH TR NTRANS PRLT2 PRLT4 PRLT15 PRGT15 ARESP1)
SEL R(Y=81 & TM)                      TM:   This month
PRINT
                                      IMS  TRANSACTION  STATISTICS
```

MONTH	TRANS	I	NTRANS NUMBER	PRLT2 % lt 2	PRLT4 % lt 4	PRLT6 % lt 6	PRLT15 % lt 15	PRGT15 % gt 15	ARESP1 sec
JUL	AAGAT01	I	200	82.78	93.33	97.22	100.00	0.00	1.24
	AOF	I	2040	75.76	81.82	81.82	84.85	15.15	1.48
	CARST01	I	275	72.03	94.07	95.76	99.15	0.85	2.30
	CESIS	I	9535	87.19	93.46	95.59	98.09	1.91	1.67
	CESISED	I	503	---	---	---	---	---	---
	CESISQ	I	22057	64.39	80.65	89.04	97.56	2.44	2.81
	CESISQAL	I	7532	---	---	---	---	---	---
	CESISREP	I	16285	68.53	88.06	94.72	99.30	0.70	1.92
	COMSEC	I	450	58.13	86.64	90.42	97.77	2.23	3.81
	CRELK01	I	1	---	---	---	---	---	---
	CRELT01	I	1222	56.65	79.42	89.84	99.07	0.93	2.70
	CRELV01	I	2	100.00	100.00	100.00	100.00	0.00	0.60
	C15001	I	3180	80.60	88.89	93.95	97.29	2.71	2.93

```
Page:          0001
Date:     81 Jul 15
Time:        13:43:29

Year=81
Month=JUL
```

- The original print was slightly edited -

Figure 26. SLR data for IMS service agreements feedback.

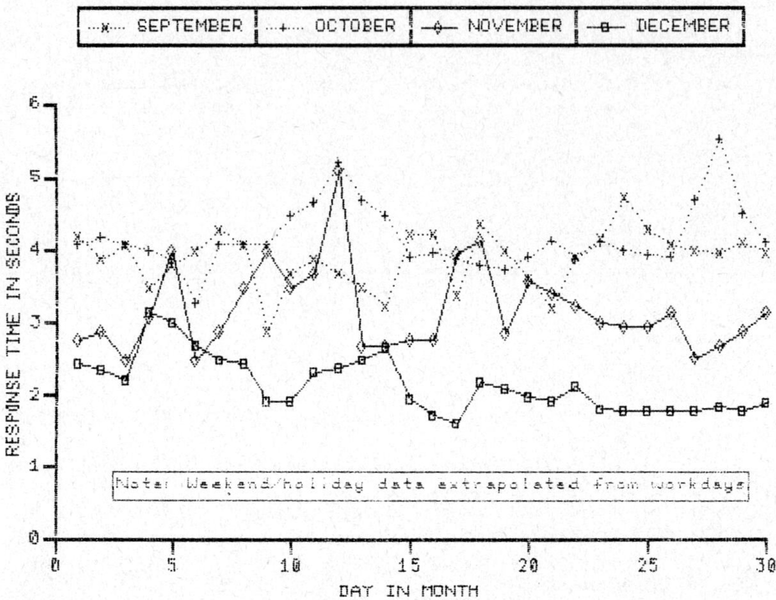

Figure 27.   SLR IMS average response time trend.

```
   Number
   of
   primary
   transactions

        |                      BB
  60000-                       BB
        |                      BB
        |           GG         BB
        |           GG         BB
        |           GG         BB         GG
  50000-            GG         BB         GG
        |           GG         BB         GG
        |           GG         BB         GG
        |           GG         BB         GG
        |           GG         BB         GG
  40000-            GG         BB         GG
        |           GG         BB         GG
        |           GG         FF EE      GG          FF                    DD
        |   DD FF         EE      EE      FF FF EE GG    FF CC        EE EE EE EE DD CC
        |EE DD FF EE HH EE FF DD      HH FF HH DD DD FF CC CC CC EE EE DD FF CC FF
  30000-EE BB DD EE HH AA EE DD BB HH CC BB EE DD FF CC CC CC AA EE DD FF BB FF
        |HH AA BB HH HH AA GG DD CC HH CC AA AA AA FF AA CC BB AA AA DD FF BB GG
        |HH AA BB HH BB HH AA DD CC CC BB AA CC AA DD BB CC BB AA AA DD AA AA GG
        |DD AA BB BB BB BB HH GG AA GG BB AA CC AA AA BB BB BB AA GG AA GG AA GG
        |DD AA BB BB BB BB HH AA AA GG BB AA CC AA AA BB GG BB AA GG AA GG AA GG
  20000-DD AA BB BB BB BB HH AA AA GG BB AA CC AA AA BB GG BB AA GG AA GG AA GG
        |DD AA BB BB AA BB HH AA AA GG BB AA CC AA AA BB GG BB AA GG AA GG AA GG
        |DD AA BB BB AA BB HH AA AA GG BB AA CC AA AA BB GG BB AA GG AA GG AA GG
        |DD AA BB BB AA BB HH AA AA GG BB AA CC AA AA BB GG BB AA GG AA GG AA GG
        |DD AA BB BB AA BB HH AA AA GG BB AA CC AA AA BB GG BB AA GG AA GG AA GG
  10000-DD AA BB BB FF BB HH AA AA GG BB AA CC AA AA BB GG BB AA GG AA GG AA GG
        |DD AA BB BB FF BB HH AA AA GG BB AA CC AA AA BB GG BB AA GG AA GG AA GG
        |DD AA BB BB FF BB HH AA AA GG BB AA CC AA AA BB GG BB AA GG AA GG GG GG
        |DD AA BB BB FF BB HH AA AA GG BB AA CC AA AA BB GG BB AA GG AA GG GG GG
        |DD AA BB BB FF BB HH AA AA GG BB AA CC AA AA BB GG BB AA GG AA GG GG GG
       0-DI-AI-BI-BI-FI-BI-HI-AI-AI-GI-BI-AI-CI-AI-AI-BI-GI-BI-AI-GI-AI-GI-GI-GI
         1  2  3  4  5  6  7  8  9 10 11 12 13 14 15 16 17 18 19 20 21 22 23 24
                                                              DAY------>

   A: JAN    E: MAY       YEAR= 81
   B: FEB    F: JUN       DAY ne TOT
   C: MAR    G: JUL       MONTH ne TOT
   D: APR    H: AUG                    The original report was slightly edited
```

Figure 28.   SLR IMS Primary transaction load trend - daily load

4.3.2   TSO

TSO response times in SLR are calculated from the RMF workload activity
records (type 72). They indicate elapsed time in the MVS system and correspond to the RMF 'average time of end of transaction':

          Transaction elapse time = swapped in time plus
                                    swapped out time plus
                                    long wait time

Thus, what is measured is a system response time, it does not include VTAM
or transmission time.   It is directly a valid measurement for locally
attached TSO terminals, but often **indicative** of response times experienced
by remotely attached users.   See references 24 and 46 for further information.

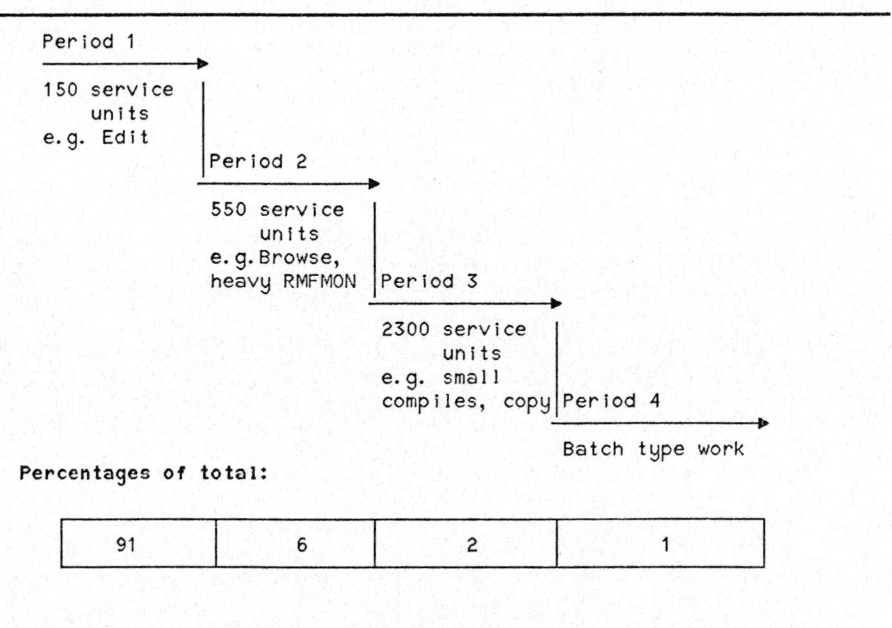

Figure 29.   TSO performance periods

Performance definitions as indicated by Figure 29, divide response times
into four periods dependent on the resource usage of the corresponding TSO
transaction.   However, it' is difficult for a terminal user to estimate
when a transaction/command falls into each category especially as the
definitions may vary.

The command examples and the percentages shown are obtained from relatively small samples.   The figures and examples are valid only in **one particular** environment and only for those workload patterns selected.

They are, however, useful indicators for any TSO environment.

Performance definitions sometimes count real storage residency as part of
service.   Real storage is an important resource, often dimensioning.   The
same TSO command may therefore land in different performance periods
dependent on system paging load.   Four such periods are shown on
Figure 29.

```
                    TSO RESPONSE TIME STATISTICS

SYS  MONTH DAY I   NTRANS PRLT02  PRLT04   PTLT06    ARESP
               I             %        %        %
**************I*******************************************
7033 JAN   TOT I   1728613  76.38   89.80    94.98     2.21
     FEB   TOT I   1832236  74.77   89.80    94.95     2.42
     MAR   TOT I   1628689  74.91   89.74    94.42     2.40
     APR   TOT I   1717639  73.96   89.13    93.60     2.60
     MAY   TOT I   1827819  85.61   93.20    96.05     1.57
     JUN   TOT I   2121668  91.72   94.52    96.81     1.25
     JUL   TOT I   1941916  91.90   94.93    97.32     1.16
```

Figure 30.   SLR TSO response time feedback - monthly

To reflect the users perception of the system, and to find **one number** to
express TSO service, it may be better to present average responses, perhaps divided into categories as for IMS. Figure 30 and Figure 31 show
this.   The different reports show different aspects of control.

Figure 30 shows trends.   There seems to be a significant improvement in
TSO response times, conveniently following heavy adjustment activities in
April and May. Some of those adjustments were primarily intended for IMS,
but as a welcome side effect improved even other services.

```
                    TSO RESPONSE TIME STATISTICS

SYS  MONTH DAY HOUR I    NTRANS  PRLT02   PRLT04   PRLT06    ARESP
                    I              %        %        %
*******************I*******************************************
7033 AUG   4    8 I     4582    92.56    96.42    97.69     0.65
                9 I     7106    91.98    95.55    97.12     1.10
               10 I     7969    91.27    96.39    97.99     0.85
               11 I     6322    90.56    92.90    97.69     1.24
               12 I     5609    93.06    96.83    96.83     0.91
               13 I     7757    94.20    97.38    98.30     0.70
               14 I    10933    92.20    93.04    96.94     1.29
               15 I     8072    64.14    81.55    84.38     3.58
               16 I     5130    94.21    96.59    97.62     1.02
               17 I     2763    96.09    98.66    99.46     0.37
               18 I     2965    94.27    97.67    99.16     0.66
               19 I     2451    93.43    96.49    96.65     0.96
               20 I     2058    95.04    98.45    98.45     0.43
               22 I      489    98.77    99.39    99.39     1.29
               23 I      460    95.22    99.35   100.00     0.32
```

Figure 31.   SLR TSO response time feedback - hourly

The TSO response time development, is expressed as a single number. Even
if this number is the average on a monthly basis, it **seems** to reflect user
experience of the system. A fluctuation of a half second in the average
monthly response time recorded meant the difference between what the user

perceived as 'horrible' response times, and acceptable responses.   Mostly
this was found to be due to better responses of long/heavy commands.   Figure 151   on page 249 shows in colour the development of TSO monthly
response times for each of three processors.

TSO responses are presented to SLR as (e.g. 15 minute) samples, and this
is the basis for the displayed averages.   Therefore the averages do not
directly reflect **user** experience.   Still they provide an indication of
system behaviour towards the user.   Percentiles are also wrong for the
same reason, but still give a fair indication of any tendency.

Figure 31   on page   67 shows the situation for one day.   Note the significant variations both in the number of transactions in one hour, and the
response time differences.

The hour 14 shows long response times. This is actually the time between
1400 and 1500, and includes some of the peak period that normally occurs
around 1500 hours.   Another period of prolonged response is between 2200
and 2300 hours.   At that time we can assume that all TSO activity stems
from operations.   The prolonged responses may occur because 2200 hours is
peak time for batch.   More likely, the longer response is due to a breakdown between 2100 and 2200; there is no TSO recorded during this period.

4.3.3   VSPC

To evaluate a VSPC environment, it is important to understand how VSPC is
implemented under MVS.   Figure 32 on page 69 shows the overall aspects of
the virtual storage implementation.

VSPC (main) is the address space taking care of logons and logoffs.   When
a user logs on, the programs in this address space check userid and pass-
word, and selects a dependent address space where the user can run.

The selection criteria are not clearly described in accessible literature,
including the system programmer's guide (1981).   It **seems** to work as follows: The lowest id address space where the user fits, assuming space for
copy etc., is chosen.   In this way the address spaces are filled up from
the lowest (id).

When not enough space can be found in any address space to allocate a
logged on user, VSPC service is refused.   Because the maximum number of
expected address spaces must be allocated at system startup time, it is
necessary to estimate this number reasonably accurately.

One method would be to allocate a large number of address spaces.
However, this needs extra space in virtual storage (CSA, SQA), thus limiting the virtual storage for user address spaces.

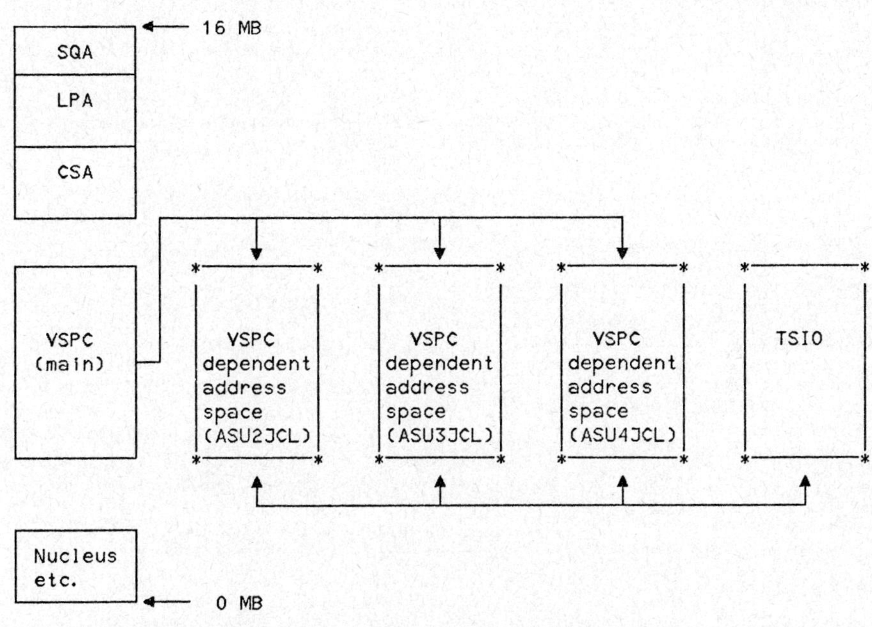

Figure 32.   VSPC virtual storage implementation

Virtual storage in MVS is used for:

      1. Nucleus e.g. paging routines and configuration
      2. SQA (system queue area) for virtual storage tables
      3. LPA (link pack area) for frequently used routines
      4. CSA (common service area) for communication between
         address spaces.

Even without further knowledge of MVS, it can be stipulated from the above
list that virtual storage need increases with system complexity and performance requirements.

VSPC uses: SQA for address space control blocks
            LPA for VSPC modules, compilers & similar.
            CSA for inter address space communication

Whatever remains of 16MB maximum virtual storage can be allocated to each
user address space. In the user address spaces, space is set aside for
control blocks and for compilers (that may reside in LPA but this does not
improve the virtual storage situation)

Tests indicate that in a complex environment roughly one fourth of the
user address spaces for VSPC is the net allocatable to users.

Having successfully logged on, the user can apply basic VSPC commands that deals with the library and the environment.

To do programming or to execute programs, the user enters a **foreground** environment, for instance APL.

Under the foreground processor, **auxiliary processors** may be called, for instance disk read/write or fullscreen edit under APL.

Currently (1981) VSPC records the response time for a **VSPC service**. For a user executing VSPC commands, this corresponds to response time as experienced in TSO or CMS.

VSPCD
START DATE
1 6 81

TRANSACTIONS RESPONSE PER HOUR (MS)										
DATE	1		2		3		4		5	
HOURS	TRAN	RESP	TRAN	RESP	TRAN	RESP	TRAN	RESP	TRAN	RESP
9-10	54	277	4184	796	3442	652	3733	270	3996	217
10-11	4232	333	5482	703	6084	711	3828	592	3980	279
11-12	4908	554	4676	379	4275	441	4354	441	3581	433
12-13	3279	256	4490	404	2794	305	5446	290		
13-14	3942	445	4381	651	2444	382	6419	395		
14-15	4804	287	7349	702	5493	404	9052	287		
15-16	4644	388	5433	589	6327	380	5319	444		
16-17	3373	373	4079	313	2015	295	2855	333		
TOTAL	29236	364	40074	567	32874	446	41006	382	11557	116
PAGES PER SECOND	26		45		33		31		30	

NUMBER OF HOURS WITH RESPONSES OVER 1 SECOND				
THIS WEEK	0	0	0	0

NUMBER OF HOURS WITH RESPONSES OVER 1 SECOND		
LAST MONTHS: APR	MAY	JUN
4	2	0

Figure 33.   VSPC transaction report

However, a user running for instance APL or BASIC under VSPC will still be recorded for the time to perform **VSPC services** that does **not necessarily** correspond to the time from entering a transaction/command till the output appears.

It is doubtful whether VSPC 'response times' are meaningful to the user. Empirically, they provide a good indication on how well the system is run-

ning: average   hourly   response   times   over 1 second indicate problems.
Either overload conditions or anomalies exist.

To   produce reports, it is necessary to define special 'report groups' for
VSPC.   These   report   groups could be, as in our case, overall groups for
VSPC,   and   one report group for each department or external user of VSPC.
A sample output from the corresponding APL report program is shown in Fig-
ure 33 on page 70, and online display is presented in Figure 54 on page
98.   The latter half of June 5 is a holiday - the Danish constitution day.

See Figure 46 on page 84 for an example intergrating response times into a
total service report.

The exceptions recorded in Figure 33 on page 70 constitute an important
aspect of service recording.   The number of hours where service was over 1
second could be an item in the service agreement, and followed continually
- see Figure 34.

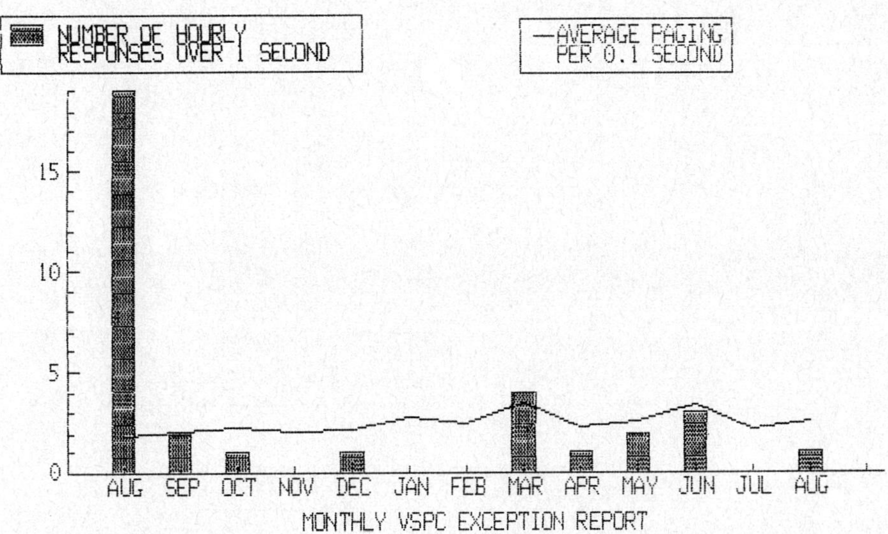

Figure 34.   VSPC exception report

4.3.4 Batch

Overall batch service is shown on Figure 35 on page 72.

```
REPORT JOBSTAT
SEL COL(MONTH TOT_JOBS FAILED_JOBS AVG_CPU LOST_CPU AVG_TAT AVG_EXCP -
DISK_MOUNTS TAPE_MOUNTS)
SEL ROWS(YESR=81 AND SYS=TOT AND MONTH¬=TOT)
PRINT
```

BATCH
PERFORMANCE CHARACTERISTICS

MONTH	TOT_JOBS	FAILED_JOBS %	AVG_CPU MINUTES	LOST_CPU %	AVG_TAT MINUTES	AVG_EXCP NUMBER	DISKM NUMBER	TAPEM NUMBER
JAN	23735	8.3	0.40	18.1	3.52	7855	228	11123
FEB	19976	8.7	0.50	13.4	2.63	7939	139	8230
MAR	23606	8.0	0.45	12.3	5.28	7531	338	12223
APR	23599	7.9	0.43	11.4	5.38	7712	348	15933
MAY	25995	6.9	0.44	7.6	7.38	7986	388	16783
JUN	35288	5.9	0.42	7.3	5.16	7446	233	14322
JUL	30155	5.8	0.42	5.8	5.48	7558	211	11232
AUG	28633	6.5	0.43	0.2	7.53	5667	198	10322
SEP	33633	6.8	0.49	12.9	5.22	7111	99	11238
OCT	33480	6.6	0.47	0.1	8.30	7403	78	12342
NOV	35585	6.2	0.36	11.5	8.21	6180	34	12937

```
TOT_JOBS:      Total number of batch type jobs
FAILED_JOBS:   Failed batch jobs (having abend code)
AVG_CPU:       Average allocated problem program time
LOST_CPU:      TCB time lost due to failure (among FAILED_JOBS)
AVG_TAT:       Average time from job read to job 'printed'
AVG_EXCP:      Average number of EXCP per job (IMS is also a 'batch' job)
               EXCP=EXecute Channel Program=a logical I/O request
DISKM:         Total disk usage - not necessarily disk mounts
TAPEM:         Total tape usage - not necessarily tape mounts
```

The data and the layout have been edited

Figure 35.   SLR batch management report

Tape mounts show the effect of an MSS installation during the first half year.

The report gives raise to a number of questions. Have the percentage failed jobs really gone down, and why? Why is there almost no lost CPU in AUG and OCT? Is there a downward trend in the number of EXCP?

Currently disk and tape mounts are not correctly represented. A tape or disk needed in several steps will be recorded as needing a mount for each step even if this is not physically true. The value can be used for a rough overview, though.

A closer analysis usually means an investigation per job class.

On Figure 36, a batch job is assumed to go through three stages. First the job is read through the **Reader**. This is a JES defined reader program, reading possibly from a physical card reader, but currently usually reading the job cards and data from previously created data sets. Thus the time to read the data on Figure 37 on page 74 is normally insignificant, and there is no queuing registered. Reader time includes time to interpret and syntax check submitted job control statements.

Next the job is selected by an **initiator** set up with the job's class, when one such initiator runs and is free. Initiators are started by the operators, according to specifications by the operations planner(s). Each initiator runs in a separate address space. One initiator can be set up with several classes. Jobs are always selected for the highest priority first. If there are no jobs with the highest priority class, jobs with the second highest class are requested, and so forth. Allocation of devices takes place in JES2 after the job has been started in an initiator; in JES3 it is done before.

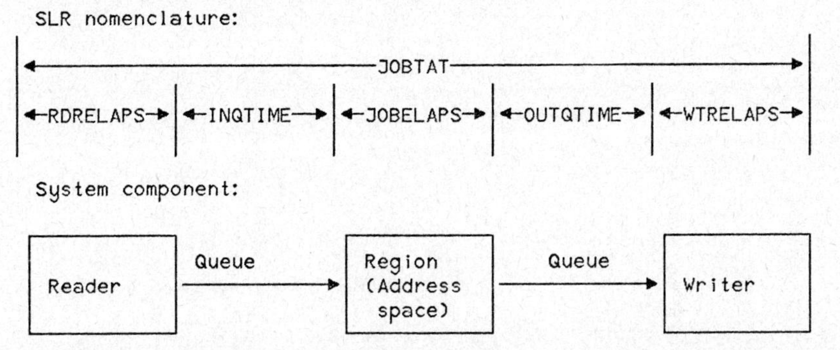

Figure 36.   Batch SLR nomenclature related to system components

After the job is finished, it is written by a **JES writer**. Often this is to a (TSO) dataset on disk only, requiring no printer action.

Jobclass 5 as followed on Figure 37 on page 74, contains text processing jobs. Some OUTQTIMES are very long. In the same connection we note that WTRELAPS time is 0 on all but one of the jobs.

This structure is quite normal in an interactive environment. The users route the output to some TSO dataset, and ask MVS to HOLD it there till they have time to inspect it. The job is not considered finished until the output is released and printed, or - most likely - purged.

Queuing can occur before the initiator, and the job can take long even after having been selected by an initiator. These are the two major parameters to investigate (INQTIME and JOBELAPS). However, to search for anomalies, all components are suspects.

To the user of traditional EDP, total turnaround most interesting: JOBTAT. This assumes that the job is queued, processed and printed like in the good old batch days. If a large proportion of all jobs are not printed,

but held,   the JOBTAT statistics is misleading, and the JOBELAPS time is
more interesting, possibly supplemented by INQTIME.

INQTIME   is misleading where operators start (production) jobs **before** they
are expected to execute, HOLD them till execution time and then RELEASE
them.   INQTIME includes the HOLD time.

Due to the large and inhomogeneous volume of batch work in many computing
centres, exception reports are suitable for user feedback.   The report can
conveniently be   concentrated on user class assuming that each user class
represents a different type of service.

An example of such a report is presented on Figure 38 on page 75.   Jobs in
class J with JOBELAPS over 1800 seconds are selected.

There are relatively few jobs taking over one half hour - a good result.
The few jobs shown all have a low CPUTIME (problem program time).   Consequently execution time should be short.   On August 20 there was a problem
- perhaps high priority service did not leave processing power for batch
jobs?   The service pattern can be found on Figure 56 on page 102 and Figure 57 on page 103

```
SEL C(JELAPSESTART JOBNAME RDRELAPS INQTIME JOBELAPS -
OUTQTIME WTRELAPS JOBTAT)
SEL R(JOBCLASS='5')
PRINT
```

JELAPSESTART TIME	JOBNAME	RDRELAPS SEC	INQTIME SEC	JOBELAPS SEC	OUTQTIME SEC	WTRELAPS SEC	JOBTAT SEC
08:48:03.72	IS20JUNP	1.14	2	52	430	---	485
08:55:41.07	IS20JUNQ	0.33	6	69	10172	---	10247
09:02:39.89	IS20JUNR	1.37	1	42	9790	---	9834
09:23:12.20	IS20JUN	---	---	2	10	---	---
09:35:27.44	IS20LEJZ	0.16	4	21	82281	66	82305
10:29:51.79	IS20JUN	144.14	2	7	15	---	167
10:27:03.78	IS20JUN	---	---	3	22	---	---
10:27:49.68	IS20JUN	---	---	4	13	---	---
10:30:00.24	IS20JUN	---	---	2	20	---	---
10:38:24.23	IS20LEUJ	0.75	2	46	82264	---	82313

The report was slightly edited

  Figure 37.   SLR batch detail report

```
SEL C(TIMES JOBNAME JOBCLASS CPUTIME JOBELAPS CC NTAPE)
SEL R(JOBCLASS=J & JOBELAPS>1800)
PRINT

JELAPSESTART              JOBNAME  JOBCLASS   CPUTIME JOBELAPS CC   NTAPE
DATE      TIME                                SEC     SEC
**********************************************************************
81  AUG 06 19:10:09.68    IS10JEBB J         4.68    5356 0000      0
81  AUG 07 12:48:11.94    IS10BFRO J         1.88    2219 0000      0
81  AUG 20 10:20:09.30    IS10MSK1 J         4.22    1896 0000      0
81  AUG 20 10:51:53.57    IS10RVN5 J         0.98    1958 0016      0
81  AUG 20 14:07:21.68    J100G129 J         4.81    4125 0000      2
81  AUG 20 15:16:08.89    J100GMSK J         4.26    4115 0000      0
```

The report was slightly edited

    Figure 38.   SLR batch exception report

The report contains completion codes (CC - 0000 means OK), and number of
tapes mounted (NTAPE).   The listed class J contains GIS (Generalized
Information System) jobs.   An objective could be to give less than one
half hour turnaround (JOBELAPS) on the majority of the terminal based
jobs. The table then represent misses on this - i.e. very few in August.

GIS is a typical **end user tool**. This means that users, without much data
processing experience can easily knit together a powerful information
tool.   This is good for the centre's service image. On the other hand,
the knitting may not be done in a manner primarily considering system performance.   GIS and similar types of jobs therefore often need special surveillance.

The above remark has been include because end user tool develop rapidly,
and will soon be a normal - and large - workload for any computing centre.

Figure 39 on page 76 shows average elapse time for some selected jobclasses during parts of day and night shift.   There is a problem with class A
turnaround at 1000 hours. There could be a hangup on class A's machine
(see problem reports). The delay could also occur because there was suddenly a burst of jobs in class A (see SLR frequency report) or the job(s)
in class A exceeded their allotted time (see SLR exception report).

Class J has long turnaround at 1900 hours, but at that time day rules for
class J do not apply, and long jobs may have been submitted.

Class F has quite predictably longer turnaround than class A.

When comparing SLR (=SMF) elapse and CPU times with those obtained on job
outputs, slight differences are often encountered. These differences are
due to the recording mechanism, and have negligible influence on overall
statistics.

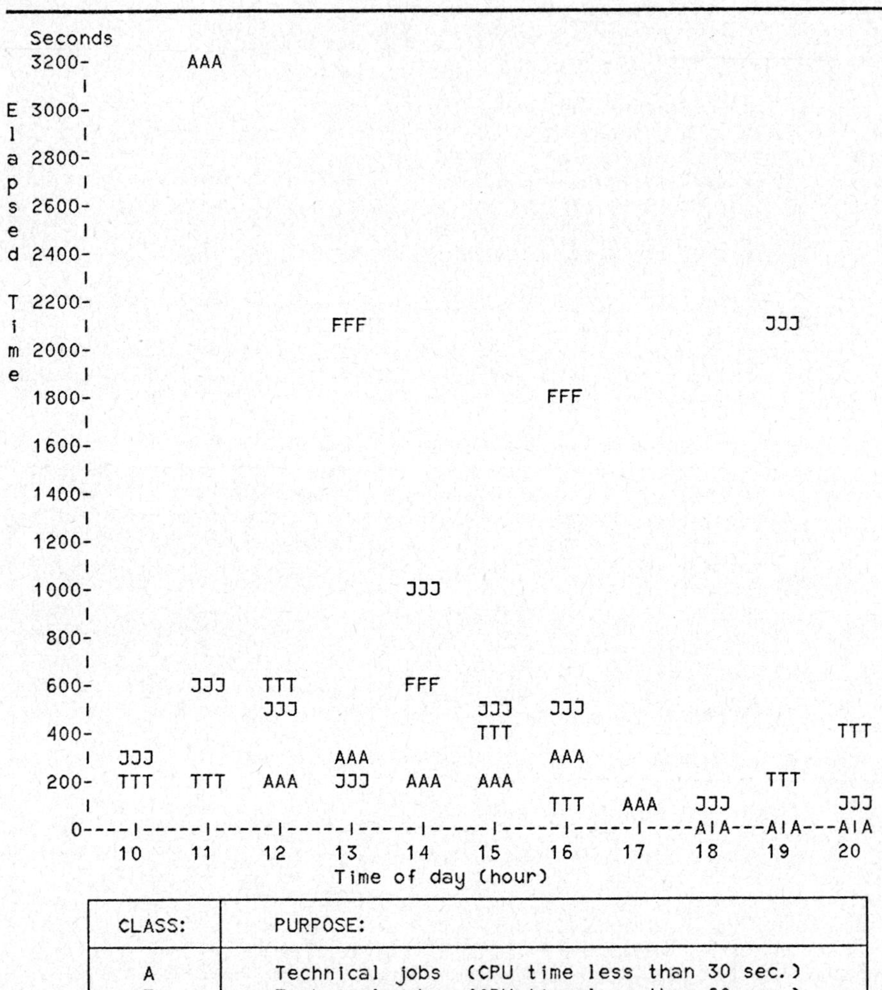

CLASS:	PURPOSE:		
A	Technical jobs	(CPU time less than 30 sec.)
F	Technical jobs	(CPU time less than 60 sec.)
J	GIS	(CPU time less than 30 sec., day)
F	Programming	(CPU time less than 30 sec.)

Figure 39.   SLR batch elapsed time for selected jobclasses

4.4 COMMUNICATION NETWORK

A (data communication) network is the set of communication link(s) that
can transfer data between the user at a terminal and a requested application. The network consists of hardware and software. Normally the network
consists of several links and nodes - defined by hardware or software or
both. The physical and logical implementation of the network should however be of little concern to the user; the network merely serves as a
'delivery vehicle' for data, as indicated on Figure 40.

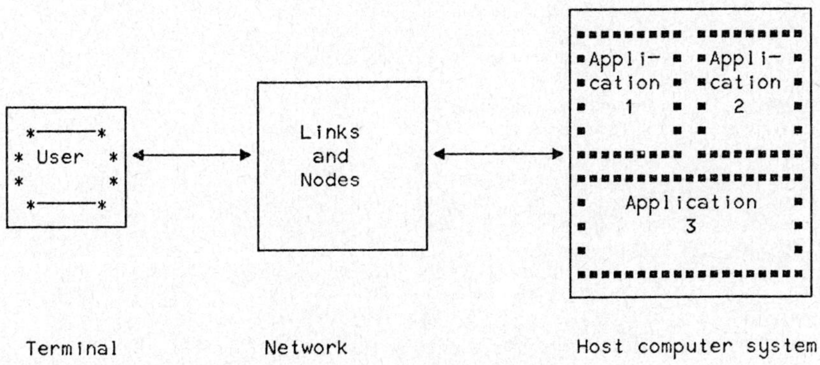

Figure 40. Communication network - logical placement

Some performance analysis programs for networks are described in chapter
2. Some idea on what to expect from such programs (NPA in the example)
can be derived from Figure 41 on page 78.

From Figure 41 on page 78 we may deduce that the 3705 with NCPA, despite
having a CPU percentage of 15 has slowed down (= total hang up during half
the measurement period (57/2=23.5 seconds). This is due to buffer shortage. According to the figure, slowdown starts when 48 buffers are left,
and we are here down to 38 buffers.

Buffer shortage may occur because the 3705 has insufficient storage or/and
because there is a sudden burst of error messages.

NPA in total presents a mixture of secondary and tertiary performance
indicators.

```
          **   NETWORK PERFORMANCE ANALYZER **
   10:11:52                DISPLAY RESPONSE                    05/08/79
NCPA  NCP    00.12  % CPU UTIL=15  % IN SLD= 50 CHHLDQ= 24  CHINTQ= 10
      NCP BUFFERS   FREE= 80  HIGH= 94  LOW= 38  MAX= 255 SLD LIMIT= 48


NAME TOT    MIN.SC OUTQ MSG/M CH/S PLN% SLN% PLL/M %NEG ERRS REMSG RECHR


bsc25 LINE  00.57    10   67   190  31  NONE 101    83    8    7   1280
SDLC1 LINK  00.57    10   67   190  21  NONE 101    83    8    7   1280
NPALI LINK  00.57    10   67   190           101    83    8    7   1280
```

Explanation:

```
CPU UTIL:     3705 CPU utilization
% IN SLD:     Percent of time with 3705 slowdown (due to overload)
CHHLDQ:       Channel hold queue length
CHINTQ:       Channel intermediate queue length

NAME:         Resource and type
TOT:          Number of records
MIN/SC:       Interval size in minutes and seconds
OUTQ:         Resource outbound queue length
MSG/M:        Messages per minute
CH/S:         Characters per second
PLN%:         Primary line utilization percent
SLN%:         Secondary line utilization percent (not if bisynch)
PLL/M:        Polls per minute
%NEG:         Negative poll percent
ERRS:         Temporary error count
REMSG:        Retransmit count
RECHR:        Retransmit byte count
```

Figure 41.   NPA display sample (adapted from reference 37)

The logical structure on Figure 10 on page 31 conveys that in future systems (NSRS), data will be collected from different relevant sources, and
load and availability data can be provided **per application,** using this
system that is already available; however two components, VAMP and NSRS
are (1981) only for IBM internal use.

To obtain response times, one can use the equivalent of another IBM internal product, a Canadian system, TRMS , that uses an IBM series 1 minicomputer to gather response statistics.   Response data are planned to be
available both online and historically.

4.5 AVAILABILITY

4.5.1 Service feedback report

```
*--------------------------------------------------------------------*
I ROLLING AVERAGE FOR WEEK 8126 TO 8135      I     QUARTERLY AVERAGE   I
I                    +===============================================I
I (XX) = OBJECTIVE   I AVAILABILITY I  STOPS  I 1. Q I 2. Q I 3. Q I 4. Q I
I===================================================================I
I IMS                I  97,3 % (97)  I 1,7 (3) I 94,4 I 97,8 I ---- I ---- I
I-------------------------------------------------------------------I
I Network softw.      I  99,1 % (98)  I 1,5 (3) I 96,6 I 99,3 I ---- I ---- I
I-------------------------------------------------+-----------------I
I MVS A ( 3033 UP )   I  97,6 % (98)  I 0,8 (2) I 1.  Q = 8051 - 8111   I
I-----------------------------------------------I 2.  Q = 8112 - 8124   I
I TSO A               I  97,4 % (98)  I 0,9 (3) I 3.  Q = 8125 - 8138   I
I-----------------------------------------------I 4.  Q = 8139 - 8150   I
I MVS B (168 UP)      I  99,9 % (98)  I 0,4 (2) I                       I
I-----------------------------------------------+-----------------I
I TSO B               I  99,6 % (98)  I 0,9 (3) I EXCLUDED WEEKS :      I
I-----------------------------------------------I IMS/Net :             I
I VM    ( 158 MP )    I  99,1 % (98)  I 1,6 (2) I MVS/TSO :             I
I-----------------------------------------------I                       I
I VSPC  ( 3033 UP )   I  99,2 % (98)  I 1,3 (2) I                       I
*--------------------------------------------------------------------*
```

Figure 42.   Management availability report

In Figure 42, the rolling average is taken for the 10 last weeks recorded.
The rolling average is just one example of a presentation technique, with
drawbacks(e.g. non-specific) and advantages (e.g. compact).   Most parameters in Figure 14 on page 42 are reported in the figure.   IMS details are
provided in a separate report similar to Figure 43 on page 80.

4.5.2 Detail reports

Figure 43 on page 80 shows a detailed report for the network part of the
system.   The centre is connected to two centres abroad, and the traffic to
the MVS systems is routed through two 3705 communications controllers.

Figure 44 on page 81 shows the central system in more detail with major
services apart from IMS that is given a separate, detailed report not
shown here.

Including VM response times is a step towards a more complete status
report shown on Figure 46 on page 84.

```
    C C C          A V A I L A B I L I T Y   S U R V E Y              C C C

                      WEEK:   8128   ( 810706 - 810710 )

*------------------------------------------------------------------------------*
 |   1981      |  VTAM  |  NCPF  |  NCPG  | CONCPH | CONENG | CONHOL |
 |-------------|--------|--------|--------|--------|--------|--------|
 | 10-WEEK     |        |        |        |        |        |        |
 | AVER.AVAIL %|  99,9  |  99,9  |  99,9  |  99,9  |        |        |
 | OBJECTIVE  %|  98,0  |  98,0  |  98,0  |  98,0  |        |        |
 | AVER. STOPS |   0,2  |   0,2  |   0,2  |   0,4  |        |        |
 | OBJECTIVE   |    2   |    2   |    2   |    3   |        |        |
 |-------------|--------|--------|--------|--------|--------|--------|
 |             |        |        |        |        |        |        |
 |    MONDAY   | 100,0  | 100,0  | 100,0  |  99,7  |  74,7  |  99,7  |
 |    TUESDAY  | 100,0  | 100,0  | 100,0  | 100,0  | 100,0  | 100,0  |
 |    WEDNESDAY| 100,0  | 100,0  | 100,0  | 100,0  | 100,0  | 100,0  |
 |    THURSDAY | 100,0  | 100,0  | 100,0  | 100,0  | 100,0  | 100,0  |
 |    FRIDAY   | 100,0  | 100,0  | 100,0  | 100,0  | 100,0  | 100,0  |
 |             |        |        |        |        |        |        |
 | WEEK  AVAIL | 100,0  | 100,0  | 100,0  |  99,9  |  94,9  |  99,9  |
 |             |        |        |        |        |        |        |
 | NUMB. STOPS |   -    |   -    |   -    |    1   |    1   |    1   |
 |=============|========|========|========|========|========|========|
 | PLAN HOURS  | 55,00  | 55,00  | 55,00  | 55,00  | 55,00  | 55,00  |
 | STOP HOURS  |  0,00  |  0,00  |  0,00  |  0,03  |  2,78  |  0,03  |
 | AVAIL HOURS | 55,00  | 55,00  | 55,00  | 54,97  | 52,22  | 54,97  |
 |-------------|--------|--------|--------|--------|--------|--------|
 | MTBF        | -----  | -----  | -----  | 27,48  | 26,10  | 27,48  |
 |-------------|--------|--------|--------|--------|--------|--------|
 | MTTR.       | -----  | -----  | -----  |  0,03  |  2,78  |  0,03  |
 | OBJECTIVES  |        |        |        |  0,50  |        |        |
 |-------------|--------|--------|--------|--------|--------|--------|
 | MAX. STOP   |  ----  |  ----  |  ----  |  0,03  |  2,78  |  0,03  |
*------------------------------------------------------------------------------*
 |  DAY     |   PERIOD     |   APPL.   | C |           REASON              |
 |----------|--------------|-----------|---|-------------------------------|
 | MONDAY   | 08.40-11.27  | CONENG    | S | AFTER BREAKDOWN IN            |
 |          |              |           |   | INTERNATIONAL CENTRE.         |
 |          | 11.25-11.27  | CONCPH    | S | CON STOPPED FOR SAME REASON   |
*------------------------------------------------------------------------------*
NCPF    : Network Control Program in 3705 F.
NCPG    : Network Control Program in 3705 G.
CONCPH  : Copenhagen network concentrator
CONENG  : English network concentrator
CONHOL  : Dutch network concentrator
MTBF    : Mean Time Between Failures
MTTR    : Mean Time To Repair
```

Figure 43.   Availability report - network

```
WEEK:  8128  ( 810706 - 810710 )
PRIMARY SERVICE PERIOD : 8.00-19.00
*---------------------------------------------------------------------*
I    1981      I MVS A  I TSO A  I MVS B  I TSO B  I VM/370 I  VSPC  I
I--------------I--------I--------I--------I--------I--------I--------I
I 10-WEEK      I        I        I        I        I        I        I
I AVER.AVAIL%  I  99,9 I   99,8 I   99,8 I   99,4 I   99,1 I   98,3 I
I OBJECTIVE    I  98,0 I   98,0 I   98,0 I   98,0 I   98,0 I   98,0 I
I AVER. STOPS  I   0,3 I    0,4 I    0,6 I    1,0 I    1,0 I    1,4 I
I OBJECTIVE    I     2 I      3 I      2 I      3 I      2 I      2 I
I--------------I--------I--------I--------I--------I--------I--------I
I              I        I        I        I        I        I        I
I     MONDAY   I 100,0 I  100,0 I   98,5 I   96,5 I  100,0 I   92,1 I
I     TUESDAY  I 100,0 I  100,0 I  100,0 I  100,0 I  100,0 I  100,0 I
I     WEDNESDAYI 100,0 I  100,0 I  100,0 I  100,0 I  100,0 I  100,0 I
I     THURSDAY I 100,0 I  100,0 I  100,0 I  100,0 I  100,0 I  100,0 I
I     FRIDAY   I 100,0 I  100,0 I  100,0 I  100,0 I  100,0 I  100,0 I
I              I        I        I        I        I        I        I
I WEEK  AVAIL  I 100,0 I  100,0 I   99,7 I   99,3 I  100,0 I   98,6 I
I              I        I        I        I        I        I        I
I NUMB. STOPS  I    - I      - I      1 I      1 I      - I      1 I
I==========================================================================I
I PLAN HOURS   I 55,00 I  55,00 I  55,00 I  55,00 I  48,50 I  51,00 I
I STOP HOURS   I  0,00 I   0,00 I   0,16 I   0,38 I   0,00 I   0,71 I
I RUN HOURS    I 55,00 I  55,00 I  54,84 I  54,62 I  48,50 I  50,29 I
I--------------I--------I--------I--------I--------I--------I--------I
I MTBF         I ----- I  ----- I  27,42 I  27,31 I  ----- I  25,15 I
I--------------I--------I--------I--------I--------I--------I--------I
I MTTR.        I ----- I  ----- I   0,16 I   0,38 I  ----- I   0,71 I
I OBJECTIVES   I  0,50 I        I        I        I        I        I
I--------------I--------I--------I--------I--------I--------I--------I
I MAX. STOP    I  ---- I   ---- I   0,16 I   0,38 I   ---- I   0,71 I
I--------------------------------------------------------------------I
I   Day    I   Period     I   Appl.   I C I          Reason          I
I----------I--------------I-----------I---I----------------------------I
I MONDAY   I 10.00-10.43 I VSPC       I S I MLPA error                I
I          I 10.22-10.32 I MVSB       I S I 168UP RE-IPLed  (MLPA)    I
I          I 10.16-10.39 I TSOB       I S I TSO DOWN, (MLPA)          I
```

VM BENCHMARKING TRANSACTION REPORT					
Date	%0-2 sec	%2-4 sec	%4-6 sec	%6-60 sec	%gt 60sec	Number
Jul 6	92	6	1			600
Jul 7	97	3				1200
Jul 8	99	1				1200
Jul 9	99	1				1200
Jul 10	99	1				1200
Jul 11	100					1200
Jul 12	100					1100

Figure 44. Availability service report

In Figure 44, 'Number' is the number of benchmarking responses (indicates
period length).   Including the VM response report leads up to the total
service report as shown in Figure 46 on page 84.

When VM response times are not continually recorded (needs monitoring
resources), the benchmark program is the main service feedback mechanism
for VM.   Experience found a significant correlation between user dissatis-
faction and the number of benchmark responses over 2 seconds. This
applies to one implementation of a benchmarking program, and is therefore
not portable to another centre unless that other centre uses the same program.   A more direct approach to service recording is to use the Predictor
program.   An example of this is presented in chapter 10, Figure 149 on
page 248.   The problem with the Predictor report is that it requires a lot
of data to be stored; also VM cannot monitor to two datasets simultaneously,   so that to obtain data for the predictor it may be necessary to stop
ordinary monitoring and concentrate on Predictor monitoring for instance
during peak hour. With ample disk space the two monitor datasets may be
reduced to one containing all incidents.

4.5.3 Unavailability reason report

Figure 45   on page 83 shows availability losses on one processor with reason codes.   Such reports are prepared for major components:

        Network hardware
        Network software
        Central hardware
        Central system control program
        Major Application - for instance IMS or VSPC
        Transaction - if applicable

The figure shows the result of an availability drive during the first half
of 1981.   By analysing each of the unavailability occurrences, and by concentrating total systems design on availability, impressive results were
obtained.

Note the large number of 'Miscellaneous' occurrences. Most of these were
power breaks.   A better classification procedure could be desirable.

Each component should be analyzed in more detail.   For instance the heading 'Hardware' could be broken down into:

        Processor
        Storage
        Channels
        Disk storage controllers
        Disk string controllers
        Disks
        MSS and MSS paths
        Teleprocessing attachments
        Other peripheral equipment
        Environmental factors such as power breaks

```
Reason codes:

*    The software component itself
S    Other systems software
H    Hardware
O    Operator error
A    Applications
D    Miscellaneous


====0     25    50    75   100   125   150   175 Minutes lost=====0 Stops  10
1981+----+----+----+----+----+----+----+----+----+----+----+----+----+----*
W  1 IDDDDD          .                                             ID.
E  2 I*HHHHHH        .                                             I*H
E  3 I                    +                                        I .
K  4 IS               .                                            IS.
   5 I*******HHHHHHHHHHHH                                          I**HH
   6 ISOOOOOODDDDDDDDDDDDDDDDDDDDDDDDD                             ISOD
   7 I**              .                                            I*.
   8 I*DDDDDDDDD  .                                                I*DD
   9 I*******SSDDDDDDDDDDDDDDDDDDDDDDDDDDDDDDDD                    I***SDD
  10 I                    +                                        I .
  11 IS                   .                                        IS.
  12 I                    +                                        I .
  13 I                    +                                        I .
  14 IHHHHHHHHHHHHHHH                                              IHH
  15 I                    +                                        I .
  16 IHHHHH           .                                            IH.
  17 IDDDD            .                                            ID.
  18 I                    +                                        I .
  19 I                    +                                        I .
  20 ISSSSSSS         .                                            ISS
  21 ISSHHHHO         .                                            ISHO
  22 I                    +                                        I .
  23 I                    +                                        I .
 >24 I                    +                                        I .
 >25 I                    +                                        I .
 >26 I                    +                                        I .
 >27 I                    +                                        I .
 >28 I**              .                                            I*.
 >29 I                    +                                        I .
 >30 I                    +                                        I .
 >31 IS                   .                                        IS.
 >32 I                    +                                        I .
 >33 ID               .                                            ID.

Figure 45.   Availability losses and reasons - one total MVS system
```

4.5.4 Total service report - VSPC example

Figure 46 on page 84 shows different aspects of service integrated into
one report. Currently it is an experiment that could be carried over to
other service categories.

```
Sample report VSPC week 34 1981.

   Availability: Weekly        100 %   10 week average        99.4%
                 Stops           0    10 week average         1.1

   Number of incidents during week (VSPC supervision) :    6

   Performance:  Perfect     >> <<    Quality:  Perfect     >>X<<
                 Good        >> <<               Good        >> <<
                 Acceptable  >> <<               Acceptable  >> <<
                 Critical    >>X<<               Critical    >> <<
                 Uacceptable >> <<               Uacceptable >> <<

Performance and quality ratings are based on subjective evaluation of
comments and data received.

Error log from VSPC supervision:

Format is: date (dd/mm, ), from hr.(hh.mm, ), text:

19/08 10.35: Storage temporarily unavailable (20 users online).
Error report.

19/08 11.20: Response problems (24 online). Error report.

19/08 12.45: Response problems (17 online).

20/08 13.50: Resources temp. unavailable (21 online).

20/08 14.15: Response problems(supervision stopped a batch job
running on wrong system)

Response times:

For an example, see Figure 33 on page 70.

Comments:

Batch and TSO will be limited until installation of larger machine

Oustanding error reports:

Selected PTFs added to system. Several problems concluded.

User help:

Number of calls:  14   Average time to complete: 4 min 30 secs.
Number of unresolved calls at week end:   2
Number of calls unresolved from last week: 0

Figure 46.   VSPC total service report
```

One important property of availability reports is that they can help planning.   For instance if an availability increase of 1 percent of total
uptime (from 98% to 99%) is planned, it may be useless to spend resources

- e.g. manpower - on projects accounting for only a small fraction of the lost time. Figure 47 on page 85 is an example of such a yearly report.

Monthly availability status for MVSA (3033A) Per. 14-01-1982.

```
--------------------------------------------------------------------------
I YR *                          3 0 3 3 A                                 I
I 1 *---------------------------------------------------------------------I
I 9 *NON *   *   R E A S O N :  * STOPS IN  * 10-WEEK AVE.  AVAIL. %      I
I 8 *SCH.*PER*                  * PERIOD    * AT MONTH END   FOR : I
I 1 *IPL *DAY*HW*SW*MIS*IND*OPEN*08-17 17-08* IMS       TSO        SYSTEM I
I*************************************************************************I
I                                                                         I
IJAN * 10 0.48  4  3  0  3   0    8      2   93.7(96) 97.1(98) 97.7(98)I
I-------------------------------------------------------------------------I
IFEB * 17 0.85  7  4  3  3   0    6     11   93.6(96) 96.5(98) 97.3(98)I
I-------------------------------------------------------------------------I
IMAR * 09 0.41  5  3  0  1   0    2      7   95.0(96) 97.5(98) 98.8(98)I
I-------------------------------------------------------------------------I
IAPR * 12 0.63  4  1  7  0   0    5      7   96.2(96) 98.0(98) 99.2(98)I
I-------------------------------------------------------------------------I
IMAY * 03 0.16  2  0  0  1   0    0      3   97.4(96) 99.2(98) 99.7(98)I
I-------------------------------------------------------------------------I
IJUN * 04 0.19  1  0  3  0   0    1      3   98.0(96) 99.7(98) 99.9(98)I
I-------------------------------------------------------------------------I
IJUL * 01 0.04  1  0  0  0   0    0      1   98.6(97) 98.7(98) 98.8(98)I
I-------------------------------------------------------------------------I
IAUG * 10 0.48  4  2  4  0   0    7      3   97.3(97) 97.4(98) 97.6(98)I
I-------------------------------------------------------------------------I
ISEP * 04 0.18  1  2  1  0   0    0      4   98.2(97) 98.5(98) 98.7(98)I
I-------------------------------------------------------------------------I
IOCT * 01 0.05  0  1  0  0   0    0      1   98.5(97) 99.3(98) 99.7(98)I
I-------------------------------------------------------------------------I
INOV * 04 0.19  4  0  0  0   0    0      4   97.7(97)   ---    100.0(98)I
I-------------------------------------------------------------------------I
IDEC * 02 0.10  1  0  1  0   0    0      2   98.4(97)   ---     99.9(98)I
--------------------------------------------------------------------------
```

```
+------------------------------------------------------------------------+
| Out-of-line situations DEC 1981:                                       |
+------------------------------------------------------------------------+
|  NO out-of-line situations.                                            |
+------------------------------------------------------------------------+
```

Figure 47. Yearly availability status

For each application a report like Figure 47 is prepared. Monthly status on (unscheduled) outages are given with reason area. MIS is miscellaneous, IND, independent of component. The incidents marked OPEN are still under investigation.

For each month, the ten week average status at the end of that month is given as a feedback on the service objectives. The numbers in parenthesis are the service objectives for each component.

Figure 48 on page 86 gives additional information to planners. The yearly loss to the different components can be referred to different groups or

persons that perhaps themselves can subdivide the reasons based on problem
reports.

STOP REASONS
FOR IMS   WEEKS 8101 TO 8153

REASON	STOP		TIME LOSS	
HARDWARE	24	20.0 %	15 HOURS 38 MINUTES	
SOFTWARE	40	33.3 %	22 HOURS 31 MINUTES	34.3 %
OPERATION	11	9.2 %	2 HOURS 21 MINUTES	3.6 %
IMS-ERROR	11	9.2 %	9 HOURS 2 MINUTES	13.8 %
APPLICATION	20	16.7 %	5 HOURS 36 MINUTES	8.5 %
MISCELLANEOUS	14	11.7 %	10 HOURS 27 MINUTES	15.9 %
TOTAL	120		65 HOURS 35 MINUTES	

PLANNED TIME	2280 HOURS
AVAILABILITY	97.1 %
STOPS PER WEEK	2.3
MTTR	33 MINUTES
LONGEST STOP	175 MINUTES

(WEEK 8109)

MTTR: Mean Time To Repair

Figure 48.   Yearly availability status by break reason

The availability reports could be used to compare one system to similar
systems.

Figure 49 on page 87 shows an example of such a report. For diplomatic
reasons, the actual numbers are not given. The centres are IBM internal
computing centres, that have a certain degree of similarity and therefore
are comparable.

Country	Loss reason area (% of theoretical availability)					
	Hardware	Network	VSPC	MVS	Other	External
Belgium	1.13	.33	.45	.10	.31	.02
Denmark	1.01	.21	.09	.31	.02	.20
France	.64	.01	.07	.13	.66	.59
Italy	.94	.44	.33	.37	.00	.07
Holland	.78	.17	.50	.50	.12	.00
Spain	1.12	.22	.03	.63	.00	.00
Sweden	1.23	1.12	.28	.10	.31	.12

Figure 49.   VSPC un-availability comparison (fictitious values)

To evaluate the data on Figure 49, we need information on how much VSPC each centre is running. Besides that it is necessary to know what hardware components are involved, their coupling, software components and level, workload mixture etc.

If all this is known, experienced technical people could extract important information, like stability of a new release or machine, fixes advisable, workload mixes to avoid etc.

4.6 COMBINED REPORTS

For a full overview of centre activities, a report combining the different
services e.g. for a month can be helpful. For instance a layout like in
Figure 50 can be used:

Service type	Responsitivity		Availability		Problem management		Info management	
	Number trans/ sec.	Response time (sec)	%	Number of breaks	Incoming problems	Solved problems	Incoming help requests	Solved help reqst.
IMS	2.2	1.8	97.3	6	4	3	25	25
VSPC	3.1	0.4	99.3	5	5	4	43	41
VM	8.1	0.6	99.2	1	1	1	13	13
TSO	3.3	1.5	98.3	4	0	0	4	4
Network	17.3	1.2	99.3	2	4	4	8	7
Batch**	0.1	220	98.3	4	16	12	3	3

** For batch the number of transactions is the number of jobs
   and the response time is the job elapse time.

   Figure 50.   One month total service report - prime shift

Figure 50 should be used with caution. For instance the definition of
transaction varies between the systems. Besides, the reports originate
from different sources/software products. At present, the table must be
hand made, in itself a source of errors.

The need for a combined report seems to be realized, and for instance SLR
version 2 features combination facilities features that can supply the
numbers for availability and responsitivity. Network data are more
tricky, but with tools as described in the previous chapter, possibly
reduced by SLR, a comprehensive approach is possible. Note that SLR version 2 (1982) as announced does not immediately support for instance the
reduction of network response data; in theory, however, these data represent 'Other logtapes' (Figure 19 on page 53), and can be integrated with
other SLR data. The practical implementation in a complex network may be
more than a trivial task, though.

Another way of combining the data would be to include the network response
and/or unavailability in the figures for each interactive service, giving
(close to) the total response times experienced by the user.

4.7 CONCLUSION

Measuring service requires a good understanding of what service means to
the end user, how service is rendered by the system and in what manner
service components are measured and recorded.

It is not advisable to measure service if these prerequisites are not ful-
filled. Costly misunderstandings and grave conflicts may follow.

Ideally, service should be measured in the same manner in any interactive
system. This is difficult in today's environment and another approach is
presented. The current chapter describes different approaches to measuring, and this provides the reader with a selection of methods.

In the future service measuring should be integrated into one system, for
instance SLR that is designed for this purpose. In addition, integrated
reports for each major application, like VSPC (Figure 46 on page 84)
should follow, and perhaps a reference table showing each service compared
with its objectives as a total status for the centre.

This would be distributed as follows:

Management:

    1. One page status

    2. One page per major application

    3. Service trends per major application

Users and user support groups:

    2 and 3 (only relevant applications)

    4. Service rendered for major applications per subcomponent
       (for instance transaction or project).

    5. Service rendered per major application - hourly

    6. Service and resource consumption by individual users
       - only in exceptional cases

System support and production:

    1 through 6 (selected per system)

    7. Detail reports per application, time period and possibly
       user - user group, including resource consumption

CHAPTER 5

RESOURCE CONTROL

A heart untouched by worldly things, a heart that is not swayed.
By sorrow, a heart passionless, secure - that is the greatest
blessing

> Sutta Nipata
> After C. Humphreys:
> Buddhism

Thoth, the judge of right and truth of the Great Company of the Gods
who are in the presence of Osiris(the deceased - here the scribe
Ani), saith: Hear ye this judgement. The heart of Osiris hath in
very truth been weighed, and his Heart-soul has borne testimony on
his behalf, his heart hath been found right by the trial in the great
balance. There hath not been found any wickedness in him, he hath
not wasted (or stolen) the offerings which have been made in the tem-
ples, he hath not committed any evil act, and he hath not set his
mouth in motion with words of evil whilst he was on earth.

> The Egyptian Book of the Dead
> After E. A. Wallis Budge:
> The Book of the Dead

5.1   INTRODUCTION

5.1.1   Chapter contents

From the many different resources that all are necessary to provide adequate user service, some are selected that experiencewise have an important impact on user perception of centre performance.

Guidance and examples are provided on how to measure the resources, and the implementation of MVS performance resource management parameters to adjust a complex environment to its various tasks. Emphasis has here been placed on simplicity and continuity; meaning that the examples do not depict optimal implementations, but rather approaches that can be introduced in most computer production environments without MVS internals expertise. Some selected theory is included, and should enable **production** people to acquire an adequate understanding of the system they are monitoring and handling.

The resources selected for further study are those that empirically impact performance most. Notably real and virtual storage are followed. These are both important resources in interactive systems. Secondary (disks) storage and tertiary storage (MSS) naturally extend real storage and are therefore also extensions related to performance.

MSS is given an especially thorough treatment. Partly this is because the mass storage concept is not covered in many publicly accessible documents, partly because the case presented highlights many salient points (for instance doubts) of a performance study.

5.1.2 Selecting resources for control

The following major resources should be carefully controlled:

<table>
<tr><td colspan="2">Dimensioning resources:</td></tr>
<tr><td></td><td>Processing time (CPU time)
Real storage usage at acceptable paging rate
Virtual storage usage - maximum
EXCP rate - i.e. logical I/Os</td></tr>
<tr><td colspan="2">Vital components:</td></tr>
<tr><td></td><td>Terminal controllers
Communication lines
Communication controllers
Channels
Disk storage control
Disks: traffic (SIO = physical I/Os)
Disks: busy time
Disks: space allocation
Mass storage subsystem
Printers, tapes etc</td></tr>
</table>

Other types of restricting resources are sometimes encountered:

<table>
<tr><td colspan="2">Miscellaneous resources:</td></tr>
<tr><td></td><td>Systems programmers
Operators and system supervisors
Programmers - and their test facilities
Skills, especially skill level of the above categories
Documentation - for instance what to do if the terminal fails
Education - to make the best use of new products,
              e.g. text processing
Supervisory equipment - hardware or software.
Space - e.g. to run parallel systems during hw installation.
Procedures - for instance lack of change management routines.</td></tr>
</table>

The list may be extended to suit each particular environment.

DEPT	ACTUAL KWU 1H80 per average working day						FORECASTED INCREASE %		
	Jan	Feb	Mar	Apr	May	Jun	2H80	1981	1982
PR BATT	4.3	4.2	4.2	4.2	4.8	4.0	20	10	10
BATP	9.1	9.6	9.1	7.7	5.9	5.9	20	25	20
TSOT	4.9	4.9	4.8	4.9	5.1	5.1	10	10	10
TSOP	1.1	1.2	1.2	1.3	1.0	1.2	20	20	20
IMS	13.2	13.5	14.4	14.9	13.3	14.5	30	43	37
Net	5.4	5.6	5.4	4.5	6.9	7.2	10	30	20
GIS	.2	.9	.4	.4	.1	.2	20	30	30
VSPC	1.1	.9	.9	1.1	1.6	1.8	30	30	20
DC BAT	5.4	5.7	4.9	4.8	2.0	1.9	10	10	5
TSO	.6	.8	.9	.9	1.0	1.1	20	10	5
VSPC	.0	.0	.0	.0	2.7	4.2	40	71	43
TC BAT	.2	.6	.7	1.0	.7	.7	30	60	25
TSO	.5	.5	.8	.6	.9	.7	30	70	25
CC BAT	5.9	8.4	6.3	4.6	4.0	4.0	10	5	5
TSO	1.6	1.9	1.5	1.5	1.6	1.7	20	10	10
TOTAL	53.0	59.8	55.8	52.6	51.5	53.8			

The unit is Kilo Work Units (KWU) that reflects the problem program
processing time (TCB (Task Control Block) time), converted to a scale
that compensates for uneven processing powers. For instance 3033 TCB
time (seconds) is multiplied by 4.5, 168 TCB time is multiplied by 2.6.

Figure 51.   Resource usage by forecast unit.

As indicated in reference 1, resource usage may be broken down by forecast
group as shown in Figure 51.

The example shows the actual and forecasted resource usage for the forecasting departments: PRogramming, Data Centre , TeChnical division and
Computer Centre, and the breakdown into services for each department.   The
figure relates to the Complex Computer Centre, described further in chapter 10.

The percentage increases are usually given as increase over average utilization the first six months of 1980. For sharp increases, the June value
is taken as the base, and the value compared with the forecast for December.   This is the case for VSPC, IMS and Net(work).

Figure 142 on page 241 shows a similar report, one year later, now with
some actual values to compare against the forecast.

5.1.3 Time frame for control

Resources should be controlled:

>   Online - to identify non-desirable user mixes, potential bottle-
>   necks.
>
>   Daily/weekly - to identify bottlenecks, potential load problems.
>
>   Monthly/yearly - to establish trends.

This section concentrates on the latter two, leaving online control or monitoring for chapter 6.

5.1.4 Recording tools

As Figure 52 on page 96 indicates, control is primarily planned for the main components in the path of interactive services.

This may sound obvious. Looking at Figure 52 on page 96 in more detail leaves a slightly different impression:

* Many and different tools are needed
* Not all recording tools can be run continually
* Not all components are controlled - e.g. terminal
* It is a major effort to integrate the input from all tools

As an example, a TSO text processing user needs to find response times to his/her transaction. That involves:

* Central response (SLR - is the text processing transaction
               recorded separately in SLR?)
* Possible mass storage response (MSS data interface)
* Possible disk seek times (GTFPARS)
* Communication system time (TRMS - will it know the user?)

For services like IMS and VSPC, service time is even more difficult to piece together. Due to the nature of IMS, however, a large number of users may be expected, and the system may be envisaged as an assembly of transaction types. Even then the analysis is complex.

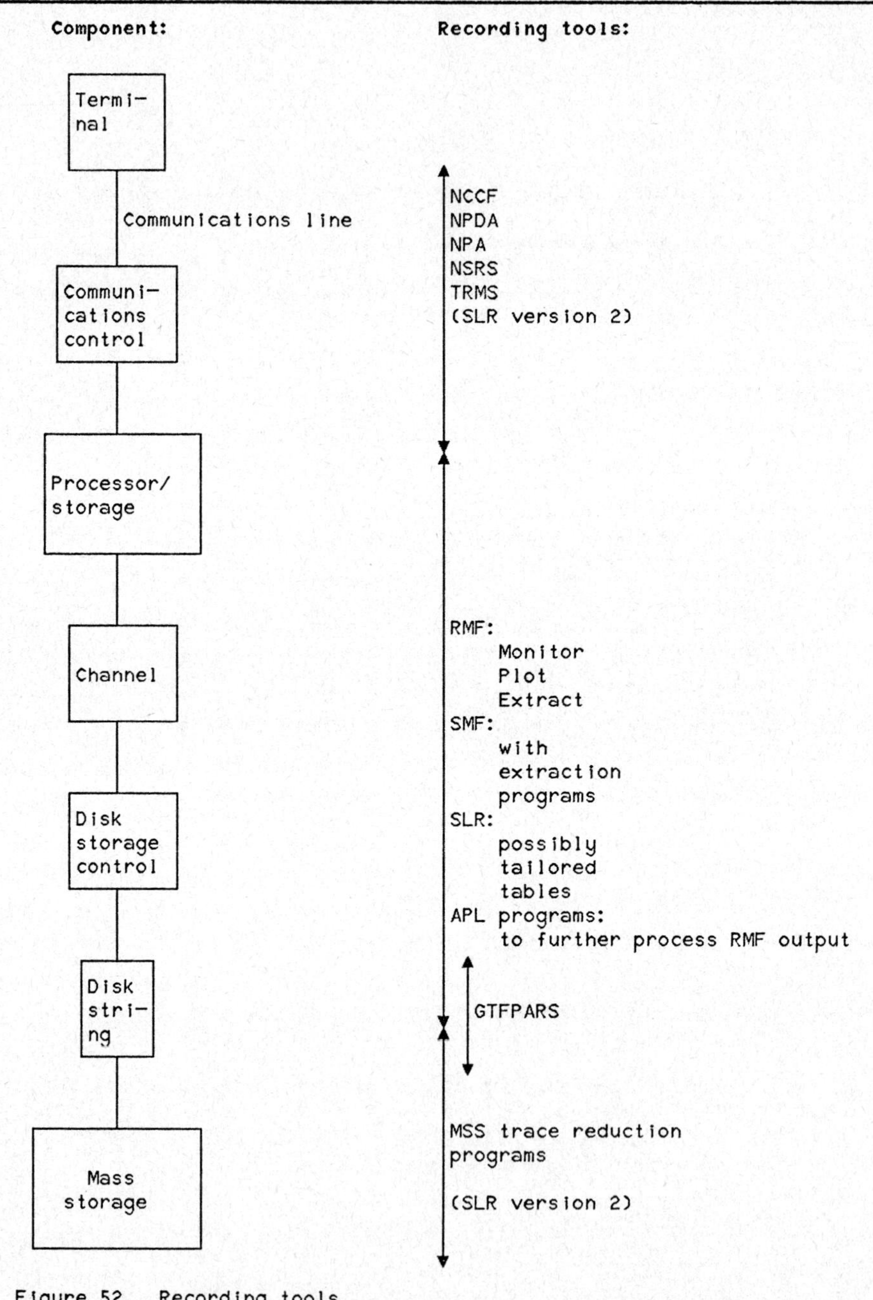

Figure 52.   Recording tools

5.2 CONTROLLING RESOURCE USAGE.

MVS provides different ways of controlling a complex environment. The primary parameter datasets involved are:

Name	Full name	Description
IPS	Internal Performance Specification	Controlling priority, multi-programming, allocating resources, controlling resource usage
ICS	Internal Control Specifications	Specifying transaction recording groups and transaction control groups
JES2PARM	JES2 startup parameters	Specifying job classes and their relation to IPS. Specifying max service for class.

Figure 53.   Control relevant system parameter datasets

In Figure 53 only the datasets mostly and directly involved with control are listed. Of these, IPS is by far the most important. The following discussion assumes a level of MVS corresponding to System Extension release 2 or above; however most parameters exist even in lower releases.

IPS and ICS provide input to the Systems Resource Manager (SRM) component of MVS. SRM's purpose is to distribute resources between its 'users'. The 'users' that SRM perceives are mainly address spaces. This means that systems like IMS and VSPC are treated on an address space basis, and there is little differentiation in SRM of single user or transaction requirements. TSO on the other hand allocates one address space per user, recognizes each new transaction, and is therefore well controlled by SRM.

Not all control procedures provided by MVS are included here. We have selected those that seems most appropriate to **our** task: the strict control of the CCC. One facility **not** included is the ability to control performance groups by ICS. This is as a valuable property, but considered too refined for the current environment.

5.2.1 Internal Control Specifications (ICS)

In later versions of MVS, special report groups may be defined in ICS. Work defined in such a report group may be separately controlled by MVS.

```
 09:21:50   ICS=IEAICS00      PERF  PERF    TRANS   AVG TRANS TIME
 SUBSYS  TRXCLASS   USERID     GRP   PER     RATE    HHH.MM.SS.TTT

 VSPC                          R300    1     1.417   000.00.07.193

 VSPC               1061(3)    R362    1     0.139   000.00.05.305

 VSPC               3634(3)    R381    1     0.194   000.00.05.337

 VSPC               3802(3)    R383    1     0.194   000.00.05.146

 VSPC               6032(3)    R394    1     0.027   000.00.19.087

 VSPC               6221(3)    R395    1     0.111   000.00.02.130

 VSPC               8981(3)    R404    1     0.111   000.00.07.392

 VSPC               8988(3)    R406    1     0.139   000.00.03.313

USERID:    The 4 first numbers in the VSPC userid (starts at position 3).
PERF GRP: The report performance group given in ICS
PERF PER: Performance period - always 1 for our VSPC
TRANS
RATE    : Transaction rate for those transactions that finished
           during the measurement period.
AVG TRAN: MVS internal response time for those transactions

 Figure 54.   VSPC report groups feedback from RMFMON
```

Report performance groups for VSPC users as shown in Figure 54 on page 98 can be created. Group R300 contains the sum of all VSPC work. This is used to control overall VSPC usage. When the response time, as here, is over 2 seconds (momentary), the system is in trouble. The transaction rate, 1.4, is not very high, and other load is probably disturbing VSPC.

The USERID given is the first four digits in the VSPC userID provided by the data centre. A 6 digit ID is given in total, but the two last digits represent individual users within a certain group or a certain customer. Subdividing on this basis restricts the number of entries on the monitoring screen, and also the number of performance groups listed in the RMF Extract Workload report.

The 3 in parenthesis refers to start character of the userid. VSPC presents to MVS a 8 character ID. If only the last 6 are used, then MVS should start comparing at character 3.

The R in the performance group ID indicates that this is a Report performance group (in practice defined in ICS rather than IPS). The performance group **number** given to each VSPC group has no intrinsic value for the described system apart from defining the listing sequence.

A **control** performance group may even be specified, such that different transaction types, or users, land in different SRM performance groups with different specifications. Thus may Education class work be given special priority.

Performance groups and performance periods will be further discussed in next chapter, IPS.

5.2.2 Internal Performance Specifications (IPS)

Controlling a large interactive system is a complex task, and this is fully reflected in the complexity of IPS. It is a skill given few, if any, to know all parameters and their effects on a live system.

IPS contains the specifications from the performance controller to MVS on what relative priority and handling different work types should receive.

When skills are scarce, and where are they not?, a simple approach to IPS can be chosen. Of the many control possibilities offered by IPS the three major ones are suitable for controlling most environments:

       1.   Multiprogramming level control (domain)
       2.   Dispatching priority control
       3.   Real storage control

5.2.3 Multiprogramming level control

In IPS each group of work should be assigned to a **domain**. For each domain, multiprogramming level is specified.

In Figure 55 on page 101, domain 1 is reserved for ordinary batch jobs. The parameters in the 'dmn' specification mean:

  1. parameter: At high system activity, 0 jobs can run in this domain
  2. parameter: At low system activity, 30 jobs can run in this domain
  3. parameter: A value to be used selecting the domain where
                    multiprogramming should be increased/decreased.

MVS decides in which domain to adjust multiprogramming level (MPL) according to a **contention index**. The contention index is calculated from:

Formula 1:

Contention index=(Average ready users x Weight)/Target MPL

- where 'Weight' is identical to parameter 3.

When the system is highly loaded ('over-utilized'), target MPL is decreased for the work with the lowest contention index.

When the system is lightly loaded ('under-utilized'), target MPL is increased for the work with the highest contention index.

I.e. the system attempts to provide the highest possible MPL to the domain having the highest contention index.

Note that there are alternative ways of specifying domains. In the presented case, an 'old-fashioned' approach was retained for compatibility with previous production patterns. According to online monitoring impression, the system is behaving as specified and expected. By the philosophy of management by exception, there is then no reason to change.

The 'average ready users' are those queued for a certain domain or running in it.

In the example on Figure 55 on page 101, if 'medium TSO' is running two users, and one is waiting to be run, and there is one batch job running, there must be 51 ready batch jobs waiting in order for domain 1 to be expanded first.

Selecting a low minimum MPL for a TSO domain may cause unnecessary swaps. SRM needs time to adjust to further increases in MPL, even if the system has surplus capacity. For a major TSO service computer, the lower bounds for the TSO domains can therefore be increased over the values in Figure 55 on page 101.

IMS, VSPC, TSO education, Network control and Systems control run 'non-swappable', meaning that they are not swapped even if SRM perceives that multiprogramming level is too high. These components will therefore always retain some pages in real storage.

When interactive services are intensively used, SRM MPL control is de facto inactivated, because no work can be swapped.

5.2.4 Dispatching control

The numerical value of 'dispatching priority' on Figure 56 on page 102 and Figure 57 on page 103 determines the priority. An 'F' in front of the value means that the value is absolute. An 'M' stands for 'mean time to wait', causing the work unit that has **waited most** to have highest dispatching priority in that group. 'M7' means that work in this group have priorities from F61 to F70 depending on wait time.

The magnitude of the difference between two dispatching priorities is of no consequence to the dispatcher. The gaps were kept partly for continuity, partly to be able to insert new work.

In a batch based service centre there is a tendency to specify 'M' type priorities (throughput oriented). When running mainly online services there is often more advantage in specifying 'F' (specific priorities), because you know what you get. Management usually has in mind a definite priority structure, and this should rigidly be reflected in internal performance specifications.

Another aspect of IPS is that it <u>can</u> screw up the system. Completely. In a highly loaded production system not even minor inconveniences caused by 'playing with' system parameters can be tolerated. Therefore changes ought to be introduced a few at a time, with controls in between. This means that an **optimal IPS** never exists, but always a working one.

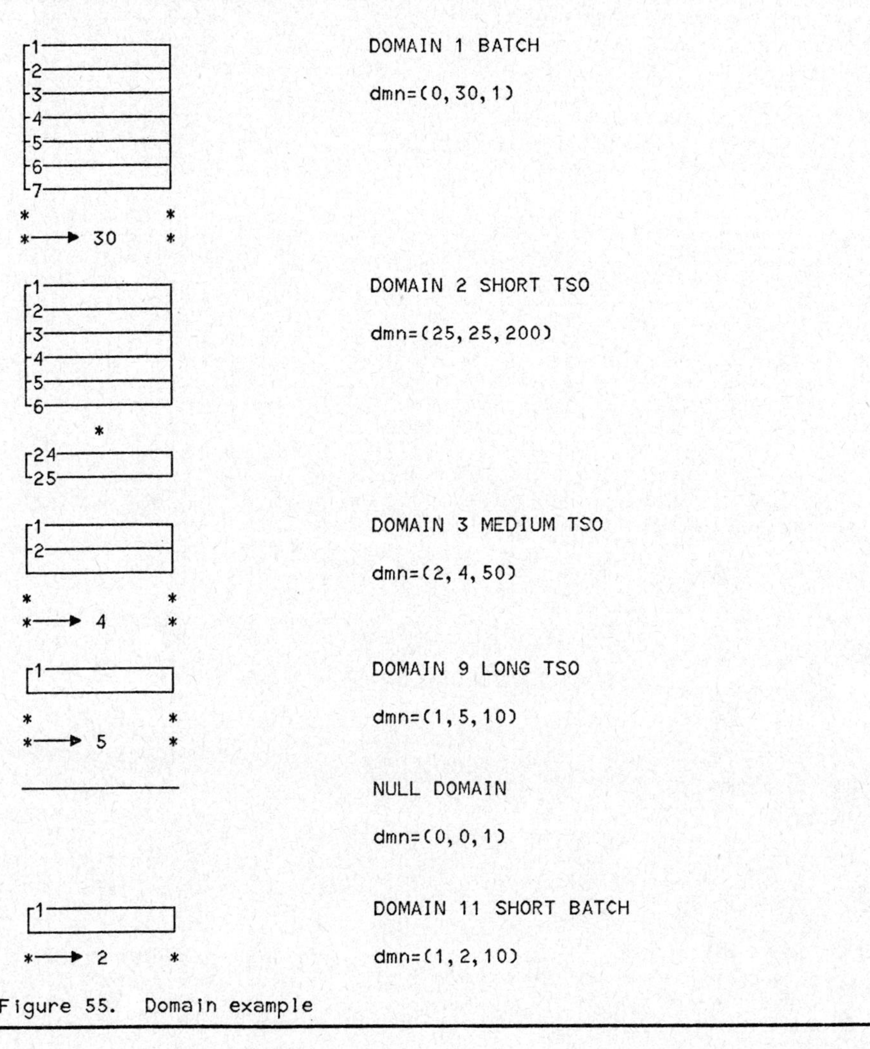

Figure 55.   Domain example

MVSA	Dispatching priority	MVSB
Master, JES2		Master
Measuring Optical read	F93	Measuring Optical read
IMS ctl	F92	VSPC dep. AS
	F91	TSIO
IMS MPP high prty	F83	VSPC main JES2
IMS MPP long	F81-F82	
IMS MPP prt.	F75	
TSO demo 1. period	F74	TSO educ. 1. period
TSO demo 2. period / TSO other 1. period	F73	TSO educ. 2. period / TSO other 1. period

Figure 56.   Priority structure example, part 1

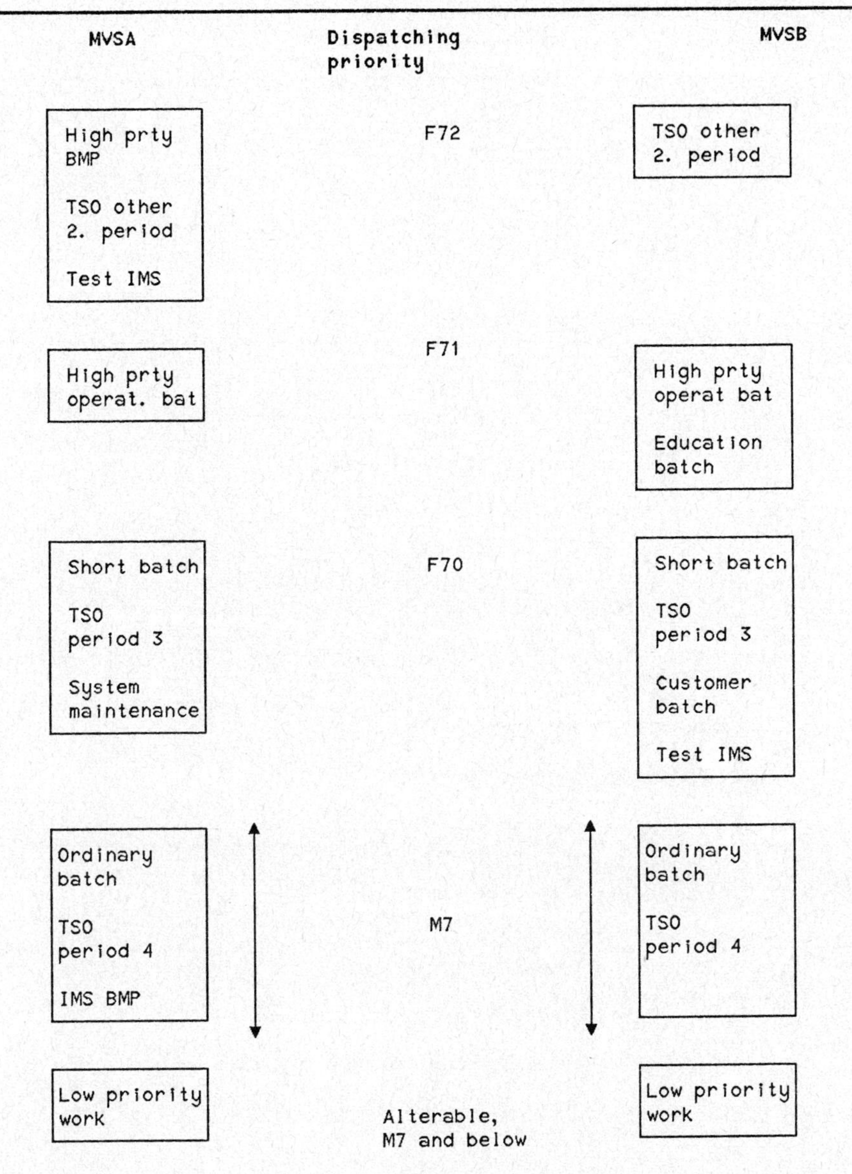

Figure 57.   Priority structure example, part 2

5.2.5 Performance groups

```
PGN=2,(DMN=2,DP=F73,DUR=150,OBJ=1,ISV=151)      /* TSO short
      (DMN=3,DP=F72,DUR=550,OBJ=1,ISV=701)      /* TSO medium
      (DMN=9,DP=M7,DUR=2300,OBJ=4,ISV=3K)       /* TSO long
      (DMN=1,DP=M7,OBJ=1,ISV=10K)               /* TSO batch type


DUR  :  Service in this period (DURation)
ISV  :  Interval Service Value = service before swap
OBJ  :  Relative importance in domain (OBJective)


Figure 58.   IPS performance group example (TSO)
```

Figure 58 shows the service specifications for TSO corresponding to
Figure 29 on page 66. TSO is allocated to PGN = Performance Group Number
2.   The performance group specification defines to MVS what relative service should be given to that performance group.

The four lines each represent a performance period, and are internally
numbered in the given order.

The duration is here given in service units, calculated according to formula 2.   A certain amount of service is given between each swap. As we
see from the specifications, the TSO user will not normally be swapped
before reaching performance period 4 unless there is a problem fitting
into the given MPL. But once in period 4 TSO is treated as batch, and may
be severely downgrading, using domain specifications, Figure 55 on page
101.

Service is calculated according to:

Formula 2: Service= A × CPU + B × EXCP + C × MSO + D × SRB

Where: CPU   is CPU time in seconds multiplied by a factor depending
                   on processor speed.

         EXCP   is number of EXCPs issued

         MSO   Main (real) storage occupancy in page-seconds

         SRB   Time spent performing systems service for an identifyable
                   address space

         A,B,C,D Coefficients provided in IPS

A × CPU gives CPU service and so forth.

The objective within the domain is hardly used in this specification. In
the example this is used in only one connection: when there are several

high priority batch jobs competing, and one class is 'more equal' than the
others.

One fact limiting the use of the domain parameter, is that the collective
result of swap decisions based on service and MPL are difficult to
predict. A predictable system that fulfills service objectives is normally superior to an 'optimal' one.

5.2.6 JES2 parameters

JES2 - the Job Entry Subsystem 2 - performs miscellaneous services on
incoming **jobs** and outbound 'print' datasets.

JES2 receives all batch jobs for all MVS processors (JES2 Multi-Access
Spool). The JOB cards are decoded and flushed if there are errors - for
instance in passwords (default jobclass is then SCAN - see Figure 59).
Thereafter the jobs are queued for the initiator(s) that may be specified
explicit (class parameter) or implicit (PGN is given). An initiator is
started up with one or more jobclass(es), and selects these in the order
specified. This means that several MVS based processors may run identical
jobclass(es), and it often necessary to specify <u>where</u> a specific job
should be run.

The batch jobs may be input over teleprocessing lines, and JES2 also handles these lines, in addition to possible channel-to-channel adapters
(with the Network Job Interface software package).

When the class parameter is given in the job, the JES2 parameters are con-
sulted to see if there is a specification in JES2PARM, as in Figure 59.

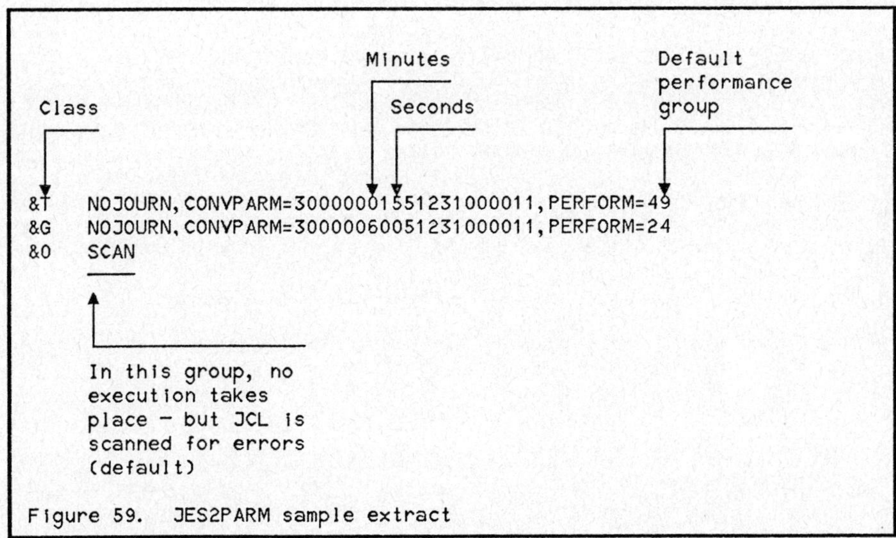

Figure 59.   JES2PARM sample extract

Only the parameters most relevant for control is highlighted on Figure 59.
The 'minutes' and 'seconds' refer to execution time per jobstep. When the

allotted time (TCB time) has expired, the operator is asked whether this
job should continue.   To avoid errors, the general rule is that jobs
should be cancelled.

This setup can be overruled by specifying performance group(PGN) or execution time(TIME) in JCL (MVS's Job Control Language). Misuse can be
controlled by way of SLR, for instance by listing jobs in class T with
more than 15 seconds of execution time. This has a significant drawback
because standard SLR lists **jobs** and JES2PARM contains **jobstep** limits.

If system programming time is available, it is possible to create a program (JOB exit) that scans for PGN and TIME parameters and performs the
relevant reset.

5.2.7 Real storage control

IPS offers few facilities to control paging. In some cases a 'fence' can
be established around a certain performance group. The fence can be specified as a minimum and a maximum. The system attempts to allocate enough
pages to work in that performance group so that the group owns a number of
pages between the minimum and the maximum, dependent on paging load on
that group.

This can be established as a 'negative fence' to prevent certain work from
beeing too greedy on real storage. A negative fence can for instance be
established around a test IMS system, preventing a sudden outburst of
energy from interfering with the higher priority work - for instance VSPC
- on the same processor.

A 'positive fence' can favour selected applications. An example of this
could be the IMS control region:

pgn=240,(dmn=7,dp=f92 .....),PWSS=(175,400),PPGRT=(20,30)

PWSS is the potential real storage size, from 175 to 400 pages. When paging - for pgn=240 - is over 30 (PPGRT) the 'working set' is increased. It
is decreased when paging is less than 20.

The values are changed quite slowly. This is good in one respect, because
it stabilizes the system. However, the method may allocate frames to pages that are no longer in use, so that the total system is uneconomical.
Figure 100 on page 164 shows an example of online monitoring of fencing.

5.3 MEASURING RESOURCE CONSUMPTION

5.3.1 Processing time - total

RMFPLOT provides a neat way of following processor busy time on a weekly basis. Figure 60 on page 108 shows one processor followed over (nearly) a week.

There seems to be spare capacity on CPU 0. However, a busy percentage exceeding 70 during peak hours gives reason to be cautious when an inter- active system is involved - as it was here.

This kind of plot can be supplemented with SLR, e.g. Figure 143 on page 245. Processor busy time has decreased since January. Less efficiency may be one reason - perhaps caused by system bottlenecks. A more likely (and true) explanation is that interactive services on that machine has expanded, tending towards a less processor-efficient load mix.

IPS is normally implemented to lower batch multiprogramming level at high paging rates. Heavy TSO is treated as batch.

When interactive systems load the machine beyond a certain point, no - or almost none - batch is allowed. Batch is very efficient in absorbing wha- tever processing power may be left from interactive services.

Less processor power used may not be an unhealthy sign in an interactive environment, in terms of fulfilling service objectives.

5.3.2 Processing time - problem program time

Figure 51 on page 94 shows 'TCB' or problem program time. This is the net time that the processor is working on applications.

The total processor time consists of problem program time and system time, or the time that MVS needs to administrate its users and perform services for them.

The system overhead varies according to service type, but is in general higher for interactive services.

For newer releases of MVS, system time spent on working for a particular application can be recorded (called SRB time, SRB = Service Request Block). An article by Cooper (reference 18) can be used to assess the influence of recording either TCB time or TCB + SRB time.

Even with TCB + SRB time recording, the full MVS overhead cannot be allo- cated to users. Paging and dispatching for instance are done on a system wide basis and must be allocated separately. The same concerns as for TCB only recording are valid, and we therefore later in this book consider only TCB recording, meaning either TCB recording or TCB and SRB recording.

```
                 CPU BUSY PERCENTAGE - CPU 0
              0       20.0      40.0      60.0      80.0     100.0
              |---------|---------|---------|---------|---------|
 8/12 21:00I*********************                 .         .         .
      22:00I*****************    .                .         .         .
      23:00I***************      .                .         .         .
 8/13 00:00I****************     .                .         .         .
      01:00I*************        .                .         .         .
      02:00I***********          .                .         .         .
      08:00I*********************.                .         .         .
      09:00I************************************* .         .         .
      10:00I*************************************** .       .         .
      11:00I******************************** .      .       .         .
      12:00I******************************** .      .       .         .
      13:00I******************************** .      .       .         .
      14:00I************************************** .        .         .
      15:00I**************************************** .       .        .
      16:00I************************************** .         .        .
      17:00I************************************  .          .        .
      18:00I*******************************************  .    .        .
      19:00I***************************** .                .         .
      20:00I**********************************************,.          .
      21:00I*******************************************    .          .
      22:00I*************************** .                  .          .
      23:00I**************************** .                 .          .
 8/14 00:00I*****************    .                .         .         .
      01:00I***************      .                .         .         .
      02:00I****************     .                .         .         .
      03:00I*************        .                .         .         .
      04:00I********     .                .         .         .
      08:00I************************ .              .         .        .
      09:00I*************************************** .         .        .
      10:00I*********************************************** .          .
      11:00I******************************** .               .        .
      12:00I*********************************** .            .        .
      13:00I************************************ .           .        .
      14:00I*******************************,.                .        .
      15:00I*********************************** .            .        .
      16:00I********************************,.               .        .
      17:00I*************************** .                    .        .
      18:00I**************************************************** .     .
      19:00I****************************************************** .   .
      20:00I************************************************ .         .
      21:00I************************************************ .         .
      22:00I***************** .                   .         .         .
      23:00I********************** .              .         .         .
 8/15 00:00I*************        .                .         .         .
      01:00I***********          .                .         .         .
      02:00I**********           .                .         .         .
```

Figure 60.   RMFPLOT total processor busy time recording

5.3.3 Real storage

The data on Figure 61 on page 109 was obtained in the manner suggested in Figure 8 on page 27.

Data for the common areas (SQA, LPA, NUCleus, UNUSed) are averages obtained from the **Paging report** of the RMF Extract program.

Data for the private areas, the rest, are found from service consumptions in the **Workload report**. Alternatively corresponding values may be found in SMF record 30 (pageseconds).

```
      PAGED
START DATE
      14 9 81
NUMBER OF DAYS
      10
CPU [3033 OR 168]
      3033
```

GROUP – PAGES									
DATE:	14	15	16	17	18	19	20	21	22	23
TSO	188	145	179	171	198	0	0	196	249	224
SYSTEM	181	152	161	136	158	0	0	163	142	131
NETWORK	554	553	585	546	555	0	0	570	562	550
IMS BMP	365	316	322	350	322	0	0	355	327	365
CC	59	22	28	19	37	0	0	49	91	59
HSM ETC	66	65	68	72	74	0	0	72	70	78
IS	243	222	123	183	274	0	0	301	180	217
IMS MPPS	1154	1137	1175	1173	1128	0	0	1130	1180	1177
SQA	203	201	195	209	205	0	0	208	213	209
LPA	505	496	483	482	490	0	0	495	491	496
CSA	515	533	526	530	535	0	0	534	540	547
NUC	190	190	190	190	190	0	0	190	190	190
UNUS	109	109	126	111	117	0	0	123	115	114
TOTAL:	4332	4139	4160	4172	4283	0		0	4385	4349	4358
PAGING:	95	87	84	92	106	0		0	113	113	107

Figure 61. Real storage usage table, major components

To find the amount of <u>pages</u> used by each application, each separate application must be run in one or more dedicated IPS performance groups. The number of pages for each performance group is found by:

Formula 3:

PAGES=(Transaction rate x MSO service x A x 50)/ CPU service x C

A and C are defined in the IPS, and are listed, together with the other parameters in formula 3, in the workload report.

Data like on Figure 61 on page 109 can be plotted over time. This highlights any tendencies in real storage usage.

An example of this is shown in Figure 62 on page 111. Note the relative stable level of real storage usage, and also the changes in page usage by CSA and IMS MPPs (and the control region) around July 20. At that date a new version of IMS was introduced (IMS 1.1.6 with the Local Storage Option - LSO). The version was introduced to relieve strain on virtual storage, especially IMS CSA usage.

The objective was achieved, but naturally had a similar effect on real storage. A minor net real storage expense can be read from Figure 61 on page 109.

```
        Pages

        1250-                                      N
            -
            -
            -                        I                    I        I I
            -                   I         I I I         I
        1000-                        I                             I
            -
            -
            -        I
            - L L       L L L I L      L I
        750L               L          L
            -
            -
            -                    K       L           L    L    L   L L
            -               K K         L L        L L   K        L
        500K K K     K K K       K    K K K      K K K   K      K   K K
            C              C          C C C             L
            - C C     C   C C C     C C         C C C
            - D D         D         D             D      C     C C C D
            -         D D D   D          D        D    D   D     D D
        250D                   D    D   D                          D
            M M M     M M M M M     M M M M M     M M M M M     M M M M
            N H H     H H H A B     H B H B B     B B H J H     B H B B
            - N N     N N N N N     N N N N N     N N N  N     N N N N
            G G F     E G F G F     E G G F F       E F G F     G G F F
            OE   E-N N -   E-E E N N  -    E E N-N E - E H-E N N   E-E   -
            45        50        55        60        65        70        75
                                      Day from 17 5 81----->

        A =   TSO
        B =   SYSTEM
        C =   NETWORK
        D =   IMS BMP
        E =   DCS
        F =   CC
        G =   HSM ETC
        H =   IS
        I =   IMS MPPS and control region
        J =   SQA
        K =   LPA
        L =   CSA
        M =   NUC
        N =   UNUS
```

Figure 62.   TRX real storage usage plot, major components

When using this approach, caution should be observed because:

- Work could be moved to another performance group.

- Abnormal conditions (especially at high transaction rate) may cause pages allocated to be wrongly estimated. The check on total systems usage is necessary. Anomalies ought to be corrected online (for instance using APL).

- Because Common and Local real storage usage originate from different reports, the sum is not necessarily equal to real storage in the system. Offline or bad frames may also disturb the picture (can be included in the plot).

Figure 144 on page 245 shows one processor followed over several months. VSPC was removed from the processor in October, and some testIMS ran in November. After October, the major interactive service was TSO.

The plot shows the real storage history of the machine; how it is used for what.

The large 'system' area contains many pages used for interactive work (mostly LPA for VSPC/TSO, mostly CSA for IMS). This could be divided out to the requesting applications as is done for Figure 157 on page 252.

Figure 144 on page 245 contains paging because real storage allocation depends heavily on the paging rate. Paging was low in the example when VSPC was run, because it needed good response times as it was used for external customers. The high paging load in November caused problems for TSO (internal programmers) and had to be lowered to give acceptable service.

5.3.4 Paging

Paging is found by a specially prepared SLR table, adding **page ins** to **page outs** to obtain **total paging**. This is the parts of the paging system that load the I/O paths.

Note that **demand paging** is often referred to. This is equal to the amount of page ins corresponding to the **page faults** in the system. A page fault occurs when the system control program cannot find a referenced page among the pages currently defined as resident in real storage.

However, the page may still physically reside in real storage - it has only been released by the page supervisor in order that a needy address space may obtain its frame. Such a page may be **reclaimed** by the earlier owner. In this case physical paging is saved.

In the case of VSPC many reclaims occur. When a VSPC transaction is finished, all its real storage pages are released. However, the user issuing the transaction may rapidly originate another transaction that can use the same pages. It would then be wrong to judge the system by the amount of page faults occurring.

Non page fault paging occurs due to swaps and VIO. VIO (Virtual Input Output) is a software simulation of real DASD IO, using paging instead of DASD space management. This is often faster for (temporary) small datasets.

MVS (SRM) uses page fault input/output (excluding reclaims) as the demand paging rate.

SLR defines demand paging rate as the sum of page fault page in rate and
page reclaim rate.

MVS demand paging is used to determine MPL. At high swap rates (heavy
TSO),   it may be wise to stop batch or limit TSO.   Current MVS only reacts
to high swap rates indirectly - if the page delay time is constantly high.

Figure 63 shows paging over an average day (including weekends).   Two typical 'humps' occur at peak periods before and after lunch.

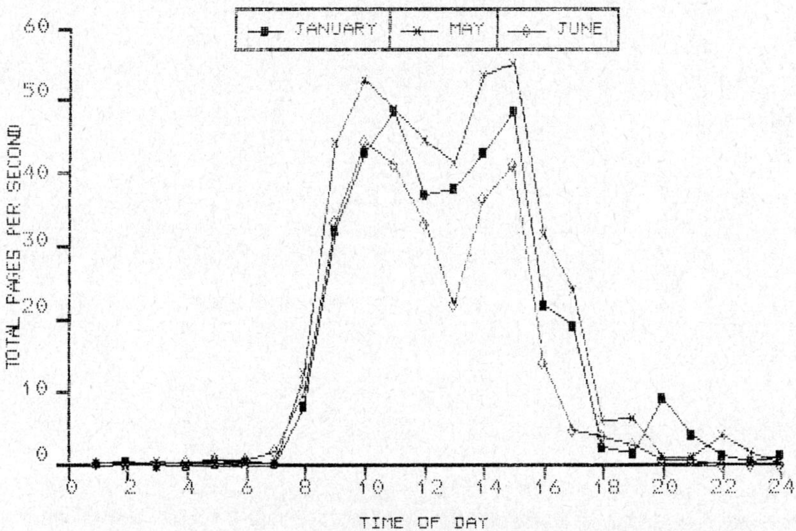

Figure 63.   SLR total paging distribution by hour

Figure 64 on page 114 shows paging rate in one of the peak periods.   Paging on that machine has obviously been reduced somewhat in May.

In the example, paging reduction was obtained by restricting the maximum
number of simultaneously active TSO users (MAXUSER).

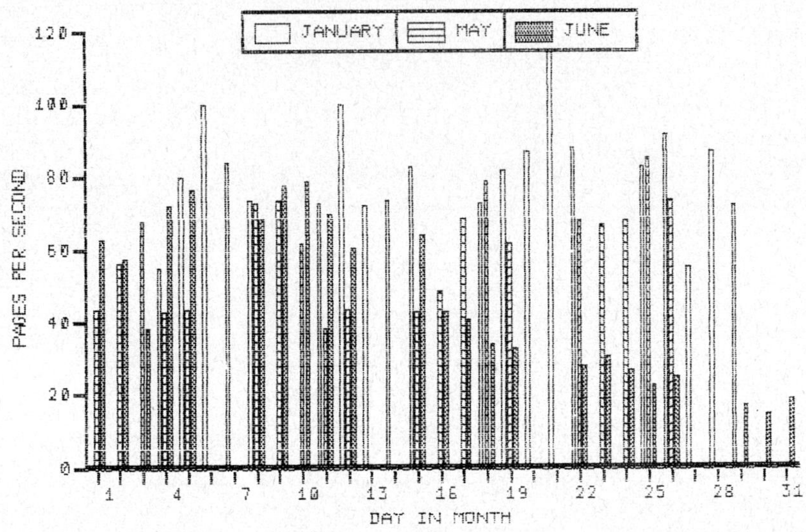

Figure 64.   SLR paging rate at 1500 - 1600 hours by day in month

5.3.5 Swapping

The term 'swap' derives from times when two work items changed places in
the scheduling system to give better service, or to alleviate an overloaded component.

Currently, swaps are mostly 'one way' (unilateral). The most frequent
reasons for swaps are that at TSO command is finished or MPL adjustment.

Swap out involves 'quiesceing' (i.e. orderly stopping ongoing work with
status saving), and writing changed pages out to disk. **Swap in** reads back
into real storage (some of) the pages held by the program when it was qui-
esced.

Sometimes there is ample real storage even if a swap is requested. This
is common in a lightly loaded TSO system. Only quiesceing is then done at
swap out; however the pages are physically written out when they are not
referenced again for an interval - normally 30 seconds. The system of not
writing out the physical swap pages is called **logical swap**. To investigate the influence of TSO swapping on paging, a further analysis of swaps
is informative.   Most swaps in our environment originate from TSO.   Figure 65 on page 115 shows that swaps vary more wildly than paging over the
day, and even that there are local swapping peaks outside paging peak
periods.   Such occurrences would be well worth investigating, preferably
armed with more detailed data on TSO behaviour, exemplified by Figure 29
on page 66.

Swaps are currently divided into two logical parts. Address space control blocks are written to the **swap dataset** using one physical I/O.

The remaining, changed, parts of the user's real storage are written out using the page supervisor to the page data set - i.e. it competes with other paging.

The user's real storage - or 'working set' - may be trimmed somewhat when written out and swapped in again. The method seems to change rapidly with new MVS releases, and a detailed description of the algorithm is therefore not included.

MVS/SP3 will   treat   the   TSO swapload homogeneously. This loads the I/O paths more, but the load is directed to one or more predefined disk(s). The system designer will consider this and find a suitable placement to avoid interfering with other, vulnerable, subsystems.

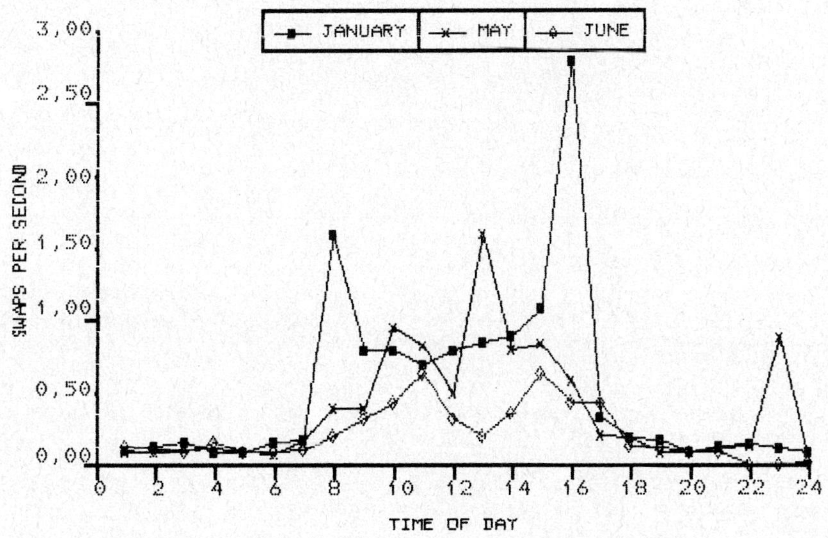

Figure 65.   Maximum swap rate 0000 - 2400 hours per day over months

5.3.6 Channels - input/output paths

Channels are part of most input/output paths, notably for (remote) mes-sages to and from the computer, and for main or real storage to communi-cate with secondary storage devices such as disks or tape.

The Central Processing Unit (CPU) can only handle data that it finds in real storage, also called main storage or main memory. Other storage with direct access to main storage, like disks and tape can therefore be called **secondary storage** that serves as an extension to **primary storage** i.e. main memory. The extension is needed partly because main storage is too costly to contain modern, large databases, but also because main storage usually is volatile and is erased when power is switched off.

The Mass Storage Subsystem, MSS acts as a backup for secondary storage, and can therefore be regarded as **tertiary storage.**

Disks are the most used secondary storage. Due to its direct access capability, disk storage is a feasible extension of main storage.

When we consider channels, the channels where disk are attached are usually most important in performance connections. Disks contain important and highly active data like pages, databases, command modules and programs. When a record is read from or written to disk, the disk arm is normally left to work alone, first to **SEEK** for the correct cylinder, afterwards to **SEARCH** for the record or the write position. Immediately before the record is found, the disk informs the channel that it wants to read or write data. The disk then wants to **reconnect** to the IO path. If the path is busy, the disk has to wait one whole revolution (=16.7 millisecond on disks used as examples here) before attempting to reconnect again. The formula for lost time is the sum of a geometrical progression:

Formula 4: Reconnect loss=(Path busy/(1-Path busy))×16.7 milliseconds

---

Path busy is therefore an important performance parameter. Normally disk IO time is in the order of 25 - 50 milliseconds. When Path busy is 0.5 (or 50%). reconnect loss is alone 16.7 milliseconds or one third. For database transactions we may estimate that at least 3/4 of the internal transaction time is used for disk IO, meaning that at Path busy 0.5 (50 percent) and disk response time 50 milliseconds, we add 20 - 30 percent to database response times. Percentagewise more is added to disks with previous faster response.

Note that this is the instantaneous value. Path busy of 30 percent over one day may cover over 60 percent during the busiest hour and 90 percent during a 5 minute interval.

C H A N N E L   A C T I V I T Y

OS/VS2 SYSTEM ID 7033 START 10/26/81-10.40.08   INTERVAL 000.09.59
RELEASE 03.8 RPT VERSION 05 END 10/26/81-10.40.08 CYCLE 0.750 SECONDS

TOTAL SAMPLES =   799
PHYSICAL CHANNEL ACTIVITY

CPU/ CSID	CHANNEL NUMBER AND TYPE		CHANNEL ACTIVITY COUNT	PERCENT CHANNEL BUSY	PERCENT CHAN BUSY & CPU WAIT	ACTIVITY PER SECOND	AVERAGE SERVICE TIME
0	0	BYTE MPX	14,477			24.145	
	1	BLOCK MPX	18,939	29.29	11.64	31.586	0.009
	2	BLOCK MPX	15,352	33.29	13.27	25.604	0.012
	3	BLOCK MPX	15,104	15.89	5.01	25.190	0.006
	4	BLOCK MPX	10,394	11.26	3.88	17.335	0.006
	5	BLOCK MPX	211	0.75	0.13	0.351	0.019
	6	BYTE MPX	84			0.140	
	7	BLOCK MPX	19,215	29.91	1.39	32.047	0.009
	8	BLOCK MPX	9,855	22.40	8.51	16.436	0.013
	9	BLOCK MPX	14,178	19.02	6.63	23.646	0.008
	A	BLOCK MPX	318	0.00	0	0.530	0.000
	B	BLOCK MPX	5,507	22.15	.8	9.184	0.024
TOTAL/ANY/AVE			123,634	85.73	30.66	206.199	0.010

Figure 66.   RMF physical channel busy report

Figure 66 and Figure 67 on page 118 show channels on one processor that
runs database, interactive programming and batch. The reports are
extracted for 10 minute periods. Physical channel busy is seldom over
30%, and therefore acceptable. There is a potential problem on channel 2
that may be followed separately with a plot (obtained easily from
RMFPLOT).

Figure 68 on page 119 shows that channel 2 is a block multiplexor channel
used for disks, i.e. one of the vulnerable performance items. Logical
channel 2, consisting of physical channels 2 and 8, also has difficulties,
with an average queue of 0.36.

For a corresponding anomaly condition, regard Figure 111 on page 183, where queuing is over 1.

For disk channels, percent busy in the example gives about the same numerical value as channel activity count/second (example channel 1: 18939/599
= roughly 30). This can be used to evaluate the influence on channel load
from one or a few specific disks. More important, it can be used to evaluate head of string busy, and perhaps disk storage control load.

```
                      C H A N N E L    A C T I V I T Y

OS/VS2 SYSTEM ID 7033   START 10/26/81-10.40.08   INTERVAL 000.09.59
RELEASE 03.8 RPT VERSION 05 END 10/26/81-10.40.08 CYCLE 0.750 SECONDS

TOTAL SAMPLES =            799
LOGICAL CHANNEL ACTIVITY
        PHYS CHAN
LOG     CPU/CSID    REQ     -   % QLENGTH DISTRIBUTION   -   AVG Q
CHN     0   1       PER         0    1    2    3    4+   LNGTH
                    SECOND
  0     0           24.145  100.0  0.0  0.0  0.0  0.0  0.00
  1     1,7         63.484   88.0  9.1  2.4  0.3  0.3  0.16
  2     2,8         26,264   72.0 22.4  4.3  0.9  0.5  0.36
  3     3,9         48.505   79.5 16.1  3.6  0.8  0.0  0.26
  4     4,A          9,079   84.0 15.1  0.9  0.0  0.0  0.17
  5     4,8         19.128   84.1 11.1  3.3  1.3  0.3  0.22
  7     5            0.351  100.0  0.0  0.0  0.0  0.0  0.00
  8     5,B          0.058  100.0  0.0  0.0  0.0  0.0  0.00
  9     6            0.140  100.0  0.0  0.0  0.0  0.0  0.00
 11     8            5.365   58.9 37.9  3.1  0.0  0.0  0.44
 14     B            9.126   88.9  8.5  2.3  0.3  0.1  0.14
```

- and continued below:

```
%REQ - % REQ DEFER DISTRIBUTION -    - % FREQ OF CONDITION     -
DEFER    CHAN   C.U.   DEV    LOG      CHAN   C.U.   DEV    LOG
         BUSY   BUSY   BUSY   BUSY     BUSY   BUSY   BUSY   BUSY
 3.85    7.89  92.11   0.00   0.00     5.13  44.81   0.00   0.00
15.27   35.90   1.62  35.95  26.53    76.10   9.26  87.36  61.58
23.22   84.03   3.53   1.48  10.97    85.73  12.64   6.76  14.02
21.98   15.82   5.07  27.93  51.19    49.44  27.91  81.48  65.46
34.48    0.96  98.83   0.00   0.21     2.13  68.96   0.00   0.38
27.30   11.59   0.38  26.86  61.16    24.53   1.25  44.43  60.83
 0.00    0.00   0.00   0.00   0.00     0.00   0.00   0.00   0.00
31.43   90.91   9.09   0.00   0.00     1.13   0.13   0.00   0.00
 0.00    0.00   0.00   0.00   0.00     0.00   0.00   0.00   0.00
13.40   71.23  28.77   0.00   0.00    18.77   8.14   0.00   0.00
18.20   61.95  38.05   0.00   0.00    43.68  28.91   0.00   0.00
```

%REQ DEFER DISTRIBUTION: Percent reasons why channel requests deferred
%FREQ OF CONDITION   : Frequency of each condition

The report has been edited

   Figure 67.   RMF Logical channel busy report

Figure 68 on page 119 does not show, however, the whole disk path. The
path to a disk consists of : Channel, Disk storage control, Disk string
control and Disk.   We do not get direct measurements of a disk storage
control and a disk head of string control. Therefore the load on these
must be calculated.   In a multi processor system, the calculation can be
difficult and a modelling tool like the one sketched on Figure 129 on page
211, is helpful.

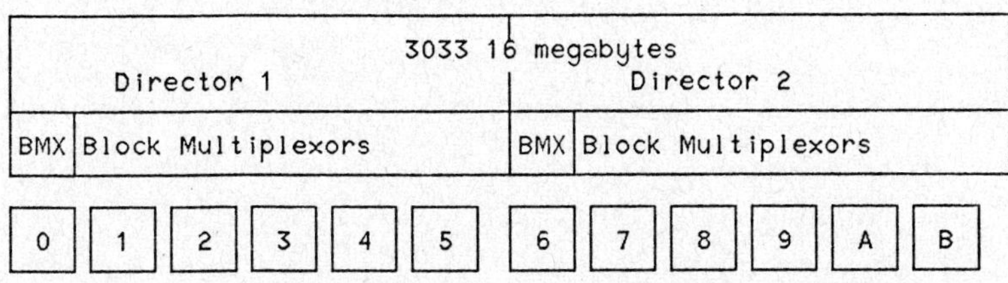

Figure 68.   Sample channel configuration

5.3.7 Job control

```
SDSF INPUT QUEUE DISPLAY ALL CLASSES                      LINE    1 TO   21 OF  76
COMMAND INPUT ===>                                               SCROLL ===> PAGE
NP C JOBNAME   JOBN PR C STAT POS JOB COMMENTS      SAFF ASYS NOTIFY  RNUM ACNT
     IS10PRW      3 1 A       1 CADG               MVSB      CADG          9275
     IS10PRW    863 1 A       2 CADG               MVSB      CADG          9275
     IS10JKL1  1102 1 A       3 JKL                MVSB      JKL           9225
     SMFCOPY1  1380 1 E HOLD    DYRHOLM                                    9905
     CCSISXXX  1384 1 E HOLD    MSS-SIS                                    9999
     ACCOSDAG  1398 1 E HOLD    DYRHOLM                                    9905
     SMFDAILY  1458 1 E         DCS-PREP,SW        MVSA MVSA              9905
     CCSISXXX  1566 1 E       1 MSS-SIS                                    9999
     CCMTOW    1701 1 E       2 CCMTO                                      9999
     CCSPAR    1517 1 G         SPA                MVSA MVSA CCSPA         9999
     JOPCDUMP  1565 1 G HOLD    IS-BACKUP AF DPC                          9905
     CCTHSA    1605 1 G       1 THORKIL            MVSA      CCTHS         9977
     CCTHA     1009 1 G       2 CCTH               MVSA      CCTH          9999
     MSVCDISB   476 1 8 HOLD    DISABLE MSVCJRNL MVSB                      9294
     MSVCENAB   482 1 8 HOLD    ENABLE MSVCJRNL  MVSB                      9294
     CPHRWS    1672 1 9         RWS                     MVSB               0004
     CCTHA      952 1 *       1 TH                 MVSD      CCTH          9999
     CCTHA      956 1 *       2 TH                 MVSD      CCTH          9999
     CCTHSZ    1681 1 *       3 THORKIL            MVSD      CCTHS         9999
```

```
JOBN:   JES2 job number    POS:      Priority position
PR :    JES2 priority       JOB
C:      Job class           COMMENTS: Description
STAT:   Status              SAFF:     System affinity
```

Figure 69.   SDSF JES2 input queue display

The JES2 input queue, shown on Figure 69 contains jobs ready to run, but
either in HOLD status by the operator, or that have not found an
initiator. Within each class the jobs are positioned, and I (CCTH) am
happy to see that I am first in class * for system MVSD. However, this
only means that my job will be **interpreted** first to find job class, priority etc. Afterwards I will join the queue for some specific class.
Figure 69 on page 119 refers to a multi-spooling system where any job may
run on any system if there is a free initiator with the appropriate class.
Normally, most classes would be restricted to to one system (processor)
only, and for cross-system classes, an affinity parameter can be specified
that limits the selection to one processor(SAFF on the figure). This is
done to avoid batch jobs constipating processors where interactive work
has top priority. Remember, even RMF has little control over I/O
priority, and a batch job can compete very successfully with interactive
work for I/O resources, especially paging and disk EXCPs. JES2 is thereby
no more an optimizing system, but that is not always needed with major
interactive systems.

```
SDSF OUTPUT ALL CLASSES    ALL FORMSLINES 1,177,632 LINE 22 TO 42 OF   59
COMMAND INPUT ===>                              SCROLL ===> PAGE
NP JOBNAME   JOBN PR C FORM FCB   UCS   FLSH  TOT REC    DEVICE ST ASYS
   ISSVAD      59  8 D STD. **** **** ****    15,564            HO
   ISMV1     2129  7 D STD. **** **** ****    22,451            HO
   J104TFU   1965  8 D STD. **** **** ****    16,530            HO
   IS10JKNN  1716  4 H STD. L12  DR10 ****        252    PRT12    MVSB
   FAKTURA   1712  4 H STD. **** **** ****        308    PRT12    MVSB
   CCTH      1105  4 H STD. 12   **** ****        504    PRT12    MVSB
   NPHVM     1087  3 H STD. L6   **** ****      2,019    PRT12    MVSB
   FAKTURA   1712  5 J 7230 6    **** ****        150
   STLI69PR  1620  4 J 0063 6    **** ****        357
   STLI60PR  1617  3 J 0063 6    **** ****      1,112
   IS20HAPT  1445  3 J 7802 6    UTNX ****      3,631
   CPHRWS     842 11 J T347 6    PN   ****        154
```

PR   : Print priority
C   : Print class
FCB : Forms Control Block - which print form requested
UCS : Universal Character Set - which print chain requested
FLSH : To be flushed (not printed)
ST   : Status (HOLD = do not print)
ASYS : System affinity

Figure 70.   SDSF JES2 output queue display

On Figure 70, I see that I (CCTH) have 504 lines scheduled for class H, a
3800 printer. There are also other jobs waiting, but few and short for
the H printer, meaning that my output should soon be available since I
specified a STD (standard) form. Some jobs like FACTURA are run for customers and need special forms.

5.4 MSS

Introduction

Assuming the configuration of the Complex Computing Centre described in chapter 10, the following MVS processors run:

    3033-A   : IMS production, batch, SCRIPT TSO, SLR.

    3033-B   : VSPC, Datacentre TSO/batch, Technical TSO/batch

    168UP   : Programming TSO/batch

    158   : IMS test and system test

Datasets frequently referenced by the online applications normally reside on disk, while MSS volumes typically are used for datasets less frequently referenced, but also for backup and 'historical' datasets. MSS is typically **tertiary storage**.

Thus the MSS contains groups of datasets such as:

    Backup and 'historical' volumes of datacentre applications,

    Backup and 'historical' IMS datasets

    'Historical' data of SLR (Service Level Reporter),

    System logs and job reports.

    HSM backups and migrated datasets

The MSS is very busy during evening and night, where most of the batch production takes place. Night batch production typically involves updating existing databases/datasets, a large number residing on MSS. In the future, virtual print is planned to reside on MSS.

MSS performance is a crucial factor for load and length of the night shift.

Poor Mass Storage System performance is, however, more directly felt by the VSPC or TSO user who has referenced a dataset residing on MSS. The MSS is usually performing better in the the daytime than in the evening; however, daytime work is more time critical.

Improving MSS performance is important both to the production manager realizing this bottleneck in the night batch production period, and to the daytime user longing for those response times that the CPU capacity seems to promise.

As with other performance improvement efforts, one should not hope to invent one brilliant change radically solving every problem. Performance improvement in a running computing centre is rather the story of small modifications, feasible within the overall framework of the computing center, inching gradually towards better service and higher profitability.

Mass Storage System principles of operations

In this section, selected principles of operations for the MSS are
described, as well as the hardware configuration supporting it.

Figure 71 shows a schematic summary of the MSS principles of operation.

Data reside on cartridges in the cartridge store. Each store has a capacity of, say, 100 Gigabytes, or 100000 megabytes. A pair of cartridges
constitutes one **virtual volume** or one **MSS volume**.

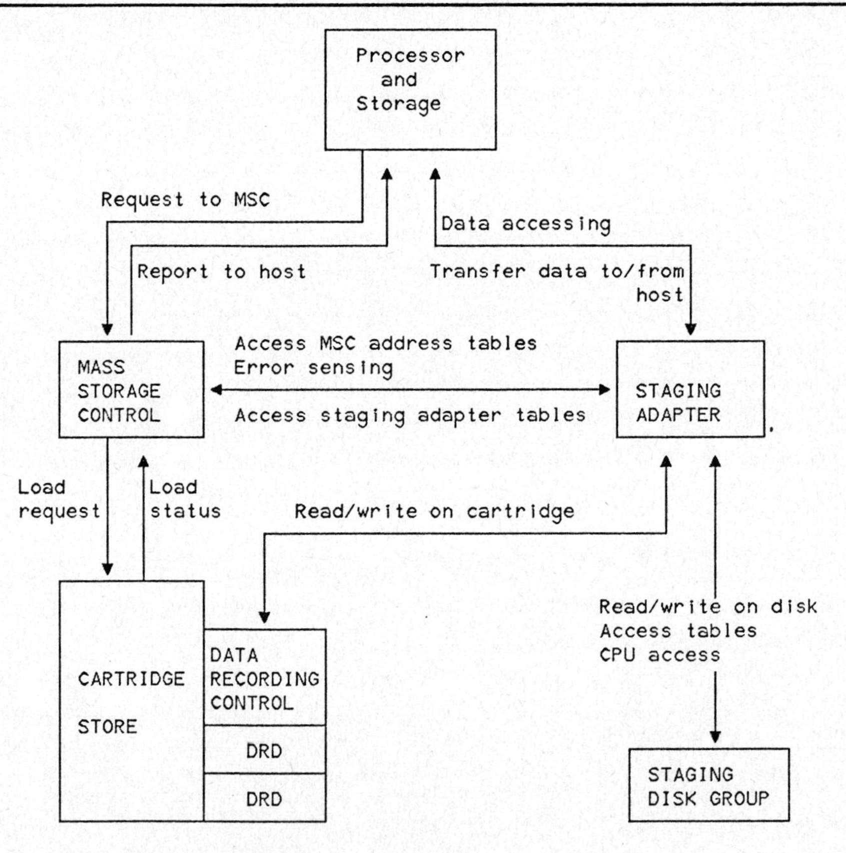

Figure 71.   MSS principles of operation

The virtual volume is referenced by the host CPU. The CPU sends a request
to the **Mass Storage Control (MSC)**, containing the reference to the virtual
volume. The request may be to read from or write to the volume.

Under the control of the MSC, the cartridge containing the Volume Table Of
Contents (VTOC) of the virtual volume is located and physically moved by

means of an **access arm** to a **Data Recording Device (DRD)**.   This process is
called **loading**.

From the DRD, data is transferred via a Staging Adapter (SA) to a disk
group working as a staging group for the MSS.   From here, data is accessed
by the CPU.

Transferring data from a DRD to staging group disks is called **staging**.   If
the contents of a virtual volume are changed, the cartridge is reloaded
and data written back to it from the staging group; this process is called
destaging.

Data can be staged in units of one cylinder.   It may then happen that the
referenced data is not found among the staged cylinders so that the cartridge has to be loaded again and another cylinder staged.   The cylinder
is said to be transferred by **cylinder fault**.   This is normally bad for MSS
performance.   Normally it is better to stage in units of **one page,** where
one page is equal to eight cylinders.   From time to time, pages are staged
by page fault, but this happens much more rarely.

If insufficient staging space is available, the MSS uses a mechanism to
clear some space, called **LRU** (for Least Recently Used).   This implies that
the least recently used cylinder(s) are cleared away before a new staging
(or destaging) can take place.   The situation prolongs MSS response times
because the normal requests have to wait for the LRU process.

The MSC treats the requests in order of arrival; however, staging has normally priority over destaging.   If more than one DRD is operational, the
MSC selects the DRD giving the least possible arm movement.   If more than
one staging group is available, the one with most available space is chosen.

MSS hardware configuration

A two MSS hardware configuration is shown on Figure 72 on page 124.   The
MSSs communicate with 4 processors, corresponding to the CCC hardware configuration in chapter 10.   There are on the figure two Mass Storage Facilities (MSFs) with the controllers:

MSC 0 : the controller of the first MSF
MSC 1 : the controller of the second MSF

Each MSF also have four DRDs. DRD 20x are the DRSs for the first MSF
(with MSC 0), where the x stands for the four numbers 0 to 3.

Each MSF has two staging adapters and two staging disk groups.

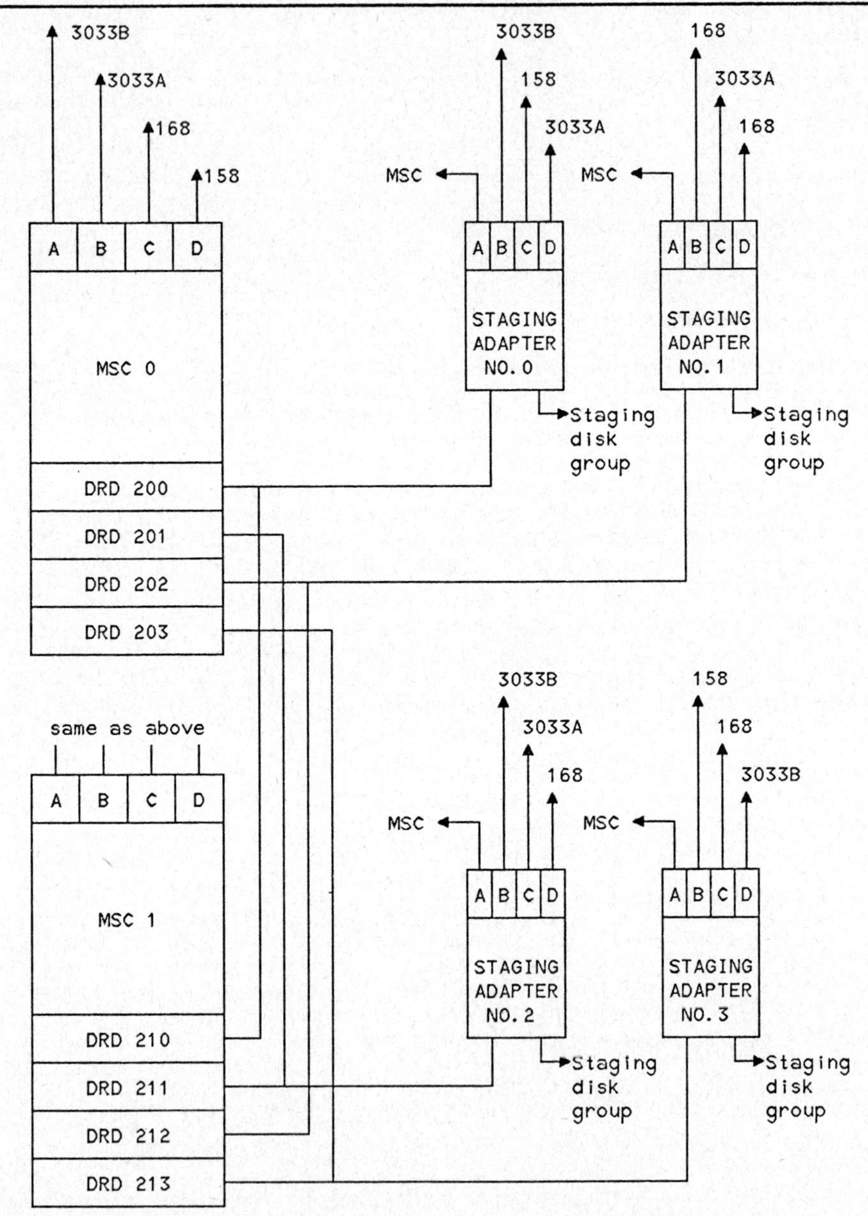

Figure 72. Sample MSS configuration - 2 MSS and 4 MVS systems

MSS measurement tools

The software tools used to monitor MSS performance may be grouped as follows:

1.   The MSS TRACE facility which logs the individual MSS transactions.

2.   A selection and formatting program that extracts required information
     from MSS TRACE and formats it into a table.

3.   Analysis and reduction programs tailored by the analyst to deduce
     meaningful correlations and - hopefully - increase the possibility of
     efficient performance improvements and capacity planning.

4.   The MSS trace/SMF Correlation Aid which logs all volume references,
     reports all references to each single volume, analyses performance on
     a five minutes basis, and summarizes performance totals.

5.   RMF giving MSC busy wait and virtual volume busy/wait.

6.   Integration with existing programs analysing channel and disk load and
     performance.

The relationship between the software tools is shown on Figure 73 on page
126.

MSS trace

Recordings to the MSS TRACE dataset are automatic and concurrent with MSS
operation. For each transaction the following information is recorded:

*   The time when the transaction was requested.

*   The volume identification.

*   The type of transaction (stage or destage).

*   The number of cylinders and pages staged or destaged.

*   The number (if any) of cylinders staged by cylinder fault, or destaged
    using LRU.

*   Identification of the MSF, DRD, staging adapter and staging group used
    in the transaction.

*   Durations of queueing for service, loading the cartridge, and staging
    or destaging the contents.

*   Etc.

A suitable amount of information (typically covering 7-8 hours) constitutes one trace 'generation'. The generation datasets are numbered conse-
qutively and may reside on MSS volumes.

The MSS TRACE report contains the transactions of all the Mass Storage
Facilities used. The host CPU does not care which MSF is used but only
how much time it has to wait for each request to be serviced. It is one
of the tasks of the analyst to use the MSS TRACE to investigate the performance of each individual MSF.

The formated trace output

A standard program is used to extract and summarize required data from the
MSS TRACE. The user specifies the time interval of interest. A module
has been created to convert from hexadecimal notation and format the output. An example of an output table is shown on Figure 74 on page 127 and
Figure 75 on page 128.

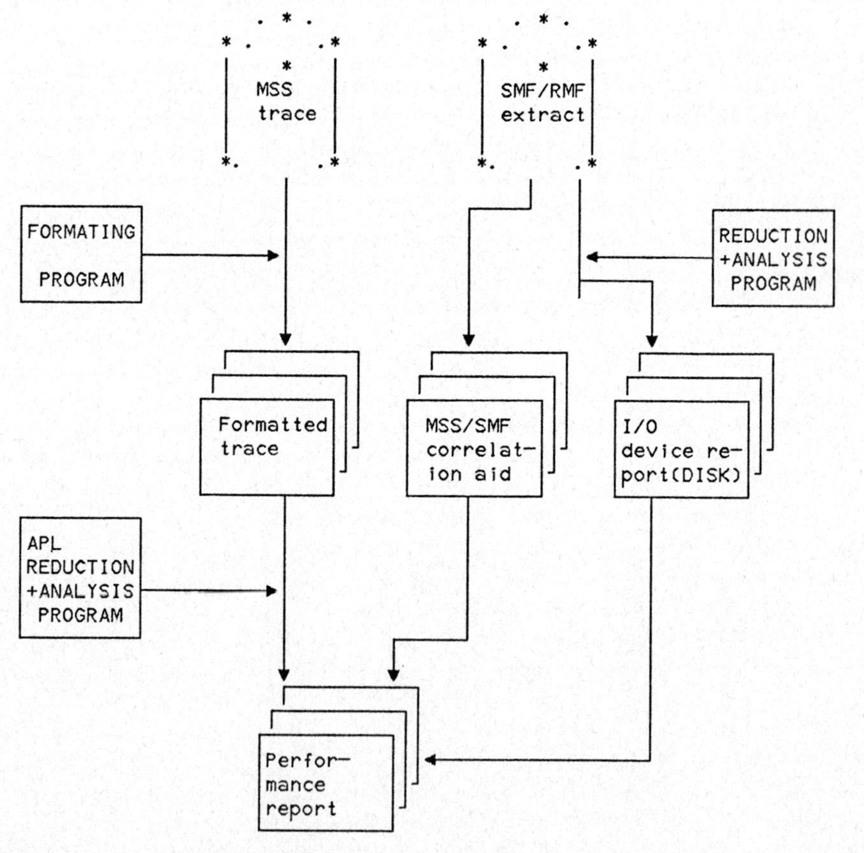

Figure 73. MSS analysis tools

<pre>
                       TRACE FROM 01/19/1982 AT 17 H 00.02 TO 01

 I   I   I STAGE/ I CYL I FAULT I LRU I PAGES I VTOC I
 I DAY I   TIME   I DESTAGE I NB   I CYL I CYL I NB   I S/D I

 I 19 I 22.54.41 I   STAGE I 07 I   07 I   I 01 I 00 I
 I 19 I 22.54.25 I   STAGE I 64 I   I   I 09 I 00 I
 I 19 I 22.55.33 I DESTAGE I 18 I   I 18 I 06 I 00 I
 I 19 I 22.56.36 I   STAGE I 01 I   I   I 01 I 01 I
 I 19 I 22.55.32 I DESTAGE I 41 I   I 41 I 06 I 00 I
 I 19 I 22.55.33 I DESTAGE I 04 I   I 04 I 02 I 00 I
 I 19 I 22.55.32 I DESTAGE I 58 I   I 58 I 09 I 01 I
 I 19 I 22.55.35 I   STAGE I 01 I   I   I 01 I 01 I
 I 19 I 22.57.48 I   STAGE I 01 I   I   I 01 I 00 I
 I 19 I 22.56.20 I   STAGE I 01 I   I   I 01 I 01 I
 I 19 I 22.55.34 I DESTAGE I 16 I   I 16 I 03 I 00 I
 I 19 I 22.56.58 I   STAGE I 05 I   I   I 02 I 00 I
 I 19 I 22.58.10 I   STAGE I 02 I   I   I 01 I 00 I
 I 19 I 22.59.24 I DESTAGE I 01 I   I   I 01 I 01 I
 I 19 I 22.59.07 I DESTAGE I 23 I   I 23 I 04 I 00 I
 I 19 I 23.00.02 I DESTAGE I 01 I   I   I 01 I 01 I
 I 19 I 22.59.04 I   STAGE I 54 I   I   I 08 I 00 I
 I 19 I 23.00.08 I DESTAGE I 01 I   I 01 I 01 I 00 I
 I 19 I 23.00.02 I DESTAGE I 11 I   I   I 02 I 00 I
 I 19 I 23.01.34 I   STAGE I 01 I   I   I 01 I 00 I
 I 19 I 23.00.09 I DESTAGE I 04 I   I 04 I 02 I 00 I
 I 19 I 22.59.29 I DESTAGE I 98 I   I 98 I 13 I 00 I

</pre>

Figure 74.   MSS TRACE record

Most data in the output record refer to standard MSS terms. 'VOLUME' is
the MVS volume identifier that makes it possible to track the job requesting the transactions, and find jobs particularly heavy on the MSS. 'LXYZ'
gives the location of the cartridge in the MSS coordinate system. 'SA' is
the staging adapter and 'STGR' the staging disk group used. 'DRD' is the
identification of the reading device used. DRDs 200-203 belong to MSF
no.1 and DRDs 210-213 to MSF no.2, referring to Figure 72 on page 124.

The durations are all in units of 1/4 seconds. To recapitulate:

* TIME SYST is the time from the request is received by the Mass Storage
  Control to the transaction is completed and the cartridge ready to be
  unloaded.

* TIME DRD is the time in which the reading device is busy. This time
  is the sum of:

  - TIME STAGE - the time needed to stage/destage the cylinder(s).

  - TIME LOAD - the time needed to physically move the cartridge from
    its position in the MSF to the DRD.

```
1/20/1982 AT 00 H 30.49
-----------------------------------------------------------------------
I          I           I SA- I       I TIME I TIME I TIME  I TIME  I
I VOLUME I    LXYZ    I STGR I DRD I SYST I DRD  I STAGE I LOAD  I
-----------------------------------------------------------------------
I CC1660 I 214 27 1 I 3-02 I 202 I 128 I 112 I  89 I 23 I
I CC1791 I 223 01 0 I 3-02 I 201 I 567 I 537 I 537 I 00 I
I CC1494 I 221 05 1 I 2-03 I 202 I 382 I 380 I 343 I 37 I
I CC2025 I 231 10 0 I 3-02 I 210 I 154 I 153 I 122 I 31 I
I CC1817 I 230 00 1 I 2-03 I 203 I 471 I 470 I 414 I 56 I
I CC1494 I 218 06 0 I 2-03 I 201 I 500 I 145 I 104 I 41 I
I CC1817 I 230 00 0 I 3-03 I 200 I 552 I 550 I 520 I 30 I
I CC1281 I 238 24 0 I 3-02 I 203 I 542 I  58 I  15 I 43 I
I CC2025 I 232 10 1 I 3-02 I 210 I  48 I  19 I  19 I 00 I
I CC1777 I 239 02 0 I 2-02 I 201 I 408 I  42 I  03 I 39 I
I CC1360 I 212 11 0 I 2-03 I 202 I 600 I 149 I 107 I 42 I
I CC1216 I 232 07 0 I 2-03 I 203 I 332 I 101 I  55 I 46 I
I CC2025 I 232 10 1 I 3-02 I 210 I  53 I  49 I  22 I 27 I
I CC1755 I 246 24 1 I 2-03 I 200 I  83 I  81 I  52 I 29 I
I CC1449 I 213 01 1 I 2-02 I 202 I 215 I 214 I 185 I 29 I
I CC1636 I 245 18 0 I 3-02 I 202 I 127 I  81 I  40 I 41 I
I CC1791 I 223 01 0 I 2-02 I 203 I 409 I 408 I 380 I 28 I
I CC1459 I 212 01 1 I 3-03 I 203 I 320 I 133 I  91 I 42 I
I CC1636 I 245 18 1 I 2-02 I 202 I 349 I 191 I 149 I 42 I
I CC2025 I 232 10 1 I 2-02 I 210 I  51 I  20 I  20 I 00 I
I CC1494 I 221 05 1 I 3-03 I 202 I 507 I 148 I 100 I 48 I
I CC1922 I 246 06 1 I 3-02 I 200 I 700 I 603 I 569 I 34 I
-----------------------------------------------------------------------
```

Figure 75.   MSS TRACE record (Continued)

The relation between these durations is sketched on Figure 76 on page 129.

Some examples of what information can be retrieved from the TRACE are:

- Staging adapters 2 and 3 seem very busy. This will be discussed further in the next chapter.

- Cylinder faults do not cause problems. This is the result of staging page by page in stead of cylinder by cylinder.

- The number of LRUs is high. This is partly because many large volumes are staged at the same time, but also because only part of the staging space is available.   The cause of this problem will be discussed later.

- The load time is relatively small, and independent of the amount of data staged, as it should be. If it is significantly larger than about 10 seconds on average, corrective action should be taken.

- The difference between the system time and the DRD time is important since this is the queue time, during which the request has been received but no DRD was available. When this duration is long, performance is seriously affected.

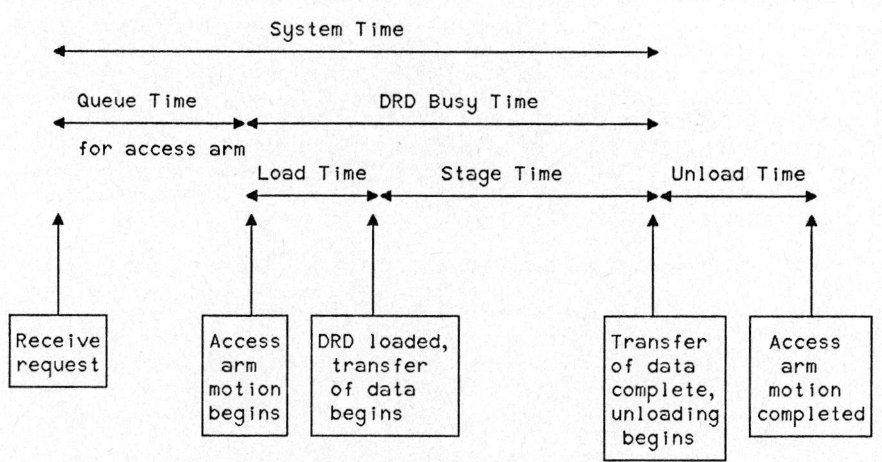

Figure 76.   Stages in MSS operation

It is useful to investigate the work of each single DRD in detail. The
following questions may be answered:

* Is any DRD overloaded compared to the others?

* Is any DRD significantly slower in transferring data than the others?

* Why is a particular queue developing?

* Does staging get priority over destaging (as it should)?

In addition to the detailed report, a summary is produced, as shown on
Figure 77.

TRACE FROM 01/19/1982 AT 17 H 00.02 TO 01/20/1982 AT 00 H 30.49

```
TOTAL STAGED CYLINDERS                        8722
TOTAL DESTAGED CYLINDERS                       9907
TOTAL STAGED CYLINDERS BY CYL FAULT            1610
TOTAL CYLINDERS LRUED                          1909
TOTAL NO OF ALLOCATED PAGES                    3910
TOTAL NO OF STAGED/DESTAGED VTOCS               886
TOTAL NO OF LOADED CARTRIDGES                  1583
TOTAL SYSTEM TIME IN SECONDS                 110337
TOTAL DRD BUSY TIME IN SECONDS               58932
TOTAL STAGING/DESTAGING TIME IN SECS         45317
TOTAL LOAD CART TIME IN SECONDS              13138
```

Figure 77.   MSS trace summary

More cylinders have been destaged than staged during the report period.
Normally, much of the batch production in the studied centre - as for many
large database services - is directed towards updating data bases. When
many destages occur and the system attempts to load the voluminous databases, the result is often a number of LRU situations. The average number
of LRUs is below 300 per hour - high, but not extreme. Some action should
be taken, see Figure 78 on page 131.

The summary is useful for evaluating average values of workload, DRD busy
time, response times etc. For example, we see that the average system
time per transaction is

TOTAL SYSTEM TIME/NO OF LOADED CARTRIDGES = 110337/1583 = 69.7 sec.

The average number of cylinders transferred per transaction is

(TOTAL STAGED CYL.+TOTAL DESTAGED CYL.)/NO OF LOADED CARTRIDGES
                                    = (8722+9907)/1583
                                    = 11.8 CYLINDERS

The average system time per cylinder processed (a useful measure of system
performance) is:

TOTAL SYST/(STAGED CYL.+DESTAGED CYL) = 110337/(8722+9907) = 5.92 sec.

5.4.1 MSS key indicators

The following (by no means exhaustive) set of key indicators of MSS performance, are suggested, see Figure 78 on page 131. For each indicator is
listed the TARGET value that the indicator should have in order for performance to be acceptable. The target values depends on the computer centre in question. Thus, a centre with twice as many DRDs and twice as much
staging space should be able to cope with twice as large a load, while the
target LRU value should be only half as large.

These key indicators are computed per shift. In this study, the period of
primary interest was Mondays through Fridays from 1700 to 0100 hours.
This is the main period of batch production. During this period, the MSS
load is heaviest, so this was the time when most problems occurred, and
where the beneficent effects of modifications are most apparent.

NAME	DEFINITION	TARGET
LOAD	(Cylinders staged+destaged)/hour	< 3000
LRU	Cylinders destaged using LRU/hour	< 200
QUEUE TIME (TOT)	(System time-DRD time)/system time for total system or MSF	< 50%
QUEUE TIME (DRD)	(System time-DRD time)/system time for individual DRD	< 50%
DRD BUSY PCT.	(DRD time+load time)/hour for individual DRD (see note)	< 80%
STAGING ADAPTER LOAD	Pct. of total load serviced by individual staging adapter	all equal
RESP. TIME	System time/(cylinders staged +cylinders destaged)	< 5 sec.

Note: The DRD busy time is the sum of load time, staging time and unload time. The reported 'DRD time' consists of only load and staging time. Thus, we approximate the unload time with the load time and add it to the DRD time.

Figure 78. MSS key indicators

During daytime, TSO users occasionally experience frustration from poor MSS performance, and will benefit from improvements.

Shift key indicators are useful for studying general trends. However, the load on the MSS shows very large variations - requests tend to arrive in lumps. It is therefore interesting to study the performance over short periods of time - an hour or even a few minutes. This will be described next.

5.4.2 APL reduction and analysis program for MSS

An APL program complex has been developed to further analyse the MSS TRACE. These analyses cover areas such as:

- Performance during short intervals, i.e. identification of bottleneck periods and how the MSS responds to them.

- Analysis of individual components:

  - MSFs

  - DRDs

  - Staging adapters

        —   Staging drives

The system may be extended to cover the following:

- Analyse the impact of different job types:

  - IMS database updates

  - Performance control data

  - Daytime batch

  - Online applications

- Statistical correlations between various factors and performance.

- ...and many others.

Standard APL can be used to produce graphical reports through APL Graphpak (see chapter 2).

Gross trends

On Figure 79, a sample summary of MSS performance measurements have been listed, covering the period October 19, 1981 through January 29, 1982, or week 43 in 1981 through week 4 in 1982. The indicators reported are defined in the previous chapter.

Week	Cyls/Hour	LRUs/Hour	Q Time (pct.)	Resp.Time/Cyl
43/81	2650	125	72.4	9.39
44/81	3091	302	75.0	9.90
45/81	2708	188	76.0	13.25
46/81	2030	225	68.2	8.80
47/81	2977	216	67.6	8.29
48/81	2439	144	54.4	6.04
49/81	2509	240	64.5	9.28
50/81	2863	187	71.2	11.64
51/81	2402	109	65.3	8.78
52/81	2709	234	58.1	7.88
53/81	2490	203	68.2	11.18
01/82	2561	172	55.3	6.38
02/82	2862	247	54.5	6.09
03/82	2672	202	52.3	5.53
04/82	2417	227	45.6	4.92
05/82	2790	192	51.8	4.99
06/82	3095	175	57.7	5.40

Figure 79. MSS performance report

The trends are apparent on the graphical representation of the report (Figure 80 on page 134).

Workload and jobmix

The workload, measured by the number of cylinders staged or destaged, reached a maximum ultimo 1981. This may be just a reflection of the end of year production load, or it could indicate an implementation of a more expedient dataset organization.

Another factor may be equally or more important. Apparently, some jobs periodically almost monopolize the MSS. Updating one particular database could on several occasions clog the system completely. On one occasion it was observed that this job alone used more than 25 pct. of the DRD time of the whole primary batch production period - more than twice the DRD time of all other day batch services taken together! It was then decided to schedule the heavy job after the busiest time of the shift. This was implemented medio November.

Because workload is a significant factor, the batch production should be planned to start the heaviest jobs well apart. The studied system seemed to get into trouble when the workload approached 3000 cylinders staged and destaged per hour.

LRUing

The number of LRUs is a prime factor determining performance, and the number of LRUs at the studied installation was high: at times, no less than 20 pct. of the destaged cylinders required LRU!

The LRU process delays staging and may be an important cause of queueing. At the end of November in the example, additional staging space was installed: 4 3350 spindles, increasing the staging capacity by about 50 pct.

It is therefore a cause of concern that this does not seem to have had the expected effect: the number of LRUs remained at the previous level.

The explanation probably is the allocation of staging space by contending data volumes.

In particular, the HSM release 2 was a prime suspect (more on HSM in next section). This HSM release does not deallocate its cylinders after use before HSM is restarted. The restart is made early in the morning, after completing night batch production but before the online applications take over.

The result is that the MSS, during the prime batch production period, has only a small fraction of its staging space available. This leads to queueing, contention between MSS stagings for staging space, and heavy LRUing.

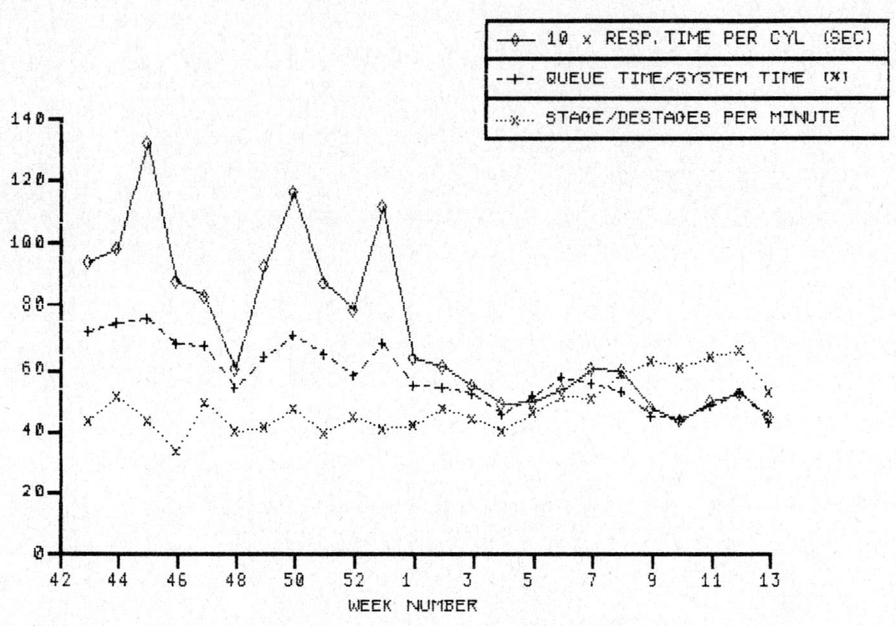

Figure 80.   MSS performance - graphical representation

The problem was solved by installing HSM release 3.   The new release automatically deallocates its cylinders after use, making it possible for the
MSS to benefit fully from all its staging space.

DRD performance.

Queue time has decreased.   An access arm is only allocated when there is
an available DRD ready to receive the MSS cartridge. Queuing physically
can therefore only occur for the access arm, but its cause may be contention for one or more of several components. Beside contention for
staging space, the largest cause of queueing is DRD unavailability. At
the beginning of the time frame under consideration, only 3 DRDs were
operational, the fourth being under hardware repair. At the conclusion of
the study, two MSFs with a total of 8 DRDs were operational, and this has
had a positive effect on the system.

5.4.3 Mass Storage Control

The Mass Storage Control is the 'CPU', the brain, of the MSS. Commands to this centre is issued from all attached CPUs. Like an ordinary CPU, the MSC can be a bottleneck for good performance.

One request from a CPU to the MSS may initiate many internal MSS commands, thereby producing queues when the same or other CPUs issue new requests.

Many internal commands occur when there is strong contention for staging space. The problem can therefore be lessened by installing adequate staging space.

This is analogous to paging in an ordinary computer system. The CPU is burdened with a lot of instructions for paging when the paging rate is high.

Response times

A positive development is reflected in the example shown, by response time per cylinder staged or destaged (Figure 79 on page 132 or Figure 80 on page 134). Obviously, the system now accomplishes its work in less time than before.

However, long wait times are still frequent, and there are still long queues that only can be found by more detailed analysis.

5.4.4 MSS hourly based analysis

A fuller understanding of the MSS performance implies a higher time resolution, as well as detailed investigation of the MSS TRACE.

Earlier in this chapter, we saw an example of how MSS TRACE pointed out particularly heavy jobs. The TRACE is also essential to understand the causes of particularly long queues. Such investigation is, however, quite time-consuming, and is therefore in practice carried out when other indicators point out the existence of a problem.

Overall MSS performance

TIME		MSS data									
HOUR	DAY	STAG	DEST	CYL	PAGS	LRU	SYS	DRD	STG	LOAD	QUEUE
17-18	3	218	398	616	152	7	21	18	11	7	15.10
18-19	3	618	932	1550	333	306	68	28	20	9	59.50
19-20	3	1454	1338	2792	560	298	100	37	28	9	63.30
20-21	3	3237	697	3934	701	152	138	48	43	8	65.50
21-22	3	1267	1284	2551	471	375	58	44	36	8	24.90
22-23	3	2535	1122	3657	649	99	88	44	40	8	50.40
23-24	3	1378	2177	3555	628	470	137	39	30	9	71.70
24-01	4	912	1488	2400	389	0	117	49	43	7	58.30

Figure 81.   MSS overall performance, February 3, 1982

Figure 81 shows an hourly analysis of MSS performance during the batch
production period on February 3-4, 1982.

Data columns 1, 2 and 3 show, respectively, the number of cylinders
staged, destaged and the total number of cylinders serviced. The fourth
column is the number of PAGeS serviced. One page contains eight
cylinders, but smaller amounts of data are also staged in units of one
page. As previously mentioned, this is done to reduce the number of cylinder faults.

Next, the number of LRUs is shown. It is obvious that this number varies
a lot during the period. There is no obvious relation between the number
of destaged and LRUed cylinders. Rather, the LRU number depends upon a
number of parameters e.g. the jobmix, the sequence of the requests and the
characteristics of the individual jobs. The arrival of requests is a more
or less random process, and the LRU number is highly sensitive to fluctuations in the arrivals.

The next four columns are average values per request of the SYStem, DRD,
STaGe and LOAD times as previously described.

The load time has been quite stable, around 8 seconds, and is not a cause
for concern.

The stage and DRD times correlate fairly well with the workload.

The system time, however, is more capricious. The difference between system time and DRD time is expressed as the QUEUE time, displayed in the
last column. This is best indicator of long MSS response times. As is
the case with the LRU number, queue time is vulnerable to small, random
fluctuations in the job load. Because load times are important to user
satisfaction/frustration, it is worth while to investigate more closely
what causes the long queue times.

It is evident that although LRUing is certainly one cause of queueing,
there must be other causes: the hour with the second largest LRUing has
very little queueing.

Part of the answer is that destagings normally have lower priority than
stagings, (although occasionally a destaging is allowed to slip in front
of a waiting staging).   Therefore, an hour with comparatively many
destagings has on average longer queue times.

In order to investigate the problem further, a more detailed study of the
individual components of the system is necessary. For instance, we might
ask how an individual MSF, or staging adapter, or DRD has performed.

Staging adapter performance

Figure 82 shows staging adapter data for the same period as shown above.

The MSS configuration (Figure 72 on page 124) shows four staging adapters:
two (number 0 and 1) connected to a 3330 staging disk group, the two others (number 2 and 3) to a 3350 staging group. In the table, the load on
each staging adapter is listed: CYLn and PCTn are the number of cylinders
serviced and the percentage of the total number serviced by staging adapter n.

HOUR	DAY	CYL0	PCT0	CYL1	PCT1	CYL2	PCT2	CYL3	PCT3
17-18	3	26	4.20	56	9.10	72	11.70	462	75.00
18-19	3	27	1.70	6	.40	592	38.20	925	59.70
19-20	3	98	3.50	281	10.10	952	34.10	1461	52.30
20-21	3	132	3.40	337	8.60	2114	53.70	1351	34.30
21-22	3	6	.20	106	4.20	994	39.00	1445	56.60
22-23	3	428	11.70	583	15.90	914	25.00	1732	47.40
23-24	3	56	1.60	345	9.70	1474	41.50	1680	47.30
24- 1	4	64	2.70	8	.30	1558	64.90	770	32.10

Figure 82.   Staging adapter performance, February 3, 1982

Based on the table one additional cause of queues can be identified:
almost all staging goes via the second staging group. The reason for this
was described in the previous section: allocation of most 3330 space by
other jobs, presumably HSM. The situation is not healthy for system performance.

DRD performance

HOUR	DAY	BUS200	Q200	BUS201	Q201
17-18	3	12.20	10.27	.00	.00
18-19	3	39.60	68.16	.00	.00
19-20	3	51.04	66.06	.00	.00
20-21	3	40.54	67.19	.00	.00
21-22	3	29.95	43.12	.00	.00
22-23	3	47.06	55.58	.00	.00
23-24	3	75.69	73.78	.00	.00
24- 1	4	44.22	62.99	.00	.00

HOUR	DAY	BUS202	Q202	BUS203	Q203	CYL
17-18	3	11.37	15.52	9.36	17.75	481
18-19	3	43.18	57.13	24.38	40.95	1513
19-20	3	53.54	67.20	54.10	65.22	2115
20-21	3	37.66	70.51	37.19	70.85	1904
21-22	3	37.38	37.09	34.31	24.55	1582
22-23	3	43.58	37.05	45.49	56.64	2140
23-24	3	81.57	75.89	52.08	70.80	3109
24- 1	4	51.17	62.80	37.83	42.08	2336

Figure 83.   DRD performance - MSF no.0

Figure 83 and Figure 84 on page 139 show the results of the analysis of
DRD performance.   According to Figure 72 on page 124, the DRD's with
addresses 200-203 belong to MSF number 0, while the DRD's with addresses
210-213 belong to MSF number 1.

For each DRD, the DRD busy percent and the queue time (as defined in Figure 78 on page 131) are calculated.   In addition, the last column contains
the total number of cylinders serviced by the appropriate MSF.   Comparison
of the two tables thus yields the relative load on the two MSFs.

Two DRDs (201 and 211) were not used.   This might indicate hardware problems.   A more plausible reason is that it is due to the configuration.

From Figure 72 on page 124, we see that DRDs 201, 203, 211 and 213 transfer data to the second staging group. This staging group has only one head
of string, so data can only flow to or from one DRD at a time.   Since
staging and destaging occupy the largest part of the DRD time (compare
Figure 81 on page 136), the result may be that the DRD is very rarely busy
while the head of string is active.   Therefore, one DRD is enough to handle the data transfer to this staging group.

HOUR	DAY	BUS210	Q210	BUS211	Q211
17-18	3	3.10	16.91	.00	.00
18-19	3	.31	2.22	.00	.00
19-20	3	11.46	57.58	.00	.00
20-21	3	34.14	76.22	.00	.00
21-22	3	35.59	3.61	.00	.00
22-23	3	43.12	40.74	.00	.00
23-24	3	11.53	1.83	.00	.00
24- 1	4	.86	2.36	.00	.00

HOUR	DAY	BUS212	Q212	BUS213	Q213	CYL
17-18	3	2.63	20.88	2.23	15.75	135
18-19	3	.85	21.15	.31	2.22	37
19-20	3	9.43	10.60	9.83	.14	677
20-21	3	38.40	55.03	47.33	35.35	2030
21-22	3	8.79	24.14	28.34	2.18	969
22-23	3	39.53	53.67	27.74	52.51	1517
23-24	3	3.54	50.24	11.78	.29	446
24- 1	4	3.65	47.03	.00	.00	64

Figure 84.   DRD performance - MSF no.1

We may thus have identified another potential bottleneck: having only one path to a given staging group may be a source of queues.

The mean queue times of the DRDs should be identical. The queue time is seen to be related to the busy percent, although one has to remember that destagings have longer queues than stagings.

5.4.5 MSS performance conlusion

Summary of the chapter

In this chapter, we have described several problems experienced with MSS and their possible solutions. To summarize:

- Workloads and jobmixes are potential problems. An analysis should be made to identify particularly heavy jobs. When this is done, production can be planned accordingly.

- Shortage of staging space shows up in two ways: Heavy LRUing, or long queue times without correspondingly large DRD busy percents. The reason for lacking staging space may be actual shortage of physical

devices.   It may also be the result of contention for staging space
with other jobs.

- The third potential bottleneck is DRD performance. It is indicated by
  long queues correlated to high DRD busy percents. Such a bottleneck
  may be the result of hardware problems. Alternatively, more MSF
  capacity may be necessary.

- MSC is also a performance factor, it is however difficult to evaluate
  the influence of commands from many different CPUs. If only one CPU
  is involved, the MSC can directly be measured and should not be more
  busy than any other CPU; i.e. the busy percent depends on the service
  level offered.

It is worth while to spend considerable time and effort developing MSS
performance study tools. The degree of detail presented in this chapter
appears sufficient to evaluate the aspects of performance.

Conserns

The primary concerns related to MSS performance and MSS capacity planning
are

- How can MSS performance be directly related to total system performance?   And what performance indicator(s) should be followed by people
  watching for signs of impending MSS problems? Candidates might be
  batch turnaround time, or the number of TSO response times longer than
  (say) 15 seconds.

- How can online RMF monitoring give clues to MSS performance? RMFMON
  (next chapter) provides information like: TSO users in 'Detected
  Wait', transaction rates for TSO performance groups, and I/O rates.

  From   this   to   telling   batch   operators   what   jobs   to
  hold/start/cancel/downgrade is some way. Many jobs in 'detected wait'
  status points to an MSS problem.

  A facility which might be useful in this respect is the Syslog Display
  and Search Facility (SDSF), that among other facilities contain information on the progress and resource utilisation of batch jobs.

- What MSS capacity should be planned for a centre of a given size?
  This planning could be based on service agreements with the users. If
  so, how is a user's request for a given amount of service translated
  into projected MSS resources?

- What is the optimal capacity and configuration of staging space? When
  planning to increase the load, which component will first become a
  bottleneck?

- What is the expected effect of increasing the use of MSS for instance
  using MSS for virtual print or generation datasets?

Conclusion

The Mass Storage System, when used, influences performance of both batch and online production.

MSS performance control should be integrated with routine system performance control. This is a natural task for I/O space management, who also monitors disk performance.

In order to control the MSS as an integral part of a computing center, we need to know the effect of bad MSS performance on primary performance indicators: response times and turnaround times.

For capacity planning a good understanding of the relation between MSS behaviour and user service is fundamental.

Another aspect of capacity planning is deciding what work should be allowed on the MSS.

In total, MSS should be controlled and planned as the critical performance resource it is.

5.4.6 The Hierarchial Storage Management system (HSM)

This is a software product designed to store data on different devices (secondary or tertiary storage) dependent on usage frequency and other parameters.

HSM use different devices for different purposes.

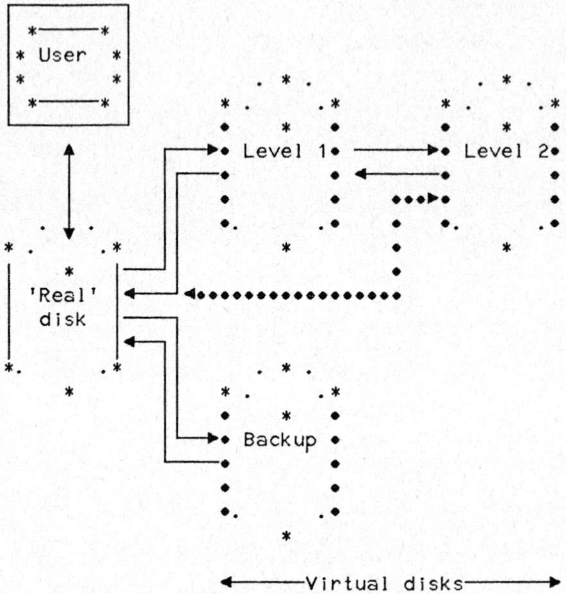

Figure 85.   HSM conceptual setup

On Figure 85, the user deals with datasets on real disks.   These disks may
have been defined to belong to a HSM set.   When the user requests it, or
when the system so decides, the data set(s) on the real disks are moved -
or **migrated** to disks further back in the hierarchy, first to level 1, then
to level 2.   Backup may be taken directly to the backup volumes, and
restored from there.

The user can also request a direct transfer of a dataset to either of the
level 1 or 2 volumes, or a copy to backup volumes, even if the originating
disk is not defined as part of HSM.   When a dataset is restored again, it
needs to be migrated anew if HSM storage is required.

Performance of such a system is difficult to analyze.   The user will feel
hang-ups when requesting a virtual dataset that cannot be staged because
the MSS is overloaded.   Most often his/her datasets have been migrated to
another level HSM device overnight.   Seldom used datasets almost certainly
are migrated.   If the user then is in a hurry, frustrations are likely.
Deciding when to back up is difficult; perhaps it is better to concentrate
on improving MSS performance that also certainly will favorably impact
HSM.

Figure 112 on page 186 shows an example of measurements for such a structure.   Because many of the virtual disks had been destaged when the sample
was taken, few of the HSM disks are reported.   However, the report can
give indications that a problem is specific to HSM rather than global to
MSS, especially if HSM disks behave abnormally over long periods.

5.5 NETWORK

The primary resources in the network are hardware: Terminals, controllers,
lines, modems etc. Controlling the usage of these needs extensions to the
software and possibly to already installed hardware.

Secondary resources in the network are programs to handle communications
and the buffers used. ACF/VTAM enables us to display buffer usage for
example as shown in Figure 86.

Related to our performance definitions, secondary resource measuring
yields tertiary performance indicators.

```
d net,bfruse
IST097 DISPLAY ACCEPTED
EE932I P00 798
IST350I VTAM DISPLAY - DOMAIN TYPE=BUFFER POOL DATA
IST632I VTAM  BUFF  CURR  CURR  MAX    MAX  TIMES  EXCP/CONT     EXCP
IST633I BUFF  SIZE  TOTAL AVAIL TOTAL  USED EXP    THRESHOLD     INCR


IST356I I000   00139 00118 00054 00226 00178 00177   00032/00068 00018
IST356I PP00   00015 00001 00001 00001 00000 00000      N/A        N/A
IST356I WP00   00144 00078 00042 00101 00080 00001   00016.......00023


IST449I CSALIMIT=0307200,CURRENT=0286808,MAXIMUM=0287608


 Parts of the original figure are left out
```

Figure 86.   VTAM buffer display (from reference 40)

The description to Figure 86 reads: 'For example in the buffer pool with
id WP00, each buffer has 144 bytes (first numerical column), 78 buffers
are currently in the pool, and 42 of those are available. The most buffers the pool has contained is 101 and the most buffers ever used at one
time is 80. The buffer pool has expanded once. If the number of available buffers falls below 16, ACF/VTAM adds twentythree buffers'.

In addition we obtain some information on CSA usage, that could be compared with monitoring results (Figure 101 on page 165).

```
IST440I   TIME=12402308 DATE 78079 LOCAL PC NAME=NCPLOC
IST441I   DLRMAX=1       CHWR=14      CHRD=15
IST442I   ATTN=15        RDATN=0      IPIU=15
IST443I   OPIU=14        RDBUF=0      SLODN=0
```

Figure 87.   VTAM tuning parameter display (reference 41)

The option TNSTAT in VTAM collects the parameters in Figure 87. The TIME
in hour down to hundredth of a second is presented with the DATE (1978,
the 79th day) for the local network controller NCPLOC.

DLRMAX shows   that there has been 1 dump-load-restart during the interval
or that one is awaiting processing.   CH relates to the network controller
channel.   RD = reads, WR = writes.

ATTN is the total number of attentions (asynchronous I/O interrupts)
received from the controller. RDATN is the number of times that VTAM was
told to read more data in a dataset already treated.

IPIU is the number of inbound PIUs (=minimum message), OPIU is the same
but outbound. RDBUF is the total number of buffers used for reads. SLODN
is the number of communication controller slowdowns during the period.
Perhaps the last item is directly of most interest to a controller.

Clearly, this kind of information is directed towards system programmers
that can follow trends in buffer usage and take appropriate action when a
resource is near to become a bottleneck.

The resource then requested is more virtual and/or real storage.   Just as
clearly, such resource usage in rapidly expanding networks must be coordi-
nated - especially in a storage constrained situation where many complex
computing centres find themselves.

5.6 HARDWARE

Hardware resource usage is measured by software in most implementations.
Another important aspect about our hardware is its availability. This
should ideally be monitored continuously. However, monitoring is expensive on manpower and financial resources. A standard software feature can
automatically control the existence of specified resources when requested.
An example of the checklist is shown in Figure 88.

```
000100 STOR 0M-15M
000200 CHAN (0-B)
000300 DEV (148,748)
000400 DEV (150,750)
000500 DEV (158,758)
000600 DEV (160,760)
000700 DEV (168,768)


The latter part of the list is not shown

Figure 88.   CONFIG(uration) display
```

The program will control the existence of 16 megabytes of STORage, 12
CHANnels (in the example) and miscellaneous DEVices - in this case disks
with alternate paths.

One problem in a complex environment is that resources may be disconnected
(temporarily?) from a processor, and somebody forgets to switch it back.
By routinely executing this program in case of performance problems, the
cause may be found, or, just as important, one possible error cause elimi-
nated.

5.7 VM RESOURCE USAGE

5.7.1 Indicate commands

---

    ind
    PROC 01-077% PROC 00-079% Q1-01 Q2-02 STORAGE-025% EXPAN-001
    PAGING-052/SEC STEAL-007% LOAD-002%

    ind user
    PAGES: RES-0040 WS-0045 READS=000592 WRITES=000322 MH -0014 FH -0031
    VTIME=000:12 TTIME=000:24 SIO=000543 RDR-000161 PRT-000504 PCH-000000

    Figure 89.   VM INDICATE command result

Any user of VM can quite easily get a feel on how the system is running
and how he/she is doing. Figure 89 shows the results of the IND(icate)
command that gives system status, and the IND(icate) USER command that
displays specific information on the user issuing the command.

The IND command tell us that the two parts of the 158 multiprocessor used
in the example are each used 77-79%. There is one interactive(Q1) user
queued for the use of the processor, and 2 heavier users (Q2). STORAGE
gives some indication of real storage use. EXPAN is the expansion factor:
how much longer a command will take due to the interactive environment.
Expansion factor 1 is ideal, but then we only have a PAGING rate of 52 per
second.   7% of all page frames are stolen - STEAL - because of real storage shortage.   The LOAD factor is 2%. This is an 'artificial' number
composed of paging related parameters. It can only be compared to itself
- here load seems quite reasonable.

The IND USER tells me that I had 40 pages resident and VM had calculated
my 'working set' to be 45 pages. The figure also presents number of page
reads and writes - next time I issue the command I can see if VM has done
more paging IO work for me. The IND commands are typically used when
there seems to be a problem. The problem could be that my program has
stopped for some reason.

MH and FH tell me how many pages I have under moving and fixed head on
disk.   Paging was here done differentially to 3350 fixed head (preferred)
and 3350 moving head areas, with migration of little used pages from fixed
head to moving head areas.

VTIME is my Virtual processing (problem program) time, and TTIME the corresponding total processing time including systems overhead. VM automatically distributes (most of its) overhead among users, leaving no need for
finding capture ratios and calculating total processing time usage.

Finally reader, printer and punch I/Os are counted. These are **virtual**
occurrences and may or may not correspond to a physical transfer.

5.7.2 VMAP

VMAP, Virtual Machine Facility/370 Performance/Monitor Analysis provides
roughly the same data as RMF. One very interesting feature is that VMAP
can display resource usage as a function of selected parameters for
instance number of logged on users. Several parameters may be shown on
one graph, such as on Figure 90. This provides a tool for understanding
the nature of the system, especially at extremes. In interactive systems,
extreme states are often the most interesting - refer to the discussion of
hang-ups in Chapter 4.

```
Au                                              First cross var.
cs
te
ir   S   C   A   L   E                          Obs   Abs%   Cum%
vs
e    1     2     3     4     5     6     7     8  9

0                                                101    5.1    5.1
1    Q     VPC         T                         166    8.4   13.6
2    Q       PCV                         T       237   12.0   25.7
3     Q      PCV                            T    226   11.5   37.2
4     Q        CV                             T  194    9.8   47.1
5     Q         VP                              T 186   9.4   56.6
6     Q          V  P                          T 166    8.4   65.0
7     Q          V  C  P                       T 156    7.9   73.0
8      Q         V   C    P                    T 115    5.8   78.8
9      Q          V    C      P                T 103    5.2   84.1
10     Q        V         C        P           T  82    4.1   88.3
11      Q      V              C        P       T  58    2.9   91.2
12       Q   V               C           P     T  48    2.4   93.7
13       Q V                    C           P  T  33    1.6   95.4
14        Q V                   C              P T 30   1.5   96.9
```

Base variable = Active users = Number of users now in dispatch list

Symbol	Cross variable	Scale	Max value	Description
P	PAGERATE	10	107.08	Page rate per second
Q	PAGEQ	1	5.00	Number of users in page wait
T	TOTCPU	10	100	Total CPU utilization
V	VIRTCPU	10	85.63	Problem program CPU
C	CPCPU	10	83.78	Control program CPU

Figure 90. VMAP VM resource usage at varying user load

On Figure 90, total CPU (T) increases to about 90% with increasing number
of users to about 7 , but after that increases no further. Problem program time (V) is even more remarkable, having a definite maximum for 4-5

users, and thereafter diminishing. Beyond that, the control program
(CPCPU) takes more and more of the (more or less constant) total CPU.

The figure lists **active users**. In VM, an active user is one that has work
currently being processed by VM or waiting for some VM resource. Many
logged on users are not actively working at their terminal, or are preparing long essays on their screens. Active users is often a better measure
of load from terminals than logged on users.

Paging increases linearly with number of users up to a rate of nearly 108.
This underlines our approach for real storage capacity planning in adding
real storage requirements for all (active) users. Page rate is elsewhere
found to be more or less linearly dependent on aggregate real storage
need.

5.7.3 The VM/370 Resource Limiter

When some resource is overloaded, we normally expect the 'system' to take
care of balancing; i.e. quiesceing or downgrading some work to best benefit the common good. As described, this is not easy in a complex system.

David M. Chess of Yorktown Heights has written an interesting program that
records resource usage for all or selected users. When a user exceeds
predefined resource usage limits, the following actions can be taken:

1. A warning message is sent to the user

2. The user's priority is downgraded

3. The user is forced off the system

This is an interesting alternative to the MVS approach where it may be
difficult for instance to differentiate between TSO users in a standard
performance setup, especially as their resource usage may vary from day to
day.

There are drawbacks with resource limiting. The most productive users
tend to use more resources; should they be punished for that? An informative message is perhaps better, accompanied with the appropriate bill.
The bill will probably be paid with a smile if the user is really productive in the sense described in chapter 1.

An interesting addition has been made to the program. Certain users
defined to the resource limiter can have selected priviledged commands
executed for them by the resource limiter address space. Normally VM
users are classified by their allowed control over VM resources. For
instance class A gives the power to FORCE somebody off the system, class E
lets you run SMART (next chapter) and so on. Sometimes a certain user
does not need all facilities within a class. By allowing access only to
selected commands, security in the total system is better.

5.8 CONCLUSION

Controlling resource usage in a complex system needs careful planning. Modern system control programs contain several facilities for both measuring resource usage and adjusting resource allocation parameters.

A prerequisite for a good performance control system, is to limit control to a few, but very useful, variables, and find values that determine when these are acceptable or that intervention is required.

In order to comprehend the results of resource recording, it is necessary to know something of the way the system control program handles resources, and how resource handling in **our** system relates to system control program concepts and the control variables that we record.

Adjustments (former 'tuning') need be implemented to ensure that the system behaves in accordance with service agreements and allocates resources in a reasonable fashion. Selecting dispatching priorities, dedicating resources (like real storage) and providing ample input/output facilities are selected means of ensuring acceptable behaviour.

Sometimes so many resources are dedicated that most control facilities are disabled, and cruder means like stopping batch or limiting TSO have to be implemented.

Extra overhead results from intensive resource management when done by the system. Because interactive systems tolerate little queuing, we have to watch both resource levels and complexity, and perhaps even specify separate objectives for peak load times like month or year end.

If service should be 'good' even at high loads, high load conditions must be investigated to find 'bottlenecks' or overloaded resources. Some examples of this are provided in chapter 8. Average values for resource usage can be quite misleading - it is often the extremes that we need to find out more about. A detail investigation of resource behaviour and usage needs a fine breakdown - 10 minutes is a good empirical value.

For any service, it is important to find out what components it is dependent on, and hence any obstructions in its path through the system. The obstructions could be a result of infrequently occurring load conditions, for instance high input/output rate on a work pack.

Trends are important to predict when dangerously high usage levels are likely.

Some aspects of performance control has interesting implementations under VM. The ability for users to see their, and the system's, resource usage here and now and easily, is psychologically important; perhaps it may also discourage some use of resources during highly active periods. Note, here the users apply the control mechanism - this can lead to a user appreciation of the problems of performance control.

The relation between different logical components in a complex system can be investigated by way of VMAP. VM also provides interesting examples on how to limit the use of the system when resources are scarce, and also on how to limit the access to resources.

Resource   control in a production environment needs a production approach.
As   much   as   possible   of the resource control mechanism should be implemented   in a manner that enable operations people to follow resource usage
on a continual, predefined basis.   An example in this chapter is MSS where
key indicators are suggested for follow-up.

CHAPTER 6

SYSTEM MONITORING

'Come, wake, wake you too, wake each other, come, wake all!
Shake off your sleep, stand up. What could that warning mean?
What has happened? Furies, we are foiled.
Who were ever as mocked as we?
Sleepless labour spent in vain!
Duty flouted, priviledge despoiled!
   See the empty snare, our prey
   Vanished, fled and free again
While we slept our right was stolen away.'

The Eumenides
Aeschylus

6.1   INTRODUCTION

6.1.1   Chapter contents

Astonishingly little emphasis has been placed on the continuous monitoring
of online (and batch) systems. Having tried it out in practice, it seems
difficult to run a complex computing centre without. The chapter provides
some examples where online monitoring has been of great use or invaluable.

The importance of online monitoring normally increases with complexity and
service requirements in a centre.   Therefore most centres will see an
increased need for monitoring systems and methods in the near future.

The chapter introduces monitoring using RMFMON with specially developed
extensions and shows how different components of the computer system can
be followed using these tools and approaches. Some theory of the MVS system is provided in order for the reader to appreciate the examples and the
monitoring methods.

The theory is also included to benefit those operators/supervisors that
will themselves monitor complex systems.

VM (SMART) is included to show how VM has introduced additional facilities
into an online monitor, altogether a long and impressive list of ordering
and selection facilities

A list of limit values of use in monitoring and performance control generally is included, and provides the reader with some starter values from
whence a tailored monitoring system may be developed.

6.1.2   Definition

By 'monitoring' in this book is meant online supervision of service or
resource usage in a computer hardware/software system.

6.1.3   Monitoring components

Figure 91 on page 153 shows major monitoring components.

1.   Configuration displays

              are needed to obtain the status of essential systems hardware
              resources, e.g. processors and channels. TV monitoring screens
              may be added, e.g. to follow IMS logtapes.

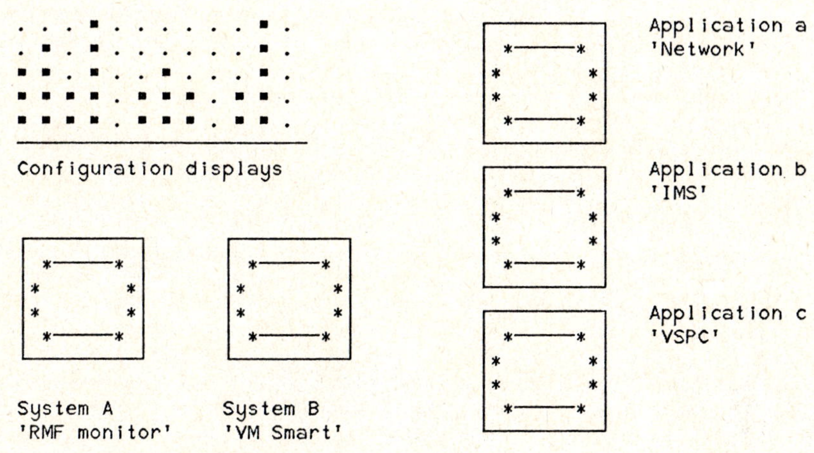

Figure 91.   System monitoring overview.

2.   System monitors

to follow global resource usage on each processor. For sensitive operation more than one screen per system may be needed.

These monitors are <u>additions</u> to system consoles. For instance
in JES3, one systems console can give the operators control over
the whole complex, and other consoles can be dedicated to different resource categories.

Operator control is an aspect of a control system. However,
software resource usage (processing time, real storage, virtual
storage, I/O etc) is not well controlled by using standard operator features, and can only be followed per system (processor)
with existing, IBM software.

3.   Application monitors.

to follow response times, load and resource usage for major
applications such as IMS or VSPC. A facility in MVS can for
instance display TSO and VSPC load and response times in real
time. This is not currently (1981) possible for IMS.

6.2 RMFMON

6.2.1 Description

Reference 15 gives a good description of the RMF monitor that is a display
facility providing online supervisory possibilities for MVS systems.

Different display screens may be called forth depending on supervision
situation.

6.2.2 VSPC example

It is sometimes impractical to run RMFMON as a continual supervisor (for
instance when lacking display terminals) and therefore the setup as shown
on Figure 93 on page 156 was implemented.

A small continual benchmark is run, based on an APL program that 'wakes
up' every 30 second, carries out a few instructions, records the time for
these and then goes to 'sleep' again.

When the time for this operation is prolonged for, say, 3 consecutive
recordings, there is a chance that the VSPC system is not running well and
more detailed investigation is needed.

The components of the RMF monitor that are considered most useful for
online supervision of complex systems are shown on Figure 92 on page 155.

RMFMON contains a facility for extending the standard screens with new
options.

SRM, QCB and SID are examples of such programs, whereas the options CSA
and SQA were added from already existing 'home made' programs. SDSF is a
standard product added in the same fashion.

Opti-on	Full name	Description	Component supervised
Supervision			
ASD	Address Space state Data	All address spaces displayed with resource consumption and status	Processing, paging, priorities, swap state
TRX	Transaction activity data	For each performance group: transaction rate and response times	Response times, transaction rates
SDSF*	Syslog Display and Search Facility	All address spaces started as batch displayed with resource consumption	Job classes, IO rates
CSA*	CSA display	Shows CSA usage by supervisor key	CSA (virtual storage)
SQA*	SQA display	Shows SQA overall usage	SQA (virtual storage)
Problem determination			
SPAG	Paging	Paging load per system component	Paging distribution on Common, Swap and Private
ARD	Address space resource data	Resource usage per address space with	Paging & IO per address space
ASD d	ASD with delta	Processing time as increment since last 'enter'	Who uses the processor
SRM*	SRM data	SRM values and the corresponding system	SRM values, real paging, paging queues
SID*	Storage inter-active display	Storage usage and paging for fenced address spaces	Control fences
QCB*	QCB values	ENQ contention, reserves	Waits for disk
UCB*	UCB values	DASD contention	Disk hangup

*   User developed or/and added program

Figure 92.   RMFMON supervisor facilities

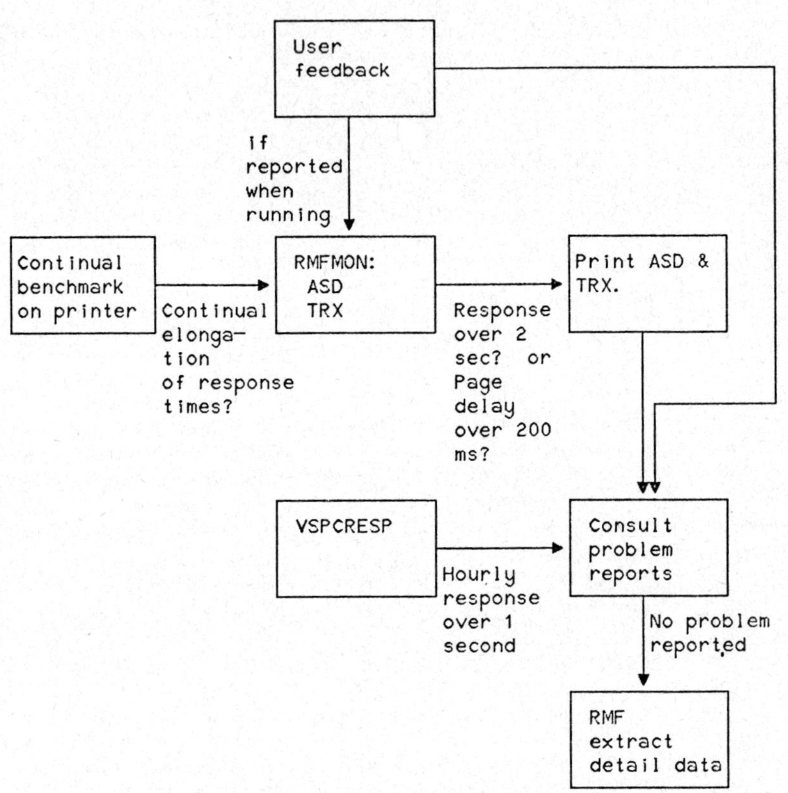

Figure 93.   VSPC monitoring example

User input may also trigger an investigation. This user input may be for-
warded directly to the supervisor or via some contact person. The input
may be formulated into a problem report

Printing the RMF monitor screens ASD and TRX helps the subsequent investigation.

6.3 SYSTEM WORKLOAD

```
F         CPU= 62 UIC= 12 PDT= 157 DPR= 53     ASD              T
  15: 46: 47          P  P    TRAN    C   R  DP DP  RS   WS         CPU
  JOBNAME   DMN    G  P    TIME    L   LS PR PO  F    IN          TIME
  *MASTER*   0     0  1 04: 58: 23 NS     FF  1  31    0        536. 48
  JES2       7     3  1 04: 57: 42 NS     BB  6  80   13        218. 19
  HSMA       7    55  1 04: 56: 42 NS     99 18   9    4         54. 86
  NET        7     4  1 04: 54: 24 NS     BF  2  25   15        135. 12
  CCJEP      1    24  1 00: 39: 13 OT US FF       0   14         25. 93
  J104FBM    6   244  1 04: 25: 34 NS     9D 14 182   23        132. 04
  ISELC      1    46  1 00: 14: 06 OT EX FF       0   26          1. 62
  J208QAP    8    15  1 04: 26: 28 NS     99 19   6   12         10. 42
  J208M6P    5   242  1 04: 31: 40 NS     B9  7   7   14         15. 81
  J208M5P    5   241  1 04: 32: 06 NS     B9  8  52   11         95. 75
  J208M4P    5   243  1 04: 32: 23 NS     B5 12  27   23        152. 25
  J208M3P    5   245  1 04: 32: 55 NS     B8 10 120   14        150. 26
  J208M2P    5   246  1 04: 33: 08 NS     B8 11  92   11        171. 47
  J208M1P    5   242  1 04: 33: 38 NS     B8  9  62   12        228. 85
  J214IBA    7    17  1 04: 49: 05 NS     96 21  44   12        154. 13
  J209VMA    7     5  1 04: 53: 37 NS     BE  4  59   22         90. 98
  J208IMP    7   240  1 04: 51: 38 NS     BD  5 587   15       1771. 2
  J209ATA    7     6  1 04: 54: 13 NS     BE  3 158   17        406. 31
  IS10FNIB   1    43  1 00: 57: 56 OT US FF       0   38         48. 72
  IS10AXN5  11    42  1 00: 01: 04 OT US FF       0   31          2. 12
  J208AIP    8    15  1 01: 12: 37 NS     98 20  18   20          6. 80

Figure 94.   RMFMON ASD frame
```

On Figure 94, the jobs J208MxP are IMS message processing regions, where x
is the number of the region.   They are all non swappable, and have
(almost) the same priority.   J208IMP is the control region.   Other jobs
starting with J20.... support either the IMS environment or control the
network.   In addition JES2, (the) MASTER (scheduler), HSMA (HSM) and NET
are system related tasks.   In sum, a lot of the total power (real storage,
processor time) is rigidly allocated to system and application tasks.   The
few batch jobs running in domains 1 and 11 are swapped out.   There is
another display frame or more to tell the whole workload story.   In the
example, the second frame contained mostly TSO.

The two jobs in performance group 242 have different priorities; this may
seem strange.   However, the dispatching priority was here given in the JOB
card, not by IPS.   These two IMS jobs were later separated so that J208M6P
ran in performance group 247, in order to better differentiate between the
services.   J208M6P and J208M5P contain group 3 IMS transactions, i.e.
slow, low priority work relative to other transactions.

Figure 95 on page 158 explains terms used in Figure 94.

The ASD option can be expanded to show even swapped out users, or
restricted to one category, for instance TSO alone.

Header line (heavy print on figure)

CPU in
heading: Total processor busy percent (problem program and system)

UIC: Unused Interval Count - number of seconds the 'oldest' page in
         the system (or address space if relevant) is left unstolen
         after use

PDT: Page Delay Time: time in milliseconds to resolve page fault

DPR: Demand Paging Rate, according to MVS definition, different
         from total paging rate (Figure 96 on page 159).

ASD: Name of RMFMON frame

T: Total - i.e. CPU time in detail lines is calculated for
         the total time of the executing jobstep.

15:46:47 Display time of day

Detail lines

JOBNAME: Name of job running in address space
DMN: Domain number
PG :   Performance group number
PP :   Performance period
TRAN
TIME: Elapsed time for jobstep
CL: Classification: NS: Non swappable
                         OT: Swapped out
                         (IN: Swapped in - i.e. part of MPL)
R LS: Reason for last swap:
         US: Unilateral swap - swapped to maintain a certain MPL
         EX: Exchange swap - exchanged with another address space to
             maintain resource balance or give service when an address
             space receives less service than its objective states
DP PR: Dispatching priority. FF is highest
DP PO: Dispatching priority order. 1 is highest
RS F :   Real storage frames allocated to address space.
WS IN: Working set- as seen by MVS, the swap in working set
CPU
TIME: TCB time for jobstep

Figure 95.   RMFMON ASD explanation of terms

```
                          CPU= 48 UIC= 20 PDT= 140 DPR= 40    USER SRM  T
      RESOURCE CONTROL                    LOGICAL SWAP CONTROL


UIC:         2 -        4 ==>       27     UIC:       20 -      30 ==>      27
ASMQ:     1000 -     1000 ==>       15     ASMQ:    1000 -    1000 ==>      15
PTR:      1000 -     1000 ==>       38     AVQ:          -     300 ==>     129
CPU:     101.0 -    101.0 ==>     82.3     TNKT     3.0 -    30.0 ==>     3.0
MSPP:     1000 -     1000 ==>      140     LSWAP ASIDS:         4


      DEMAND PAGING


DPR:        42 -       52 ==>       40
MSPP:      100 -      130 ==>      140
CPU:     101.0 -    101.0 ==>     82.3


      SWAP REASON COUNTS


TOSC:     1618 TISC:    43927 LWSC:      890 XSSC:          RSSC:
DWSC:     3120 RQSC:          NQSC:        6 EXSC:      149
USSC:      830 TSSC:       21 LSSC:    34323 LFSC:     1631


PAGRT: 112  AFQA: 129  INUS:  28
```

Header line (see also Figure 95 on page 158)

USER SRM: This is a user defined frame called SRM

Detail lines (see also Figure 95 on page 158)

RESOURCE CONTROL

```
ASMQ     : Average number of queued paging requests
PTR      : Page transfer rate - = page faults in interval
MSPP     : Mean Service time Per Page
```

LOGICAL SWAP CONTROL

```
AVQ          : Average number of available pages
TNKT         : Average think time (time between two commands)
LSWAP ASIDS : Number of logically swapped address spaces
```

SWAP REASON COUNTS

```
SC: Swap count

TO: Terminal output     TI: Terminal input      LW: Long wait
DW: Detected wait       RQ: Requested swap       EX: Exchange swap
US: Unilateral swap     TS: Transition           LS: Logical swap
LF: Logical swap failed XS: Aux. storage short. RS: Real storage shortage
NQ: Swaps to prevent enqueues

PAGRT:  Total (=real) paging rate   AFQA:   Average free frames
INUS :  Total MPL
```

Figure 96.   RMFMON user SRM frame

The resource limits specified is shown on Figure 96 on page 159 before the respective arrows.

The resource control parameters are in the example set to disable this aspect of SRM control. For logical swap control, think time and system UIC has effect. Think time is the time between the output for one command is received and the next command is entered.

If system UIC falls below 20, system think time (3 on figure) is decreased. If system UIC raises above 30, system think time is increased.

When any user's think time is higher than the system think time, that user is eligible for physical instead of logical swap. When system think time reaches 0, all address spaces are eligible for physical instead of logical swap.

This loads the physical IO paths more in a system that already is struggling.

Paging often the most vulnerable aspect of a complex computer system. In the algorithm shown under demand paging, the MPL will be **lowered** if DPR is over 52 **and** MSPP is over 130 - i.e. at high paging and/or long page delays.

The MPL is **increased** if **both** DPR is below 42 **and** MSPP is below 100.

A paging bottleneck will therefore hit batch first, and then TSO according to the specifications in last chapter.

Among swap reasons, logical swaps constitute a large part of terminal input waits, indicating that a TSO command has finished. There is no obvious problem indicated on the figure, but the system is approaching saturation.

```
    TRX  15/56/38
         PERF   PERF    TRANS   AVG TRAN
          GRP    PER     RATE    HHH. MM. SS


         C  2     1      3. 010    000. 00. 00. 813
                  2      0. 164    000. 00. 06. 778
                  3      0. 041    000. 00. 17. 782
                  4      0. 008    000. 02. 43. 622


         C 24     1      0. 005    000. 05. 08. 030


         C 49     1      0. 011    000. 01. 36. 268

    TRX    :  Identification of this frame


    PERF
    GRP    :  Performance group number
                                       2:   TSO
                                      24:   System programming batch
                                      49:   Short batch
    PERF
    PER    :  Performance period

                                       1:   Short TSO commands
                                       2:   Medium TSO commands
                                       3:   Long TSO commands
                                       4:   'Batch' TSO commands


    TRANS
    RATE   :  Transaction rate in interval, and only for those groups
              where at least one transaction ends during interval.

    AVG.
    TRAN   :  Average (internal MVS) transaction time for those transactions
              having finished during interval.

    Figure 97.   RMFMON TRX frame
```

Figure 97 shows a TSO transaction rate of about 3/second. The differentiation of response times between short commands and the more resource demanding, is quite noticeable - and planned. Figure 29 on page 66 informs us that about 90% (91) of all transactions finish during the first period.

Comparing TSO performance period 4 with short, high priority batch, leads us to guess that service is better in the latter group. The response times are in general better, and the CPU time consumption by batch and heavy TSO about the same (as seen from ASD monitoring).

Sending work to batch would have saved on average over 3 minutes terminal time waiting for execution, in addition to the better response time.

```
SDSF DA MVSA PAGING 95.98 SIO 143.00 CPU  50.45%  LINE   1 TO  21 OF  32
COMMAND INPUT ===>                                   SCROLL ===>      PAGE
  JOBNAME  STEPNAME DMN PGN POS SR DP    REAL CL EXCPR     EXCP  CPU TIME
  *MASTER*           0   0 N/S    FF    132K    2.72     39,942   555.56
  JES2     JES2      7   3 N/S    BB    220K    9.33     98,015   225.95
  ISWTR    IS        4  19 IN     97     52K    0.00     13,873    30.73
  HSMA     HSMA      7  55 N/S    99     36K    0.00     31,747    62.23
  MSSSISA  MSSSISA   7  55 OUT DW FF     0K     0.00         34     0.18
  TLCS     TLCS      4  19 OUT LW FF     0K     0.00         47     0.11
  DSPRINT  DSPRINT   4  19 OUT DW FF     0K     0.00      1,781     6.34
  TCAS     TCAS      0   0 IN     CB     48K    0.00         43     7.58
  NET      NET       7   4 N/S    BF    272K    0.00      4,144   138.68
  J209NCA  NCCFA     7  55 OUT DW FF     0K  I  0.00        509    11.28
  CCJEP    UCL       1  24 IN  US FF     0K  G  0.00     28,371    27.20
  J104FBM  C104B40   6 244 N/S    9D    816K  I 15.93     43,454   140.19
  ISELC    C2220PC   1  46 IN  EX FF     0K  U  0.00      1,752     1.62
  J208QAP  QALERT    8  15 N/S    99     24K  I  0.00        335    10.76
  J208M6P  PROCIMS1  5 242 N/S    B9     28K  I  0.00      6,528    15.81
  J208M5P  PROCIMS1  5 241 N/S    B8    336K  I  3.89     10,518    99.70
  J208M4P  PROCIMS3  5 243 N/S    B7    404K  I  0.78     19,438   159.28
  J208M3P  PROCIMS3  5 245 N/S    B8    428K  I  1.94     18,540   154.92
  J208M2P  PROCIMS1  5 246 N/S    B8    352K  I  1.17     24,816   177.87
  J208M1P  PROCIMS3  5 242 N/S    B8    464K  I  0.00     28,929   237.44
  J214IBA  IBTS      7  17 N/S    97    212K  I  3.89     43,158   163.90


PAGING    : Total paging
SIO       : Start IO rate
DMN       : Domain
PGN       : Performance group number
POS       : = MPL classification on ASD
SR        : = R LS (reason for last swap) on ASD
DP        : Dispatching priority - FF highest
REAL      : equivalent to ASD RS F, but in kilobytes
CL        : Job class
EXCPR     : EXCP rate (not necessarily equal to SIO rate)
EXCP      : Number of EXCP issued by step

 Figure 98.   SDSF frame (batch detail report)
```

Figure 98 provides additional information on batch and batch type work
when ASD etc. are too limited: For instance jobstep is given, and its
name sometimes provide information on what work goes on.

Note that IMS jobs are defined as batch, so that their resource usage -
especially EXCP can be investigated. Most EXCP seem to originate from IMS
in this sample.

SIO for this machine - a 3033 - is not particularly high, 200 - 300 is
reasonable in an interactive environment.

Class is important for batch control. Resource demanding jobs sometimes
congest the system when running in a high priority class.

6.4 REAL STORAGE

6.4.1 Real storage usage by private areas

Figure 94 on page 157 includes storage usage by private address spaces. Workload report extracts, like on Figure 62 on page 111 can be used to complement monitoring.

6.4.2 Storage usage by common areas

```
                             CPU= 65 UIC= 30 PDT=   57 DPR= 16    USER CMN T
REAL STORAGE USAGE             ** UIC DISTRIBUTION **      09:33:31
           VIRT  REAL   FIX     0    >1    >2    >4    >8   >16   >32   >64

LOCAL            809    55    345                     84   173   207
LSQA             135          135
PLPA             396    39    182                      4    16   194
SQA              170          170

CSA-KEY0 117      23     2      4                             1    18
CSA-KEY1  37      23            1                            22
CSA-KEY2 178      52           38                      2     3     9
CSA-KEY5   1       2            2
CSA-KEY6 319      92    30     58                      1    11    22

NUCLEUS          170
OFFLINE
BAD
UNKNOWN            1
AVAIL.           175

VIRT    : Virtual storage frames allocated
REAL    : Real storage frames used
FIX     : Fixed pages
0, >1..: Number of frames with UIC in this interval

LOCAL   : Frames allocated to private areas

CSA keys
0       : System (but usually also contains some application code)
1       : Job scheduler
2       : VSPC
5       : Data management
6       : VTAM
7       : IMS (not run in this example)

 Figure 99.  RMFMON user CMN frame (common real storage)
```

Figure 94 on page 157 shows that roughly one half (809 + 55 local and 135 LSQA pages) of the 8 Megabytes are used for private address spaces. The remainder is system areas: Nucleus, PLPA, CSA, SQA, unknown or available

(free). The situation is quite typical when heavy interactive work is run
(here VSPC, as indicated by CSA key 2).

According to the UIC distribution, some pages are left unstolen for over
16 seconds, showing no immediate problem with paging, underlined with the
DPR (demand paging) of only 16.

6.4.3 Storage fencing

```
**********CPU= 73 UIC= 47 PDT= 266 DPR= 53 ****************************
JOBNAME DMN  PG  ALC TAR CUR HI  MIN MAX MIN MAX     CPU
                 FRM FRM PIN UIC FRM FRM PIN PIN     sec
Common          1114         42
J208IMP   7 240  406 400  29  2  175 400  20  30 1475.13


FRM:      Frames
ALC:      Allocated, i.e. used by this address space
TAR:      Target - this is what the system attempts to allocate
PIN:      Page in - here in relation to processor time usage
CUR:      Current - during last measurement period
MIN/      Extreme values for target number of frames/page ins
MAX


CPU in
heading: Total processor busy percent


CPU in
detail:  TCB time used by address space


Common:  Real storage usage by common areas (CSA,LPA)


When  page  in  is  above the maximum, the target is increased till it
reaches the maximum.  When page in is below the minimum, the target is
reduced until it reaces the minimum


Figure 100.  RMFMON monitoring fenced pages (user SID option)
```

Figure 100 shows fencing of the IMS control region (J208IMP). It is specified up to 400 pages, but is currently using 406. A slight overrun is
'allowed' by this mechanism, but the conclusion from the figure is that
IMS should be allocated **more** pages as it is a very significant service.
The UIC of 2 underlines this decision: pages are stolen from the control
region almost as soon as they are allocated.

6.5 AVAILABILITY SUPERVISION

6.5.1 CSA monitoring

```
    ********** CSA USAGE BY STORAGE KEY ***********
    * KEY 0: SUPERVISOR..............          472 K
    * KEY 1: JOB SCHEDULER..........           148 K
    * KEY 2: VSPC...................           712 K
    * KEY 5: DATA MANAGEMENT........             4 K
    * KEY 6: VTAM/TCAM..............           1276 K
    * CSA USED......................           2612 K
    * CSA FREE......................            400 K
    * CSA SPECIFICATION.............           3012 K
    ********** CSA USAGE BY STORAGE KEY ***********

Figure 101.   RMFMON user CSA frame
```

Figure 101 complements Figure 99 on page 163 in providing a fuller view of
the virtual storage situation. When virtual storage for CSA is exhausted,
MVS might fail, and a reIPL of the system is necessary.

When availability is important - as it is for interactive systems - CSA
must be monitored, especially when close to being filled. Some applications do not always perform proper housekeeping, i.e. do not free unneeded
virtual storage.   The system therefore has a tendency to fill up the CSA
over the day.

Giving CSA space enough for no concern may restrict other virtual storage
components like user address spaces.

6.5.2 SQA monitoring

Sometimes CSA space is 'stolen' by SQA because the SQA is filled. SQA
should also be followed, but here housekeeping rules seem to be followed,
and it is relatively easy to compute storage needs (a function of number
of active address spaces and virtual storage allocated etc.) Figure 102
is otherwise regarded as self explanatory.

```
    ********** SQA USAGE ***************************
    * KEY 0: SUPERVISOR.............           512 K
    * SQA ALLOCATED.................           512 K
    * SQA FREE......................           105 K
    ********** SQA USAGE ***************************


Figure 102.   RMFMON user SQA frame
```

6.5.3 Disk hangup monitoring

Sometimes disk hangups on one processor may cause other processors using
the same disk, to stall. An online monitoring facility is then helpful,
for instance as shown in Figure 103.

```
                        CPU= 94 UIC= 15 PDT=  89 DPR= 51    USER        T
RESERVE AND ENQ CONFLICTS                              09:31:24    09:31:17
MAJOR      MINOR                      JOB            STATUS    CUU VOL

SYSZRACF SYS1.RACF1P                  CCGIOSCR SHR         RSV 36A CCSRF2
                                      ISSGL    EXCL        RSV 36A CCSRF2
SYSVTOC  IS1020                       ISSGL    EXCL SMC RSV 162 IS1020
SYSIGGV2 ISUC.VIS1020                 ISSGL3   EXCL        RSV 162 IS1020
SPFDSN   D549.TEST.WORK3              ISJHA    EXCL        RSV 372 IS1776

MAJOR:    Major resource enqueued upon
MINOR:    Minor resource
STATUS:   SHR  = Shared request
          EXCL = Exclusive control needed
          RSV  = Reserved
          SMC  = Step Must Complete, i.e. must run alone in address
                 space.  An operator CANCEL will have no effect.
CUU:      Channel and unit address for disk

 Figure 103.   RMFMON user QCB frame
```

On Figure 103, job ISSGL wants the RACF dataset with exclusive rights;
however, CCGIOSCR holds it presently, and even if CCGIOSCR is willing to
share, ISSGL wants more than a shared dataset. ISSGL is in conflict with
another job, perhaps issued by the same user, for the use of IS1020.

The example only shows RESERVE conflicts, but the program can even handle
ENQs.

Figure 120 on page 195. shows a view of which disks were busy at any one
time. This is an important addition, especially in anomaly situations.

6.6 VM MONITORING

```
            *****   SMART  COMMAND  SELECTION  MENU   *****

      1  D                  11  D    SRC        |   61  ORDER   %CPU
      2  D      I/O         12  D    VMX        |   62  ORDER   %CP
      3  D      DEV         13  D    LOGM       |   63  ORDER   %USR
      4  D      CHAN        14  D    EVEN       |   64  ORDER   ISEC
      5  D      SLOG LAST   15  D    PRIVOP     |   65  ORDER   PSEC
      6  D      ULOG LAST   16  D    IOS        |   66  ORDER   WSS
      7  D      ALOG LAST   17  D    FREE       |   67  ORDER   RES
      8  D      LOG         18  D    CP TRACE   |   68  ORDER   USEC
      9  D      IDLE        19  D    VMCF LAST  |   69  ORDER   PRI
     10  D      USER ALL    20  D    DASD ALL   |   70  ORDER   VMSIZE
                                               |   71  ORDER   Q
     80  SET CHAN ON        82  SET CPTR ON     |   72  ORDER   QW
     81  SET CHAN OFF       83  SET CPTR OFF    |   73  ORDER   ECM
                                               |_________________
                                               |   74  QUERY   INTERVAL
                                               |   75  QUERY   CPT

    90 DISPLAY     91 PRINT      92 PRTO
    97 NEXT        98 RECOMP     99 END            SLEEP  15        SEC
   Enter SMART command, or command number:
  Program Function Key 10 selected for Figure 105 on page 168.
   1=HLP  2=D L  3=END  4=DSL  5=DUL  6=DAL  8=NXT  10=RCP  11=DLM  12= EN

  Figure 104.   SMART overview picture (internally developed)
```

Like RMFMON, SMART contains a selection menu (Figure 104) showing the different options available.   A quick glance confirms that many possibilities exist. For instance numbers 61-73 request reports sorted according to the specified resource usage: %CPU gives processor time usage, PSEC pages per second, ISEC input/output operations per second, WSS real storage allocated ('working set size').   All these are helpful in performance investigations.

The D(isplay) commands show a complete set of characteristics, for instance load on all channels (CHAN) or disks (DASD ALL).

The bottom line present Program Function Key (PFK) selections, obtained by pressing the relevant PFK on a 3270 type keyboard.

To obtain Figure 105 on page 168, PFK 10 was pressed.   It provides the ReComPute selection, identical to writing 98. On the figure, the two bottom lines give ---> maximum and <--- minimum utilization during the interval of the resources presented.

The processor (CPU) is used 200 percent maximum. Not bad, well, it was a multiprocessor, but even then...

The control program (%CP) then uses twice as much processing power as the problem programs (%USR). Perhaps we should find who causes this by requesting a 'ORDER %CP' report?

```
+-------------------------------------------------------------------------------|
|                                                                               |
| USERID-> %CPU %CP %USR ISEC PSEC WSS RES USEC DRUM PRI VMSIZE Q EXCTN-STATUS  |
| KMO        57   9   48   .4   .0  54  54  .0   98  64  1024K 3 CMS,RUNABLE    |
| SMART      19  13    6   .0  2.7   2  34  .0  100  64  1280K 2 CMS,INSTWAIT   |
| DCVMHB     16  12    4   .0   21  49  45  .0  100  64  2048K 1 CMS,RUNABLE    |
| PREBEN    9.3 6.5  2.8  1.1  4.4  54   0  .0    0  64  1024K . CMS,IDLEWAIT   |
| NLJ       7.3 7.3   .0  9.1  1.2  59  45  .0   22  64  1024K 2 191,IOWAIT     |
| AUTOPAJ   5.9 3.9  2.0  3.1  2.5  32   3  .0   63  64   512K . CMS,CFWAIT     |
| KAARE     5.7 5.3   .4   .2  6.5  14   0  .0   11  64  1024K . CMS,IDLEWAIT   |
| DCS00003  5.3 3.9  1.4   .0  4.7  30   0  .0   15  64  1024K . CMS,IDLEWAIT   |
| INGE      5.2 3.8  1.4   .0  6.8  15   3  .0   32  64  1024K . CMS,IDLEWAIT   |
| KONSSTAT  4.7 4.4   .3   .0   13  12   9  .0   13  64  1024K 2 CMS,PAGEWAIT   |
| PVM       3.8 3.2   .6  2.7   .0  24  24  .0   79   0  1024K 1 CMS,IDLEWAIT   |
| RSS       3.8 3.5   .3   .0  8.8  10   0  .0   17  64  2048K . CMS,IDLEWAIT   |
| MADS      3.6 2.4  1.2  5.4   .0  42  40  .0   33  64  1024K 2 195,IOWAIT     |
|                         <-- 01 LOG ACTIONS INDICATED -->                      |
| %CPU %CP %USR %TWT %PAG %I/O %IDL %STO ISEC PSEC XPG PPAG USR IQ WQ ACT PRVS  |
| ->200 132  68    0    0    0    0   40   39  117   0 1612 105 11  0  26  177  |
| <-159  87  72   41    3   13   25   26   29   42   0 1612  86  7  0  33  239  |
+-------------------------------------------------------------------------------
```

Figure 105.   SMART resource usage sorted in CPU order

SLEEP determines the time between each change of screen, when also the
values are recomputed (RCP). The SLEEP value can be changed, for instance
to 60 seconds or 15 minutes. Handy! The RCP option forces a recompute,
providing values taken at the time of the request.

For minimum CPU during the interval (bottom line), the wait conditions are
given (they are 0 when the processor is fully loaded):

```
    %TWT              Total wait time
    %PAG              Paging wait
    %I/O              I/O wait
    %IDL              Idle - no user dispatchable
```

From this we find what causes the processor to perform less than it the-
oretically could. No immediate problem is evident from the sample, but we
notice in the user list EXCTN(execution)-STATUS that two users wait for
I/O, devices 191 and 195. A further investigation by SMART can easily be
done if I/O wait conditions deteriorate.

Other information in the bottom line is:

```
    %STO                Storage utilization
    ISEC                Non-spooled Input/outputs per second
    PSEC                Total pages per second
    XPG                 The number of CP extended pages (now used by CP)
    PPAG                Total page frames available for user paging
    USER                Number of logged on users
    IQ                  Number of users in In queue (i.e. scheduled users)
    WQ                  Number of users in Out queue (i.e. unscheduled)
    ACT                 Number of active users (= those not in idle wait)

                        - a better planning figure than logged on users.
                        Note the ratio between these two numbers.

    PRVS                Privileged instructions not handled by hardware
                        (nomally done on behalf of subsystems, like
                        VS1 and DOS).
```

The user section contain some of the same information distributed by user, and in addition:

```
RES             Number of page frames allocated to this user
USEC            Number of virtual input/output per second
DRUM            Fixed head device paging
PRIORITY        User priority - 64 is default
VMSIZE          Size of virtual storage
Q               What internal VM queue:
                1:  Interactive user - light resource usage
                2:  Non interactive - a little heavier on VM resources
                3:  Heavy user - batch type
```

User KMO is very heavy, and is quite justly allocated to queue 3. However, only few users are RUNABLE according to the frame (that only shows some of the roughly 100 users), and KMO may go on hammering the CPU, even at low priority, if not moved forcibly by VM to non dispatchable status. This happens when total resources - especially real storage - are scarce, and the 42 - 117 pages per second was seemingly not enough. High paging is a good indicator of real storage shortage.

SMART also features an exception report that for example lists the time and the three largest CPU users when the system runs 200% busy (in an MP system). This can help to identify recurrent 'sinners', the removal of which can greatly help the overall system. A problem here is that heavy users often are very productive and therefore popular. In some cases a compromise may be worked out for instance providing more disk space to one user to enable even more efficient working.

6.7 MONITORING LIMIT VALUES - CURRENT IMPLEMENTATION

Figure 106 on page 171 shows only selected monitoring values. Some may be repetitions, for example disk follow ups. However, it it easier to run the DISK program (described in chapter 7) than to follow all disks all days through RMF extract. The DISK program also stores values in a database, allowing trends to be followed.

There are few magical numbers in the survey. However, if all these values are OK, and service objectives are met, there should be no cause for alarm.

Monitoring can be started now and then, and more often when some resource seems near exhaustion.   Also, if some service is not performing up to objectives, it is natural to follow the applicable system online.

Systems resources can usually be followed well on a weekly basis, again, provided the service objectives are met. Poor performance should automatically trigger a more detailed follow up.

For disks, a set of monitoring values is suggested. When the 'danger' limits are exceeded, action is initiated. When values are less then the OK range, nothing is done unless there are specific problems.

Where to measure	What to measure	Limit value	Suggested period

Online monitoring (RMFMON)

Where to measure	What to measure	Limit value	Suggested period
TRX	VSPC response	< 2 seconds	1 minute
	TSO period 1 response	< 2 seconds	1 minute
SRM	ASMQ (paging queue)	< 10	1 minute
	PAGRT (total paging)	< 120/sec (3033)	1 minute
All	PDT (page delay time)	< 200 millisec.	1 minute
	UIC (time page left unstolen)	< 4-8 (seconds)	1 minute
CSA	CSA FREE (free virtual stor.)	> 200 K with IMS	Any time
SDSF	SIO/batch job	< 40 (3033) **	1 minute
SID	UIC/Specific work unit	< 3 (seconds)	1 minute

Systems resource follow up

Where to measure	What to measure	Limit value	Suggested period
RMF extract	Interactive work: disk busy	< 30%	1 hour
	Batch work : disk busy	< 60%	1 hour
	Disk queue average	< .04	1 hour
	Total paging per second	< 100 (3033) **	1 hour
	Disk channel busy (interact.)	< 25% **	1 hour
KWU	CPU - interactive work and work of higher priority (TCB)	< 25%	1 week
DISK (danger)	Interactive disk busy	> 30%	1 day
	Interactive disk SIO rate	> 10 per second	1 day
	Interactive disk response	> 80 milliseconds	1 day
DISK (OK)	Interactive disk busy	< 20%	1 day
	Interactive disk SIO rate	< 5 per second	1 day
	Interactive disk response	< 60 milliseconds	1 day
VSPCX	CPU maximum for 5 minute period (TCB time)	< 40%	1 day
VSPCRESP	Response time	< 1 second	1 hour
SLR	Maximum swap rate	< 2 (3033) **	1 hour
	Average IMS response	< 3 seconds	1 hour
	Average TSO response	< 3 seconds	1 hour

** If 3330/3350 disk configuration

Figure 106.   Suggested limit values for significant systems resources

6.8 OVERALL MONITORING

In a multi CPU environment, there ought to be a central control of all the resources.

JES3 har implemented a version of this concept. One terminal can for instance control all tapes (the tape pool), one can control all disks, one controls all CPUs and so forth. There are in JES3 a number of routing codes and selected routing codes can be sent to selected consoles.

In this fashion, the whole complex can be governed from one or a few terminals.

With colour terminals, this concept can be carried further. Certain messages can be highlighted, for instance using blinking red colour. Other messages, more of a warning nature can be designated blue, and so forth.

If one screen is used to supervise several CPUs, the layout of the screen could be used to designate certain CPUs and resources, and colour the degree of attention needed. When everything runs OK, the screen would be neutral. Figure 107 on page 173 sketches this concept.

As can be deduced from Figure 108 on page 173, the red is reserved for un-availability and extreme resource usage situations. Perhaps 300 SIO per second is not much for a 3033, but it easily endangers an interactive environment.

In today's environment response times, for instance for IMS, are difficult to obtain online. The figure shows conceptual monitoring, however, and the actual implementation may have to await further hardware and software developments.

The hardware checking is done against a standard configuration checklist as described in chapter 5. Possibly a high error rate on a hardware component could be a 'blue' incident; this would mean that the error count should also be obtainable online.

	CPU	Paging		SIO	TP	IMS	VSPC	CICS	TSO	Hardware		
	%	Rate	Time								Disks	Central	TP
CPU1												
CPU2												
CPU3												

Blinking red: Alert
Blue: Impending danger
Yellow: Values are high
Green: Within limits, but not scheduled for this CPU
White: Designated for this CPU, but not running

Figure 107. Overall monitoring screen, possible layout

The limit values could be selected as follows(Figure 108).

	CPU	Paging		SIO per sec.	TP	IMS	VSPC	CICS	TSO	Hardware		
	%	Rate	Time								Disks	Central	TP
Red	◄1	►200	►1s	►300	Not running					Component not up		
Blue	101	►150	►500	►250	Avg. resp over 5 sec.					◄—Not used————►		
Yellow	►90	►120	►300	►200	Avg. resp over 3 sec.					◄—Not used————►		
Green	◄—Not used————►									◄—Not used————►		
White	◄—Not used————►									◄—Not used————►		

The Paging time is the same as the Page Delay Time, and is expressed in
seconds(s) or milliseconds ('blue' and 'yellow' incidents).

Assumed time between automatic sampling: 1 minute.

Figure 108. Monitoring limits for overall monitoring (3033 UP based)

6.9 CONCLUSION

Online monitoring of complex EDP centres has received little attention in current EDP literature. This is unfortunate, because monitoring naturally deserves a place in the performance control system, similar to the control room setup for an electrical plant, or the control bridge on a ship.

Traditionally supervision has been carried out by systems programmers or similarly skilled people. This may still be advantageous when using monitoring to evaluate the impact of a systems change or identify problem areas.

Another aspect of monitoring is day-to-day supervision This could for instance be carried out by the Master Terminal Operators, Network Control, or whatever group that is in charge of delivering the daily service to (normally) online users. The system cost of such supervision is normally quite low, and the cost of terminals should easily be outweighed by the benefits to centre service.

RMFMON, a versatile supervision tool, requires a deep understanding of MVS subtleties if all aspects of RMFMON is used. However, concentrating on selected parameters, effective supervision can be taught in a matter of minutes to operators with very little previous system control program knowledge. This book can provide a first line reference, with recourse to official product literature for detail information.

As a side effect from using this approach, the systems knowledge of the people involved will increase. These operators are responsible for delivering a service based on the systems; an increase in their level of appreciating systems or services will benefit the centre, and quite likely the centre's image to the users.

Monitoring is useful to follow up changes in the computing environment. Such changes could be: a new processor, another loading pattern, a new application, disk configuration changes, new users etc etc. Changes often cause alterations in other components than the one(s) changed. Professional intuition normally identifies such effects, but monitoring is useful to back this up with proofs.

Examples of the successful use of online monitoring are:

- Splitting work between processors and ensuring that the right work runs on the selected processor

- Establishing priority levels and measuring the effect

- Selecting values for real storage fencing and measuring the result

- Verifying the influence of interactive system on each other

- Identifying disturbances caused by single, heavy users

- Resolving disk hangups

- Evaluating changes

● Early problem detection

In the future, supervision of a processor complex (the processors may be part of a distributed network), should be done centrally. The implementation may be to route selected resource or service information on to colour screens that will highlight (for instance in red) whatever components are critical, for instance a failing processor. Preferrably other sensory input could be issued, for instance sounding an alarm. This will immediately bring attention to the critical situation, and aid a speedy recovery. Near-critical components could be displayed in another colour, alerting people to potential problems. Some problems may be avoided altogether in this fashion.

In the same way as with other monitoring, this central control will identify components and values essential for the smooth operation of the centre, enabling monitoring to be steadily improved.

CHAPTER 7

ANOMALY HANDLING

Tiny points of light rose above the dark waters and drifted off, to
explode with soft, popping noises, emitting noxious odors amid show-
ers of sparks. The ground continued to shake and the dark waters
overleaped their banks in places, staining the rocks and land about
with tarlike film. A winged, monkeyfaced thing the size of a bird
flew at them, talons outstretched...

> R. Zelazny
> The changing land

If a woman be not visious nor desire men, take the members of a
woolfe, and the haires which doe grow on the cheekes and eyebrows of
him, and burne it all and give it to her to drinke, when she knoweth
not, and she shall desire no other man.

> Folklore, Myths and Legends of
> Britain

- by his benevolent exertions (has contributed) to an eminent degree
to the expulsion of fairies from the Highland hills.

> New Statistical Account 1845 (I.F.
> Grant: Highland Folk Ways)

7.1 INTRODUCTION

7.1.1 Chapter contents

In this chapter anomalies are defined and an approach to identifying and resolving anomalies is outlined.

The approach is designed for a **production** environment. There is little room for experimenting, fine tuning and elegant implementations in a modern, complex computer centre. The emphasis is therefore on **trapping** an anomaly and finding its particulars from a few reports that are designed to run relatively rarely - preferably on weekly basis. A prerequisite for this is that online monitoring is in place and functioning to trap the errors that have an 'here and now' impact.

This enables a **continuous** follow up, that can be performed by people with no heavy technical background. Also, the system is designed to trap **most** errors, i.e. not only those that are immediately evident.

A disk reporting program is described in detail because it embodies most of these ideas , and because many anomalies in a complex environment originate somehow from disks and disk paths.

7.1.2 Definition

Anomalies is a collective term indicating that some system behaviour is not as expected or as assumed. Because we primarily consider service levels, normally only those anomalies that adversely affect service levels are included in the definition.

A strangely busy disk would by this method not be investigated if no effect on service levels could be found. Quite tough, but resources needed to analyse the disk and perform resulting actions, could normally be more gainfully employed on projects with a more immediate benefit.

7.1.3 Causes of anomalies

Anomalies in the system could be due to:

        Hardware errors
        Software errors
        Application program errors
        Operation errors
        Inadequate procedures
        Bottlenecks
        Wrong load mix
        Wrong resource handling
        Wrong use of one or more system components

The five first points normally would belong to the area of 'Problem management' as described for instance in reference 1. Chapter 8 in this

book discusses the relation between problem management, other management
functions, and the control system described here.

The last item on the above list sometimes accounts for most of what the
user perceives as 'poor service'. The wrong use may pertain to hardware
(e.g. terminal), the system control program (control statements, 'Job Control Language'), or the application program used.

The problem could be overcome by a 'Help' desk service, well designed procedures, 'HELP' screens and similar. This is an important aspect of anomaly handling, even if it is somewhat out of line with the other subjects
to be treated further in this book.

'Only' three areas are then left for treatment in this chapter:

Bottlenecks:

          Meaning a lack of one or more resources causing the system to
          perform worse than expected.

          Note the definition of performance from reference 1: Perform-
          ance is a measure on how well a computing centre meets its
          objectives within a framework of economy, technology and social
          environment.

          When for instance an IMS system performs badly 2 hours on a par-
          ticular day, and acceptably for the rest of the week, there is a
          reason to suspect that the total system has a bottleneck of some
          sort - provided that the load from IMS during the 2 hours did
          not appreciably deviate from load during the rest of the week.

          Or that during those two hours we had a:

Wrong load mix:

          A number of problems arise from running work together that ought
          to be separate: for instance virtual storage intensive programs
          like IMS and VSPC. Running them together may be acceptable, but
          virtual storage may run out during high load and cause unpleas-
          ant breaks.

          Another aspect is that any work should be run according to its
          relative priority. That priority may be difficult to establish
          in a complex environment.

          Even when the priority is established, an algorithm to divide
          resources between work according to the priorities is difficult
          to implement, bringing up the next topic:

Applica-tion	processor type	processor share%	real storage%	ratio processing/storage
IMS	3033/16MB	20	40	1:2
VSPC	168/8MB	10	25	1:2.5

Figure 109.   Real storage usage by typical interactive systems.

Wrong resource handling:

Modern system control programs have impressive algorithms to divide resources between work. For instance it is quite easy to tell MVS the relative dispatching priorities of all its work. However, dispatching priorities only refer to dispatchable work (reference 1). A lot of work is restrained from using the processor because of some resource shortage. In modern interactive systems the limiting resource is often <u>not</u> processor time, but some difficult-to-control resource like real or virtual storage. See Figure 109 for a comment.

Note: The figures include **private** pages only. Frames that are used for MVS common areas like CSA and LPA are not counted. Typically an interactive system also uses common areas heavily.

The figure makes fairly obvious that interactive systems are intensive **real storage** users.   This is natural, as they need quick access to data for responsiveness.

For the same reason, interactive systems are also heavy **virtual storage** users.

Some computing centres of today (1982) appears not to prioritize and control work according to this fact; that virtual and real storage are prime dimensioning resources.

Even disks and mass storage can heavily influence service, and ought to be followed continually. Disk follow up is covered more in detail later in this chapter.

In an environment where most systems resources are allocated to interactive work and batch multiprogramming level is low, a few active batch initiators may influence other work heavily. When they are in, they work and are perhaps swapped due to high resource consumption.   Because they are swapped, resource consumption decreases, and they may be swapped in again.

Batch may load input/output paths heavily without being punished at all. The paths are not always easy to anticipate, and MVS's automatic algorithms do not always suffice.   Sometimes batch work must be delayed to second shift for this reason.

7.2 SUGGESTED ANOMALY TRAPPING STRUCTURE

7.2.1 Overall structure

Suggestions for an overall structure is given in Figure 93 on page 156.

The main components are:

        A trapping mechanism, possibly augmented by user interface input
        Problem description procedures
        Problem follow up procedures

Figure 93 on page 156 shows trapping by means of a benchmark program.

7.2.2 Channel environment

A number of errors are due to input output problems and can be found by investigating channel behaviour. On Figure 110 on page 182, channel 2 is not recorded in one period the October 12th (15:04), and is very slow during the following period (16:04). The slowness is underlined by a special character string used when a value on the graph is outside the normal graph reporting range. The number 0.070 is the average response time in milliseconds for that period (one hour). This should be compared with the normal response of 10 milliseconds. Referring to **Problem management** records, channel 2 was at that time disabled due to disk storage control errors.

Figure 111 on page 183 shows an overload on both physical channels 3 and 6. These are both disk channels, and should not be loaded more than 30 percent during the day. Notably, one of those disks have a longer average service time. 10-12 milliseconds is a high value for a channel serving 3350 disks. The channel in question did in fact also serve 3340 disks with a slower transfer speed, and those 3340s were used for paging. The page supervisor tend to string several I/O (paging) requests together to save overhead. Normally 2-3 pages are transferred together in a highly active (paging) environment.

Disk channels 3 and 6 are both on logical path 4, so why in the example was not more of the paging transferred over physical channel 6? The answer was found from configuration drawings: string switching was not yet installed on the 3340, and therefore they were attached to only one channel. When string switching was later installed, balance was achieved.

```
            CPU/CSID 0 CHANNEL 02  AVG. SERVICE TIME
        0       0.010     0.020     0.030     0.040     0.050
        |---------|---------|---------|---------|---------|
0/12 08:04|*************          .         .         .         .
     09:04|************          .         .         .         .
     10:04|************          .         .         .         .
     11:04|***********          .         .         .         .
     12:04|*********          .         .         .         .
     13:04|***********          .         .         .         .
     14:04|**********          .         .         .         .
     15:04|             .         .         .         .
     16:04|••••••••••••••••••••  0.070  ••••••••••••••••••••••••
0/13 08:00|************          .         .         .         .
     09:00|************          .         .         .         .
     10:00|************          .         .         .         .
     11:00|**************          .         .         .         .
     12:00|**********          .         .         .         .
     13:00|**********          .         .         .         .
     14:00|***********          .         .         .         .
     15:00|*************          .         .         .         .
     16:00|***********          .         .         .         .
0/14 08:04|**********          .         .         .         .
     09:04|**********          .         .         .         .
     10:04|************          .         .         .         .
     11:04|***********          .         .         .         .
     12:04|***********          .         .         .         .
     13:04|************          .         .         .         .
     14:04|************          .         .         .         .
     15:04|*************          .         .         .         .
     16:04|**************          .         .         .         .
```

Figure 110.   Channel anomaly

For an explanation of terms on the figure, refer to Figure 66 on page 117
and Figure 67 on page 118.

The overload is causing long queues on logical channel 4.   The culprit
turned out to be an ailing swap disk, resulting in excess error recovery
that congested the channels.

The channel investigation was an intermediate step in our performance
investigation.   The problem was **found** when the controller attempted to log
on to a very slow system.   The problem was **localized** when online monitoring made quite certain that the problem was a disk or disk path anomaly,
prolonging disk response times considerably.

Searching could then be concentrated on disk and disk paths, and the above
reports were requested.   In addition _monitor_ displays (RMFMON user UCB,
see Figure 120 on page 195) for disks were run, indicating that one particular disk accounted for most problems.   This was confirmed when looking
at the _RMF disk activity report_ for that disk.   It had 20 I/Os per second
for the swap disk and was 97% busy.   Thus the problem was **identified.**

The problem was **solved** by replacing the ailing disk.

```
PHYSICAL CHANNEL ACTIVITY
       CHANNEL          CHANNEL    PERCENT    PERCENT          ACTIVITY AVERAGE
CPU/   NUMBER           ACTIVITY   CHANNEL    CHAN BUSY        PER      SERVICE
CSID   AND TYPE         COUNT      BUSY       & CPU WAIT       SECOND      TIME
 0   0  BYTE MPX          4,738                                 7.876
     1  BLOCK MPX         9,592    13.09      0.12             15.945    0.008
     2  BLOCK MPX         8,922    14.84      1.12             14.831    0.009
     3  BLOCK MPX        26,636    59.35      2.87             44.278    0.013
     4  BLOCK MPX           352     1.37      0.12              0.585    0.022
     5  BLOCK MPX           682     3.37      0.12              1.133    0.029
     6  BLOCK MPX        31,444    45.76      2.74             52.271    0.008
TOTAL/ANY/AVE           82,366    84.41      4.36            136.922    0.010


LOGICAL CHANNEL ACTIVITY
       PHYS CHAN
LOG    CPU/CSID    REQ      -    % QLENGTH DISTRIBUTION   -    AVG Q   % REQ
CHN    0    1      PER      0      1     2      3     4+   LNGTH   DEFER
                  SECOND
  0    0           7.876  100.0   0.0   0.0    0.0   0.0   0.00    5.83
  1    1,2        30.722   95.4   4.1   0.4    0.1   0.0   0.05    8.99
  4    3,6        89.327   34.4  40.5  16.2    6.0   2.9   1.04   39.11
  6    4           0.585  100.0   0.0   0.0    0.0   0.0   0.00    0.00
  7    5           1.133   96.8   1.4   0.9    0.9   0.1   0.06   30.06
  8    6           7.236   93.0   6.5   0.5    0.0   0.0   0.07   38.69
```

Figure 111.   RMF channel overload condition

7.2.3 Disk environment

Based on experience and the DISK program a procedure can be implemented
to list the most probable bottleneck components. Because the disk performance is central in performance investigations, and because the implementation of the DISK program is typical for the suggested extracts from RMF,
the whole procedure for the DISK program is included.

The DISK program process:

```
            'any number of disks'
      for   4 MVS systems  - as implemented
      and   2 periods      - as implemented
      and   5 days         - as implemented
```

Because the program complex is in APL, changes are easy to implement.

The data are assembled into a weekly database, for instance to plot central characteristics for selected disks over several weeks.

7.2.4 Input to the disk reporting program

The disk data are selected from the RMF disk report. The report is extracted from the WEEK datasets, that for clarity are supposed to be on tape in this example. Disk/MSS would be more appropriate media.

The report periods are the following:

Period 1:   0900 to 1700   Extracted by job DISK1

Period 2:   1700 to 2400   Extracted by job DISK2

The requested start and finish dates (work days only) should be respecified to the RMF program for each week. The first date is normally the Monday in the week, the last date is the Friday. For example for week 1 in 1982: Week tapes requested are 155 and 156. Dates specified are 82004 (Monday) and 82008 (Friday). The dates are input to RMF.

Output from the jobs are sent to a virtual reader on your VM system (possibly a TSO print file). You read it from there by the command: READ DISKnnn VMAPL3F. This creates a file called DISKnnn VMAPL3F on your primary disk (A disk). nnn stands for a number; we suggest the following:

Period 1:   nnn is the number of the first specified dataset

Period 2:   nnn is the number of the second specified dataset

Start APL by writing:

Period 1:   DISK1

Period 2:   DISK2

This loads APL and also the fullscreen APL program DISKPROG that displays a menu screen on your terminal. If in doubt about a menu item, a HELP screen can be displayed using program function (PF) key 1.

The first choice on the menu enables the disk data to be read from the CMS file created from RMF data. The nnn number given to the appropriate CMS file should be specified.

7.2.5 Output from the disk reporting program

There are five logical parts to the list:

1. Selected disks for each day.

    The twenty most busy disks, the 10 slowest disks (highest disk response) and the grouped virtual disks are listed for each day.

    Most virtual disks are destaged at sampling time, and listed under the ●●●●●● heading. The rates and busy percentages are added, and the maximum disk response is listed.

The identifiable virtual disks, are grouped according to the following
criteria, based on the DISK ID:

DISK ID	Disk reporting	Purpose
CCxxxx	STAGIN	MSS virtual volumes
CCBxxx	BACKUP	HSM backup volumes
CCMxxx	LEVEL1	HSM level 1 volumes
CCNxxx	LEVEL2	HSM level 2 volumes

- where the x's are digits from 0 to 9.

The following columns occur in the output:

a. DISK ID

    The (normally) 6 letter ID of the disk as extracted from RMF. If
    a disk has been moved, it is the address occurring to RMF when the
    sample was taken; in our case 1700 hours (period 1) or 2400 hours
    (period 2).

b. HOST COMPUTER with identification

    The addresses for the registered DISK ID is given for each of the
    four MVS systems. If the address does not exist for a certain
    system, then it was not registered for that system when the sample
    was taken. Normally it means that the disk was offline to that
    system.

    The systems are the CCC systems described in chapter 10.

c. I/O RATE

    The composite IO rate (SIO per second) for all four systems.

d. BUSY PCT.

    The composite busy percent for all four systems (the sum of the
    busy percents).

e. RESPONSE MILLIS.

    For each system, RMF finds average response in milliseconds for a
    disk I/O operation. This is the time from issuing the SIO request
    till the disk sends an interrupt telling it is ready. It there-
    fore includes most, but not all, queues within the disk system. A
    normal job or transaction issues several SIOs, and the sum of
    these is the part of the response time or turnaround time attrib-
    utable to disks. IMS transactions may issue 15-20 SIOs in average
    per transaction. If each of these take 50 milliseconds, there is
    already about one second of response time.

```
******************* COMPLEX COMPUTER CENTRE    *****************************
******************* DISK ANALYSIS PROGRAM      *****************************
******************* DAILY REPORT, WEEK  1      *****************************

DATE:    5  1 82

DISK   HOST COMPUTER:              I/O  BUSY RESPONSE PERCENTAGE IO:
ID     158   168   3033A 3033B     RATE PCT. MILLIS.  158   168   3033A 3033B

TOP TWENTY MOST LOADED DISKS

VSLIB0 2B7   1B7   4B7   8B7       8.61 46.68    46     2    70    28    0
CCAWK1 39F   39F   29F   29F      13.31 33.44    25     0     0   100    0
IS1074 2A7   1A7   4A7   8A7       5.91 22.68    66     4    12    83    0
IS1744 373   373   373   373       5.96 18.94    32     9     3    88    0
CCMJ01 38D   38D   28D   28D       3.59 15.99    53    16    41    19   24
IS1090 2A3   1A3   4A3   8A3       2.54 15.15    65    29     4    67    0
CCBR0E 14D   14D   14D   14D       3.62 15.10    41     0   100     0    0
CCBR51 176   176   176   176       6.48 14.61    42     0    53     0   47
CCBR46       3B1   3B1             2.47 14.32    58     0    99     0    1
CCBB53 39B   39B   29B   29B       2.18 14.27    65     0     0   100    0
ISPAK1 367   367   367   367       3.23 14.13    35     1    88    11    0
CCBR47       3B8   3B8             2.44 14.07    57     0   100     0    0
CCBR48       3B9   3B9             2.48 14.01    56     0   100     0    0
IS1062 152   152   152   152       4.15 12.17    23     0    52    48    0
CCBR42       3A9         3A9       4.34 12.13    41     0    67     0   33
CCBR01 15C   15C   15C   15C       2.25 12.01    52     0   100     0    0
CCMS03 15D   15D   15D   15D       3.76 11.99    28    14    69    17    0
CCSRF3 36A   36A   36A   36A       4.54 11.76    23     3    75    22    0
CCMS02 14E   14E   14E   14E       4.74 11.56    31    11    52    14   22
CCMS01 16B   16B   16B   16B       3.66 11.16    26    14    68    17    0

TOP TEN SLOWEST DISKS

IS1712       346   346   346        .84   .65   104     0     7     0   93
IS1074 2A7   1A7   4A7   8A7       5.91 22.68    66     4    12    83    0
IS1090 2A3   1A3   4A3   8A3       2.54 15.15    65    29     4    67    0
CCBB53 39B   39B   29B   29B       2.18 14.27    65     0     0   100    0
CCBR41       3A8         3A8       2.46  9.28    60     0    62     0   38
CCBR46       3B1   3B1             2.47 14.32    58     0    99     0    1
CCBR47       3B8   3B8             2.44 14.07    57     0   100     0    0
CCBR48       3B9   3B9             2.48 14.01    56     0   100     0    0
IS1725       341   341   341        .00   .00    55     0     0     0    0
IS1729 34E   34E   34E   34E        .01   .03    53     0     0    92    8

VIRTUAL DISKS - TOTAL GROUPED USAGE

STAGIN       6FF   879   F3C       1.80  7.57    65     0    19    81    0
LEVEL1       6FE   87A   23F        .50  1.77    21     0    23    77    1
LEVEL2             862              .00   .00    17     0     0     0    0
BACKUP                              .71   .00     0     0     0     0  100
```

Figure 112. DISK program - daily report

f.   PERCENTAGE IO.

For each of the host computers, the percentage of the SIO issued
to each disk is registered. This helps identifying the user systems for each disk, and is helpful when disk problems may originate from several sources, or/and when RESERVES is a suspected
problem area.

2.   All disks for last (full) day in week, sorted by SIO rate

The information items in this list are identical to the preceding
list, but all registered disks are listed, and the sort criterion is
different (number of start I/Os). Even the MSS related disks are
listed. The purpose of this list is partly to provide an alternate
sorting, but mostly to give a total overview over connections in the
system. No example of this list is included in this book; it would be
quite voluminous (220 disks for the sample case) and are rather specific to a particular environment.

3.   Overall string analysis

For all strings, the composite I/O rate is shown, distributed on CPU,
and total. The data are weekly averages.

The address of the first disk in each string is shown. The string
identifier is read from a CMS file based on the address of the first
disk.

Disk addresses are read from RMF. Only one day, with a presumed full
recording is selected as a basis. The disks are allocated to strings
based on their addresses. Some disks could not be uniquely identified
based on any of the four addresses (sometimes blank), and are lumped
in a separate group.

```
******************* COMPLEX COMPUTER CENTRE       ***********************
******************* DISK ANALYSIS PROGRAM         ***********************
******************* I/O RATE SUMMARY FOR DISK STRINGS  *****************

STRING   HOST ADDRESS                    SIO RATE
   ID  158   168  3033A 3033B    158    168   3033A  3033B  TOTAL


STR 55 160   160   160   160     .39    .87  12.55   1.01  14.82
STR 51 2A0   1A0   4A0   8A0    1.31   1.23  11.49    .17  14.20
STR 61 398   398   298   298     .09    .58  12.84    .10  13.61
STR 56 168   168   168   168     .22   2.54   8.21    .79  11.76
STR 58 178   178   178   178     .01    .04  10.17    .23  10.45
STR 57 170   170   170   170     .16   2.49   7.06    .69  10.40
STR 14 388   388   288   288    2.99   3.49    .95   2.77  10.20
STR 52 148   148   148   148     .22   5.34    .45   1.18   7.19
STR 11 2B8   1B8   4B8   8B8     .64   1.26    .38   4.05   6.33
STR  1 360   360   360   360     .32   3.58   1.17    .81   5.88
STR  8 378   378   378   378     .38   1.54   3.40    .49   5.81
STR  3 2B0   1B0   4B0   8B0     .65   3.06   1.63    .15   5.49
STR 13 368   368   368   368     .29   2.70   1.30    .65   4.94
STAGIN 320   6F0   878   130     .44   2.04   1.72    .14   4.34
STR 54 158   158   158   158     .19   2.30    .36   1.32   4.17
       2A8   1A8   4A8   8A8    2.95   1.05    .00    .15   4.15
STR  7 370   370   370   370     .26    .48   2.28    .56   3.58
STR 53 150   150   150   150     .00    .93    .91   1.37   3.21
                                 .00    .17    .00   2.92   3.09
STR 21       3A8         3A8     .00   2.27    .00    .47   2.74
STR 23       3B8   3B8           .00   2.53    .00    .00   2.53
STR 12 180                      1.65    .00    .00    .77   2.42
STR  2 350   350   350   350     .06    .74   1.29    .02   2.11
STR 22       3B0   3B0           .00   2.02    .00    .01   2.03
STR  6 340   340   340   340     .17    .32    .06   1.21   1.76
STR 20       3A0         3A0     .00   1.61    .00    .00   1.61
STR  4 348   348   348   348     .24    .56    .31    .00   1.11
       338   138   138           .00    .14    .31    .00    .45
STR 27 3D8         3D8   3D8     .00    .00    .00    .34    .34
       358   358   358           .00    .00    .00    .20    .20
STR 26 3D0         3D0   3D0     .00    .00    .00    .12    .12
STR 14       380   280   280     .00    .00    .00    .00    .00
STR 62 290               290     .00    .00    .00    .00    .00
STAGIN       6D8   858   220     .00    .00    .00    .00    .00
STAGIN             860           .00    .00    .00    .00    .00
STAGIN             870           .00    .00    .00    .00    .00
STR 25                   3C8     .00    .00    .00    .00    .00
STAGIN       600   200   200     .00    .00    .00    .00    .00
STAGIN       608   208   208     .00    .00    .00    .00    .00
STR 24       3C0   3C0   3C0     .00    .00    .00    .00    .00

TOTAL                          13.63  45.88  78.84  22.69 161.04
```

Figure 113. DISK program - string analysis

The composite rate for each CPU is shown on Figure 113, and also the
isolation factor, on Figure 114 on page 189.

The isolation factor is computed as follows:

For each disk string, the following numbers are found:

    NRATE   = I/O rate to processor N

    TOTRATE   = I/O rate to all processors

    ISOLATION   = NRATE/TOTRATE

The isolation factor is the weighted average of ISOLATION of all strings, and is defined in the formula:

Isolation factor = sum(NRATE x ISOLATION) / sum(NRATE)

Ideally, the isolation factor should be 1 for each processor, i.e. a sum of 4 for four processors.

Recommended target for **string** isolation factors for production processors is tentatively set at **0.75**.

```
******************** COMPLEX COMPUTER CENTRE            **********************
******************** DISK ANALYSIS PROGRAM             **********************
******************** I/O INTERFERENCE SUMMARY FOR DISK STRINGS ******************

                         ISOLATION FACTOR
                158      168     3033A   3033B


                .34      .52      .75     .42
```

Figure 114. Disk program - isolation analysis

---

4. Disk group summary.

A disk group is a collection of disks (disk strings) that share disk path, and is for instance attached to the same (two) disk storage controller(s).   In MVS terminology and implementation, the disks will then share logical path. Figure 115 on page 190 shows an example of disk group usage in the presented environment. Note the high rate on group 6. A long range plan is to dedicate this to the IMS processor, but the report shows that there is still a long way to go.

Data analogous to the disk string summary is given.

```
******************** COMPLEX COMPUTER CENTRE        **********************
******************** DISK ANALYSIS PROGRAM          **********************
******************** I/O RATE SUMMARY FOR DISK GROUPS **********************

STRING    HOST ADDRESS                      SIO RATE
   ID  158  168  3033A 3033B    158     168    3033A   3033B  TOTAL


DGR  6 160  160  160   160      .78    5.94   37.99    2.72   47.43
DGR  7 2A0  1A0  4A0   8A0     5.55    6.60   13.50    4.52   30.17
DGR  8 280  380  280   280     3.08    4.07   13.79    2.87   23.81
DGR  2 360  360  360   360     1.25    8.30    8.15    2.51   20.21
DGR  5 140  140  140   140      .41    8.57    1.72    3.87   14.57
DGR 12      3A0  3A0   3A0      .00    8.43     .00     .48    8.91
DGR  1 340  340  340   340      .47    1.62    1.66    1.43    5.18
STAGIN 320  320  120   120      .44    2.18    2.03     .14    4.79
                                .00     .17     .00    2.92    3.09
DGR 10 180                     1.65     .00     .00     .77    2.42
DGR 11 3C0  3C0  3C0   3C0      .00     .00     .00     .46     .46
STAGIN      6C0  840   220      .00     .00     .00     .00     .00
                 860            .00     .00     .00     .00     .00
STAGIN      600  200   200      .00     .00     .00     .00     .00

TOTAL                         13.63   45.88   78.84   22.69 161.04
```

Figure 115.   DISK program - disk group data

5.   Detail string data

For each string the constituent disks are shown with data as for the
'top twenty' reports.   Any string with suspiciously high response
times can be found in this report, and compared with other strings on
the same controllers.

Figure 116 on page 191 shows one disk with a very high response time.
On the other hand, the report shows a lot of sharing.   The string is
mainly used for the IMS system, but 'everything else' is crowding into
it.   A very clear case for an availability improvement is presented,
for instance by removing CCCR01, a systems disk for the test system.

One observation needs to be inserted at this point.   It may sound easy
to move disks around to present a neat, healthy picture where only
minimal interference occurs.   Due to a shortage of disks that many
centres experience, the exercise is not easy.   A program like the suggested DISK program serves to build up tangible evidence that can be
used to convince management and others of the consequences of wrong
disk placements.

Any path sharing presents an availability risk.   Besides, sharing adds
to response time problems.   The disk often configuration accounts for
a major part of response time and availability problems.

```
******************** COMPLEX COMPUTER CENTRE        **********************
******************** DISK ANALYSIS PROGRAM          **********************
******************** STRING DETAILS - STR 51        **********************

DISK  HOST COMPUTER:              I/O  BUSY RESPONSE PERCENTAGE IO:
ID    158   168   3033A 3033B     RATE PCT. MILLIS. 158   168   3033A 3033B

IS1043 2A0  1A0   4A0   8A0        .50 1.53   290     0     0    88    12
IS1081 2A1  1A1   4A1   8A1       1.12 3.41    34     0     9    89     2
IS1082 2A2  1A2   4A2   8A2        .79 2.26    46    24    72     2     3
IS1090 2A3  1A3   4A3   8A3       2.85 15.82   66    16     2    82     0
CCCR01 2A4  1A4   4A4   8A4        .48 1.69    39    98     0     0     2
IS1004 2A5  1A5   4A5   8A5       1.91 5.96    34     0    16    84     0
IS1074 2A7  1A7   4A7   8A7       4.92 18.11   69     4     4    92     0
CCAWK2 2A6  1A6   4A6   8A6       1.66 4.20    31     0     0   100     0

TOTAL RATE                       14.22
```

Figure 116.   DISK program - detail string data

7.2.6 Disk reporting system - example

Figure 112 on page 186 shows a listing of the most active disks by adding
load from the (four) MVS processors.   Disk addresses on each processor are
included for facility of reading.

This enables the analysts to select the most likely bottleneck candidates.

In the example, VSLIB0 is a system disk, used for instance by TSO and IMS.
It it disturbing that it is so highly used.

More than 30 percent busy over the whole day may cover hourly usage of
twice that amount. This disk is used by four processors, and the strong-
est (3033) will always get precedence on shared paths, for instance disk
string controller, or the disk itself.

The following disk, CCAWK1, is a work pack. One should think that no wor-
ry need to be spent. However, the work packs share paths with the IMS
disks, and the high I/O rate is really a concern. A long range objective
of removing the work packs from IMS strings does not help the here and now
situation.

IS1074 contains format datasets for IMS. This dataset was moved from a
dedicated 3330 used about 10 percent. The IMS specialists are 'certain'
that nothing else is used on IS1074. This has been 'proved' by running
GTFPARS to trace disk usage. The problem here was that GTFPARS only ran
for 1/2 hour.

Quite significantly IS1074 also is high on the slow list. Something seems
wrong. (Later the format dataset was moved back with good effect).

The following disks: CCBxxx are system disks for the 168. Normally there
should be zero activity from the other systems. The sharing shown may be
cause for alarm, and points to an additional use of the report. The slow

CCBR4x disks are all 3340, and are used for paging. They serve in lieu of
3350s only because the supply of 3350 was at the time limited.

IS1090 and CCBB53 contain the IMS load libraries (the programs). Due to
virtual storage shortage, most IMS program are loaded when needed, and the
load library contention is therefore serious for IMS response. Of the
'Top twenty' list shown, the load library contention is among the most
disturbing. Both program library disks are also among the slowest.

7.2.7 Extensions to the DISK program

Extensions to this system can be implemented.

See for instance Figure 117 where selected indices are followed over
several weeks.   In this way changes - continual or abrubt - are easy to
detect and quantify.

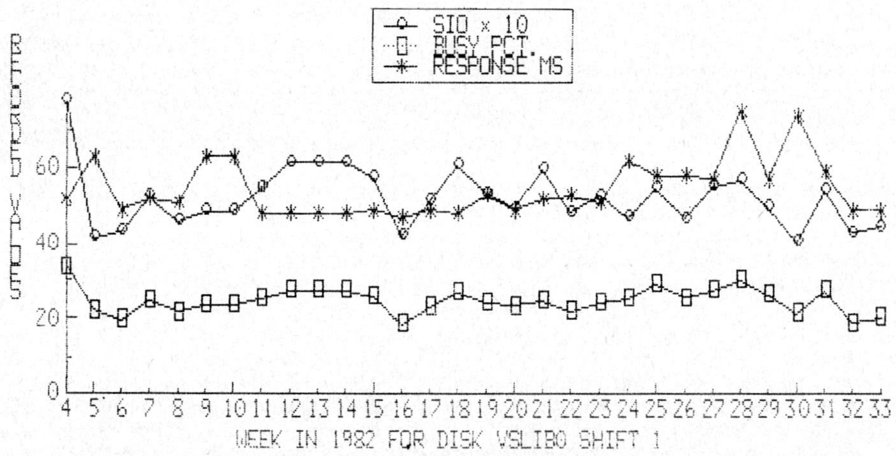

Figure 117.   Following disk performance indices

Another use is to follow the references to the disk from several processors; perhaps not all references are expected or desired. By the way, is
there a tendency in the usage pattern? Figure 118 on page 193 shows an
example of such disk access pattern for a 4-processor environment.

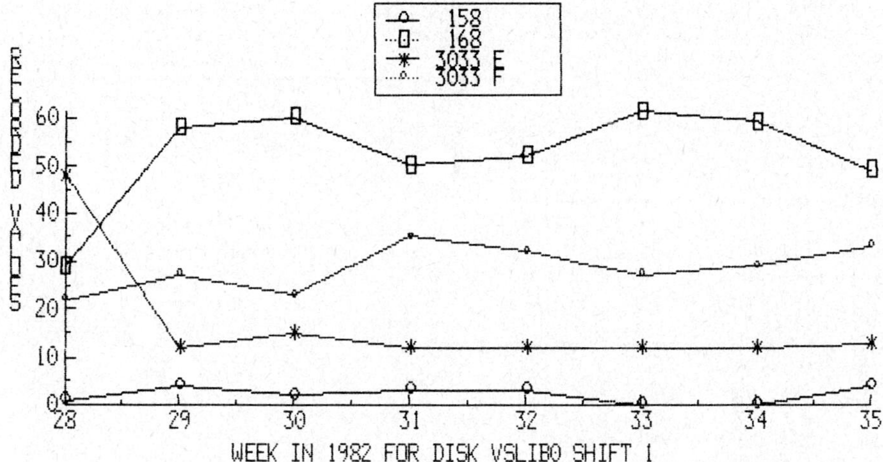

Figure 118.   Disk access pattern

Another extension would be to merge the recording programs with a disk
modelling system as described in chapter 7.   Another way, or an additional
way, is to compress the report into a few powerful performance indices.
An advantage in this case would be to start from a stable environment,
that few successful complex computer centres have today: success breeds
the desire for more success and new expansions.

7.2.8 RMFPLOT based disk analysis

Another input to supervision is naturally by way of problem reports, or
informal contacts.

In sum, some disks are identified as potential problem areas, and should
be followed in more detail.

Detail investigation is done by extracting weekly RMF plot reports for
these disks.

Figure 119 on page 194 shows output from such a plot where one disk has a
very high load during several hours.   The disk load caused batch jobs to
be prolonged by a factor up to 10 - and this was not easy to spot otherwise in a highly active batch production environment, especially as problems only occurred at night.

A similar, fairly tricky type of problem was found from RMF reports.   One
disk was suddenly one day extremely busy; exceeding 90% over the whole

day.   It was relatively easy to identify the users, two GIS batch
programs.

These programs were submitted again, and we monitored to see if there was
extreme IO activity. Monitoring, using ASD, ARD and SDSF told us that the
programs did not use much processing time, we did not catch them issuing
many EXCPs; in sum, they behaved very well.

```
               DEVICE 361              BUSY PERCENTAGE
               0        10.0       20.0       30.0       40.0       50.0
               |---------|---------|---------|---------|---------|
  8/13 00:00|••••••••••••••••••••    93.7    ••••••••••••••••••••••
       01:00|••••••••••••••••••••    79.0    ••••••••••••••••••••••
       02:00|              |         |         |         |         |
       08:00|              |         |         |         |         |
       09:00|              |         |         |         |         |
       10:00|              |         |         |         |         |
       11:00|              |         |         |         |         |
       12:00|              |         |         |         |         |
       13:00|*****         |         |         |         |         |
       14:00|****          |         |         |         |         |
       15:00|******************* |   |         |         |         |
       16:00|*********************************** |         |         |
       17:00|*************        |             |         |         |
       18:00|••••••••••••••••••••    77.8    ••••••••••••••••••••••••
       19:00|••••••••••••••••••••    95.7    ••••••••••••••••••••••••
       20:00|••••••••••••••••••••    99.5    ••••••••••••••••••••••••
       21:00|••••••••••••••••••••    99.6    ••••••••••••••••••••••••
       22:00|••••••••••••••••••••    99.5    ••••••••••••••••••••••••
       23:00|••••••••••••••••••••    91.8    ••••••••••••••••••••••••
  8/14 00:00|••••••••••••••••••••    59.3    ••••••••••••••••••••••••
       01:00|*********************************************************|
       02:00|********************          |         |         |
       03:00|*************************************          |         |
       04:00|              |         |         |         |         |
       08:00|***********           |         |         |         |
       09:00|**************        |         |         |         |
       10:00|              |         |         |         |         |
       11:00|              |         |         |         |         |
       12:00|**            |         |         |         |         |
       13:00|              |         |         |         |         |
       14:00|              |         |         |         |         |
       15:00|              |         |         |         |         |
       16:00|              |         |         |         |         |
       17:00|************************      |         |         |
       18:00|••••••••••••••••••••    81.7    ••••••••••••••••••••••••
       19:00|••••••••••••••••••••    95.2    ••••••••••••••••••••••••
       20:00|••••••••••••••••••••    78.5    ••••••••••••••••••••••••
       21:00|••••••••••••••••••••    55.3    ••••••••••••••••••••••••
       22:00|*************************.*****************        |
       23:00|••••••••••••••••••••    73.1    ••••••••••••••••••••••••
```

Figure 119. RMFPLOT disk plot

Displaying the RMFMON user UCB frame gave a different picture. A typical
example is shown in Figure 120 on page 195.

```
*************************************************************************
************** UCB              DELTA MODE *****************************
************** CPU= 45 UIC=  9 PDT= 102 DPR=   40 *********************
UCB  - DISPLAY BUSY DASD
CUU VOL     STATUS            JOBS ACTIVE/WAITING

353 IS1777 BSY               J104XJ99 J104GH77
38D CCMJ01 BSY               ISGJ
3A9 CCBR42 BSY               *MASTER*
```

Figure 120.   Disk overload example - RMFMON user UCB frame

The jobs J104XJ99 and J104GH77 simply kept IS1777 busy all the time, and
sometimes, when another job would use the same disk (a copy of a
database), there was increased trouble. We interpreted the IO situation
such that one EXCP (EXecute Channel Program); a software request for I/O,
in this case originated multiple SIO (physical Start Input Output).
RMFMON displays EXCP usage, but it is the physical input/output operations
that load the disk and the channel path and is recorded on the RMF extract
disk report.

An interesting side result came out of the same investigation. Each of
the mentioned GIS jobs had an elapse time of roughly 15 hours and exceeded
line print limits, whereafter the jobs abended providing approximately two
thirds of the print.   The user never complained about this for a year.
Not all the results can have been equally interesting, and the job should
be revised for usefulness and implementation in general.   How many other
such jobs are there in similar centra?

7.2.9 Batch

One drawback when using a standard procedure for general resource
follow-up, e.g. utilizing RMFPLOT, is that it is difficult to see what ran
at the anomaly time.   SLR may be used to produce a trace of all batch jobs
running, similar to Figure 38 on page 75.   However, the trace may be
illegible, and is expensive to run if the time frame is not very
restricted.

A more straight forward way is to investigate the system log as shown in
Figure 121 on page 196.

```
5.28.58               &HASP000      INIT 12 ACTIVE    JOB 7156 CCTHA   C=G


5.32.15   JOB 7156   IEF404I CCTHA - ENDED - TIME=15.32.15
5.32.16   JOB 7156   &HASP393 CCTHA     ENDED
5.32.18   JOB 7180   IEF677I WARNING MESSAGE(S) FOR JOB CCTHA ISSUED
5.32.18   JOB 7180   &HASP373 CCTHA STARTED - INIT 12 - CLASS G -SYS MVSB



Figure 121.   System log extract for batch job
```

In the case above, the CCTH jobs were not supposed to run on system MVSB,
and were using excessive resources.

The anomaly was found by investigating the RMFMON workload report. Performance group number 24 was shown to use excessive IO resources, and this
disturbed paging on the same IO path. According to performance specifications, performance group 24 ran classes G,5 and 7 at the time. The log
provided more exact information.

7.2.10 Procedure for VSPC

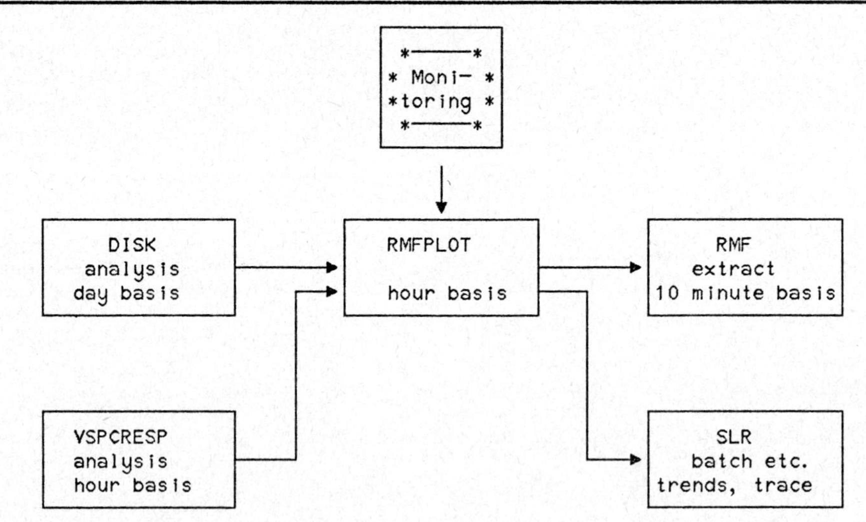

Figure 122.   Anomaly analysis structure

A VSPC anomaly analysis structure structure is as shown in Figure 122.

Operations supervision monitors VSPC continually using a benchmarking program, and RMFMON when responses seem poor.

The monitoring is supplemented by user problem reports.

Most problems are trapped in this manner, but DISK reports (Figure 112 on page 186) and VSPCRESP (Figure 33 on page 70) can be routinely checked for anomalies.

When cause for further investigation is found, usually a 10 minute RMF extract can be requested, and analyzed with reference to relevant SLR reports.

With appropriate adjustments, an analogous analysis structure could be used even for other services.

7.3 CONCLUSION

Tasks like extensive 'tuning' and constructing an 'optimal' system are
obsolete in a modern computing centre.   Instead, the normally scarce
resources should be concentrated on out-of-line situations (anomalies),
and resolving the situation to return the system to acceptable.

Sometimes the remedy is to remove or downgrade low priority work, or
postpone an installation.

Attention must be paid to history and capacity planning. When a system
runs at its estimated capacity, no further improvements designed to
extract more resources from the system need be attempted.

By keeping in mind future requirements, applications can be delayed or
refused.   Several computers in one computing centre can be logically
regarded as one facility, and then work can be moved, for instance back
and forth between VM and MVS.

Resolving anomalies are sometimes left to individualistic people known to
usually produce an answer.   How and with what resources is not always
investigated.

When handling anomalies in a complex centre, this book advocates a structure, a methodology, both for trapping and resolving anomalies. Time to
trap long responses, for instance, may be very long if nobody complains
and nobody looks.

Prophylaxis may not be as highly regarded as surgery, but is often more
effective and less painful.   Resources should be concentrated on pre-
vention. This avoids, alas, the magnificent first-aid actions suited for
story telling.   On the other hand it provides all implied parties with a
sense of trust in the service that many find more valuable.

Different people and environments need other ways and means. The important message is that there should always exist a guiding method or philosophy. Some occurrences will slip through even the best safety net, but we
ought to prepare against repetitions.

CHAPTER 8

THE TOTAL CONTROL SYSTEM

When such as I cast our remorse
so great a sweetness flows into our breast
we must laugh and we must sing
we are blest by everything
everything we look upon is blest

William B. Yeats

8.1 INTRODUCTION

8.1.1 Chapter contents

Some future avenues for performance control are described. The emphasis
is again on **production** this is no technical showcase with elegant implementations, but a list - and hopefully a structure - of pragmatic methods
and tools that without major disruptions can be implemented in most complex centres, given time and resources.

In retrospect the concepts outlined here describe not so much a 'future'
as a conclusion. Many firms have already implemented several of the ideas
given in this chapter. Some descriptions, for instance the VM predictor
model, refer to actual implementations. The reference to the future is
more a realization that in many cases the methods are not yet implemented,
at least not completely and in a structured fashion.

An important section is dedicated to challenges: performance control problem areas where a solution is not yet imminent. Defining such
'challenges' is essential in a young technology like performance control.
Our users and managers should know what we are up against, and why we -
like medical doctors - cannot automatically produce a diagnosis and a cure
for every real or imaginary ill.

The end objective is to provide a better view of centre services now and
in the future, and more buffers against degraded service.

8.1.2 Control system structure

The link to capacity planning is seen as particularly important. Sensible
performance control is a prerequisiste for successful capacity planning.
Vice versa: Capacity planning is an important way of ensuring that
resources for adequate service are indeed available. The scope of capacity planning may vary: Here we assume it to be both long and short term and
include hardware scheduling as well as software planning and application
scheduling. The latter means, expressed in more detail: finding out what
application mix should run on each processor in normal and abnormal (backup) situation. The link to performance control is immediate.

'Central systems architecture' suggests a control system like the one
shown in Figure 123 on page 201. Figure 123 on page 201 shows coordination and reporting as central functions - most likely central architecture functions - and the focal point for a number of other functions as
indicated on the figure.

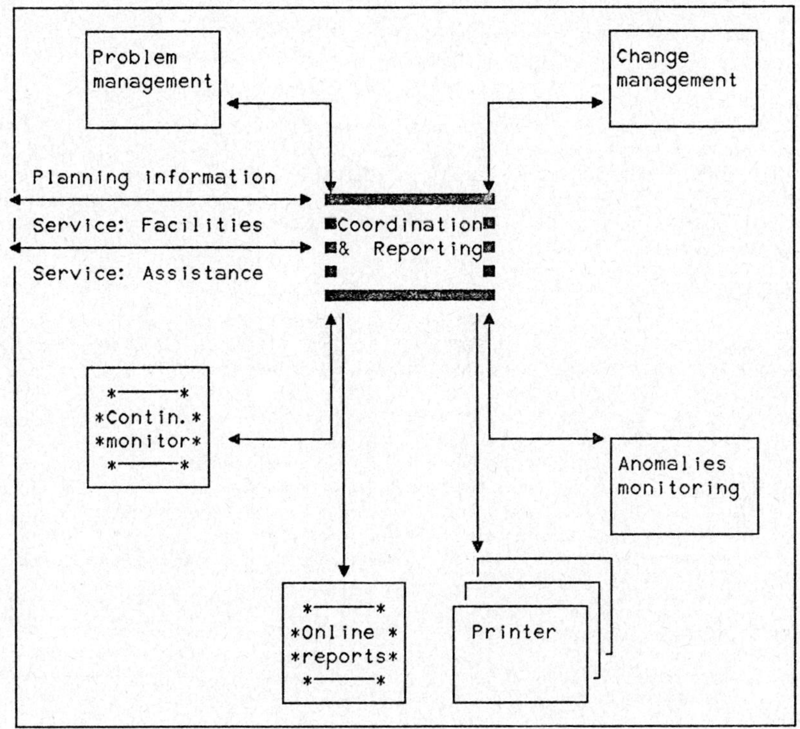

Figure 123.   Future control system

Problem management

>   provides information on what errors are recorded in the system
>   when, and what was done in each case. This enables the control
>   system to feed back to users and other involved personnel what
>   were the (likely) causes for each service disruption and what
>   was done or is being done.
>
>   Problem reports may be prepared for:
>
>   Hardware errors
>   Software errors
>   Application errors
>   Operator errors
>   Handling errors
>   Poor response times

Change management

should control any change to the system. It is therefore an important source for ideas as to the likely cause of breaks or poor response times.

Not unexpectedly there seems to be a close correlation between the amount of changes to the system and the number of breaks. A careful change management procedure can reduce the number of breaks following from changes, even if the amount of change was as complex as before the change management procedure was implemented.

Continuous monitoring

was described in chapter 6. In relation to the total control system monitoring takes on several purposes:

            Finding errors - early detection
            Finding bottlenecks - early detection
            Finding wrong uses/users of the system
            Controlling service - here and now

As in many other aspects of human enterprise, the importance of 'a stitch in time' is considerable, especially when large interactive services are run.

Anomaly monitoring

is a complement to continuous monitoring, providing a method to catch and follow up any discrepancies found.

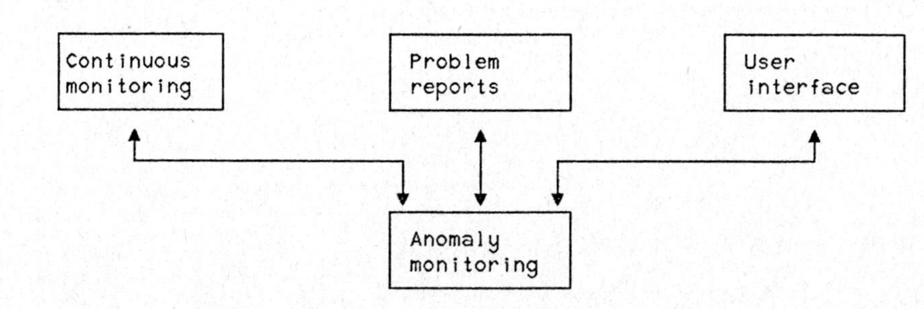

Figure 124.   Anomaly monitoring

The method is mainly as depicted in Figure 124.

On the figure, one input source to anomaly monitoring is supposed to be user interface meetings, trying to trap those situations that are not grave enough for problem reports, but still cause annoyance or may later do so.

SLR   trends   can   be compared with detailed RMF reports from the
problem area/time.   In addition, prints from the online RMF monitor may provide valuable information on the error situation.

8.2 CHANGE MANAGEMENT PROCEDURES

8.2.1 The need for an acceptance procedure

Any change in the system should be controlled. Consequently there must be procedures for **how** changes are controlled. Figure 125 on page 205 and Figure 126 on page 206 outline the requirements for acceptance data. Accept of new production components should be done by a production func- tion and be based on measurements and a standard procedure. This enables the acceptance group to say 'NO' when acceptance criteria are not met. If the acceptance criteria are not clearly defined, it is very difficult to refuse somebodys creation, that other people expect will abandon monoto- nous tasks or impatient customer queues.

Not to refuse an inferior product or a system that is directly damaging to other production, may on the other hand negatively influence far more peo- ple, and certainly the centre's image.

Most centres have some sort of acceptance procedure today; but there seems to be little emphasis on a total acceptance control procedure and its integration with performance control and change management.

8.2.2 Change Management data for IMS systems.

MVS data related to Figure 125 on page 205, can be obtained by RMF and/or SLR. The 'After' case should ideally be **before** the component is accepted for production. The Groups listed are the IMS transaction groups dis- cussed in chapter 3 and 4. The form is only an example and does not state that groups must be defined or indeed that the figure lists all the required acceptance data and only those.

The transaction data, Figure 126 on page 206, can be obtained from SLR. Response times will probably relate to a test environment. If that test environment is kept constant, any differences between the response times may point out difficulties, anomalies or perhaps an occasional success story. The SLR data on the figure are suitably complemented with DC moni- tor data.

Preferably the new systems are tested on a system ressembling the pro- duction system, perhaps the production system outside service hours, or on another system without other major services.

Follow up

The first week and first month end the new system is followed to find out if the predictions were true.

Suggested tools:

      Operator supervision
      RMF

DC monitor
SLR

Total system data (new systems - major releases only):

Component	Before	After

CPU consumption: Total
                 Control region
                 MPP
                 BMP		

Real storage - at constant =
    acceptable paging rate:
               Total
               Control region
               MPP
               BMP		

Virtual storage:
               Control region
               Private region
               CSA
               (LPA)		

EXCP - if applicable and if large difference.		
Important IMS parameters used:		

Response times: Group 1
                 Group 2
                 Group 3		

Number of transactions:
                Group 1
                Group 2
                Group 3		

Peak number of transactions:
                Daily
                Weekly
                Monthly
                Quarterly
                Yearly
                Other		

Figure 125.   Change management - system evaluation data

For each transaction:

Resource usage:

Transac.	Before				After			
ID	DB calls	DC calls	CPU time/tr	IWAITs	DB calls	DC calls	CPU time/tr	IWAITs

Response times:

Transac.	Before			After		
ID	less than 6 sec.	less than 15 sec.	Average	less than 6 sec.	less than 15 sec.	Average

Figure 126.   Change management - IMS transaction data

8.3 BENCHMARKING

8.3.1 Purpose

Benchmarking serves two major purposes in a production environment as described here:

Quality control

Performance control

The two aspects are intimately related. Control relates both to systems (new or changed) and to applications (new or changed).

A side effect would be to find bottlenecks or future problem areas.

8.3.2 Suggested system

Figure 127 on page 208 shows a conceptual benchmarking system. A benchmarking program - for instance TPNS, the TeleProcessing Network Simulator, loads the processor where the application runs. Usually TPNS should run on a separate (driver) host.

The benchmarking program needs information on what kind of terminal network it should simulate and the application load. The transaction load can be obtained from a transaction log, like the IMS logtape.

The magnitude of the imposed load can be controlled by for instance varying the number of transactions per seconds. One day's logtape may for instance be compressed into two hours.

Response times are recorded, and these are the the real response times for remote users (those that are connected to the system through a TP network).

By running SLR, RMF etc, response times for locally connected users (no TP) are obtained.

There is a difficulty in simulating these locally connected users by TPNS since it assumes a network. However, with modern VTAM, most network processing is removed from the host processor, and the error of assuming all users to be remote (or local when using other benchmarking programs) is slight.

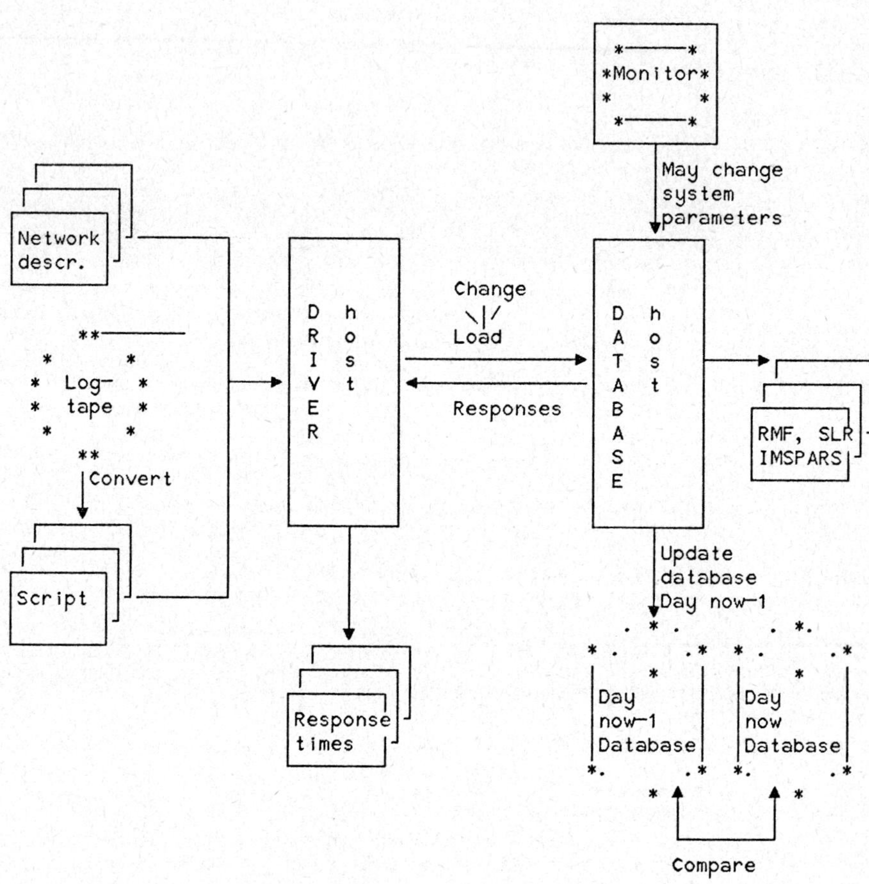

Figure 127.   Benchmarking system

8.4 MODELLING

8.4.1 Purpose

Modelling in the current context means that a software product somehow simulates the major functions in a defined part of a hardware and software system.   The accuracy should normally be within plus or minus 20 percent **for whatever it is supposed to simulate.**

Texts on computer systems modelling are usually very specific on what they model, for instance one processor, 20 terminals and 5 disks. What is not so easy to extract is: for what <u>production</u> workload, under what circumstances, with what restrictions are the findings applicable in a running environment? Do for instance the results apply only to average IMS transaction loads, do they consider batch, networking, writer programs, interactive programming, multiaccess spooling effects, or what?

Modelling can be done using a mathematical model or a simulation tool; the implementation is not a concern of this book. Usability is important, however, and the tools selected are all relatively easy to learn and use.

8.4.2 Processing time

```
      CPULOAD
GIVE PERCENT UTILIZATIONS - HIGHEST PRIORITY FIRST
      20 40 20 10
SERVICE TIMES FOR EACH LEVEL
      1 1 1 1
**************************************************
***      RESPONSE TIMES IN PRIORITY ORDER:   ***
***      1       3       13      50 SECONDS   ***
**************************************************
```

Figure 128.   CPU simulation - simple example

The utilizations in Figure 128 are assumed to be for Network control, IMS, TSO and Batch in that priority order. The percentages are total utilizations, including MVS overhead.   The MVS overhead may be approximated using **capture ratios,** telling how much of each service is recorded as TCB time. Capture ratios are listed, for example in references 1 and 13.

Service times are given as one second for all services, because we are interested in relative, not absolute, values.

The resulting responses, including queuing for the processor, are then calculated using a formula from reference 8. Even at 90% load, batch 'CPU response' is multiplied by a factor of 50.

This goes well with observations indicating that 1 second of CPU time needs one minute elapse time for ordinary batch on a fairly loaded machine with the indicated loading pattern, and provided excessive swaps do not occur.

The model uses mathematical approximations that are highly inaccurate (underestimates response time) with CPU loads over 60 percent for the same or higher priority work.   However, the significant figure we want out of this simulation is **at what load** the curves starts to bend sharply. The accuracy should in this case be within the required 20 percent.

Figure 145 on page 246 and Figure 146 on page 246 take this one step further, increasing each load type by the same factor until the machine is filled.

Figure 145 on page 246 shows that rapidly, batch responses become very poor, and even at less load, TSO suffers badly. At about 3 times original load, IMS begins to encounter problems.

Figure 146 on page 246 shows what happens if networking is moved to a separate machine. IMS can then be allowed to increase to almost 5 times the original load.

Referring to the previous discussion of applicability, the findings are only valid for processing time, and only under the given limitations. Supplementary analysis should be carried out for disk response, real storage (paging) dependency, virtual storage, influence of other workloads etc.

These arguments are useful for capacity planning, but also for daily control. During most days, traffic in peak periods will exceed 1.5 times average.

8.4.3 Disks

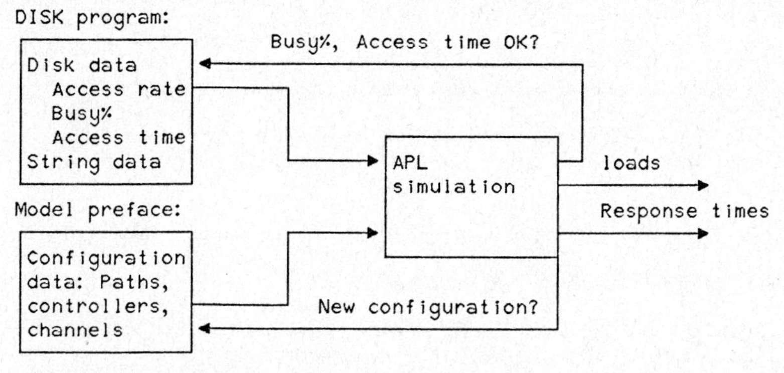

Figure 129. Suggested disk modelling system

An important part of response times for interactive applications is disk
response. In a complex environment it is almost impossible to figure out
manually the best configuration. The disk configuration should:

* Attempt to give all users on all systems access to the data they need
* Guard against unauthorised use of data on all systems
* Keep availability up by minimizing the number of connections
* Consider performance on all systems even the slow processors
* Attempt to group disks according to use
* Avoid interlocks

A fast processor will always grab a shared resource before a slower col-
league. The resulting queues may be difficult to identify.

Disk are exclusively RESERVEd by a processor when some highly vulnerable
work is carried out. This may prevent other processor from accessing
datasets on that disks.

Even interlock conditions may arise in a JES2 system because no processor
knows what the other processors do. The chance for interlocks can be minimized by running like work - e.g. TSO and batch from the same group - on
the same processor system.

These conditions could be removed with MVS/SP3, and are so already with
JES3. JES3, the Job Entry Subsystem 3, is an IBM alternative to JES2,
with more facilities than JES2.

These situations can be modelled in a system as shown on Figure 129. The
base data can be obtained from RMF reports, that even can hint to the configuration as described in chapter 7. Some parts of the configuration
must be provided by hand; e.g. the channel paths and disk types.

The model can provide response times for (selected) disks under various
circumstances, and can thus help to foresee problems or choose a favour-

able configuration.   With several processors and hundreds of disks this is
otherwise difficult.

8.4.4 Network

TPNS   can be used to directly measure network performance components in a
simulated environment.

Alternatively SNAPSHOT or another simulation/analysis program can be used
It consists of two parts:

        SNAP: System Network Analysis Program

        SHOT: System Host Overview Technique

In SNAPSHOT, the configuration can be described and different loads superimposed.   The system can be used to evaluate the current system because
utilizations and queue times are given, and to foresee the effect of
changes.   The network component is detailed and accurately described in
SNAPSHOT (1981).   The host component is sufficient for rough estimates of
system behaviour.   SNAPSHOT must currently (1981) be run by IBM.

8.4.5 VM modelling

VM Predictor provides a neat solution to some of the above questions.
Data from the VM performance monitor(the equivalent of SMF/RMF) are
digested and presented in a form (Stage I) tailored for model input.   See
Figure 130 on page 213.   Stage I output contains for instance recorded
response times that are otherwise difficult to obtain in VM.   A facility
exists for grouping users for instance into a PLI programming department
and APL user .

The modelling tool is implemented under the IBM internal HONE system.   To
construct the model, configuration data are provided in response to interactive questions.   The workload model can then be superimposed either manually from Stage I output, or directly from Stage I data.

Clearly the latter method is safer as typing and understanding errors are
avoided.   This is the method employed to obtain the model output shown in
Figure 131 on page 214.   The corresponding version of the Predictor is one
kindly provided as a prerelease (March 1982) by Yonathan Bard of the IBM
Scientific Centre in Cambridge, Massachusetts.   It features for instance a
fullscreen APL interface to modelling, and only paging disk space data
need be given to the model by the user.

Currently (1981) the Predictor stage I may be run at a IBM customer site
under special conditions; the model must be run by IBM.

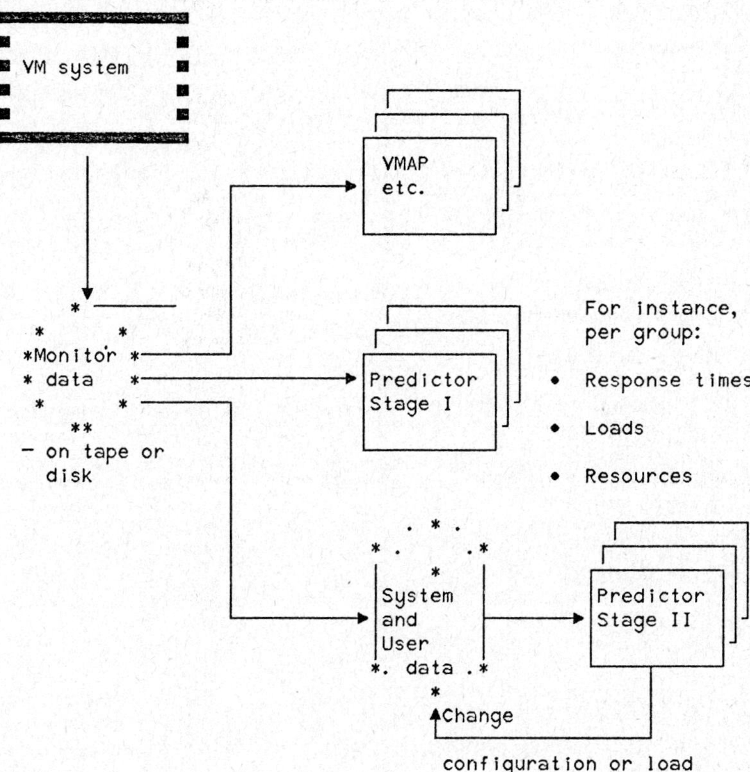

Figure 130.   VM Predictor system flow

Figure 131 on page 214 shows the result of some simple modelling. Base data was obtained from a 158MP/8MB, where the two groups: Programming and Technical experienced difficulties with heavy (Q2 - really Q2 and Q3, see chapter 6) commands.

For the model, only one parameter has been changed when going one column to the right: from column 1 to 2 only the processor speed has changed, from column 2 to 3, 4 megabytes are added.

The faster processor naturally gives better response. However, paging is heavier, and the disk channels more busy. The example is based on a daily average for an average day, meaning that load, especially paging, could be much heavier in peak periods.

Parameter	Processor type/storage size			
	158MP/8MB	3033UP/8MB	3033UP/12MB	3033UP/16MB
% CPU:	87.0	31.6	31.1	
Total paging (pages per sec.):	58.5	77.5	45.6	
Highest loaded disk channel %:	7.4x2	19.2	12.2	
Response, heavy commands (sec.):				
Technical group	2.0	.9	.6	
Programming	6.4	2.0	1.7	
External	1.8	1.3	1.0	

20 more EXTERNAL users

Parameter	158MP/8MB	3033UP/8MB	3033UP/12MB	3033UP/16MB
% CPU	90.8		32.5	32.2
Total paging (pages per sec.):	76.1		56.5	39.4
Highest loaded disk channel %:	26.7x2		43.9	34.2
Response, heavy commands (sec):				
Technical group	2.6		.7	0.6
Programming	8.4		1.7	1.7
External	2.2		1.1	1.0

The disk loads for the MP are shown with 'x2', because the model assumes
a symmetrical disk configuration. There were in the modelled 158MP 3
disk channels for each CPU, but only 3 total on the 3033.

Figure 131.   VM Predictor results for processor evaluation

Adding 4 megabytes to the model CPU gives a relief on paging and there
should even be spare capacity to take on new work on the new processor.

We see the relation between CPU and real storage.   There needs to be a
balance; a stronger processor can do more work and therefore requires more
real storage online to run at capacity speed - assuming of course that
there was balance on the slower processor.

The predictor model can even give an indication of the effect of new users
on the system.   Grouping users for instance after department or type of
work, the predictor can give resource usage and service for each group and
use the results for modelling. Consequently, we can increase or decrease
the number of people in a certain group, assuming that the group has

strong shared characteristics.   New model results can then be based on the new data.

Figure 131 on page 214 gives the result of adding 20 users (i.e. active ones) to the system.   Response times on the 168 obviously become very long.   A 3033/12MB dramatically reduces response times, but gives a heavy paging load.   Response times are not much reduced when adding another 4 megabytes, but the paging load is reduced.   It seems advisable to install more disks and disk paths for the 3033; this is another aspect of the 'balanced system' considerations.

It also seems advisable to buy the full 16 megabytes for the 3033.   Less storage also gives very good response times, but the system is likely to become clogged with paging during peak periods.

8.5 OTHER CONTROL MECHANISMS

Control over batch operations could be improved by introducing for instance MVS/SP3 with a system wide control of datasets. JES3 goes further by also providing a networking facility giving dependence between jobs and a deadline priority scheme enabling some jobs automatically to be started around certain times. Devices such as disks and tapes can in JES3 be pooled, and the operator can control each pool by a separate console.

Some of the same facilities are built into the Operations Planning and Control (OPC) program, that even can help to plan future workloads.

Programs are also available to improve tape control and extend the usage of non-paper output by a virtual print program. Virtual print can be routed to MSS, but then requires proper MSS planning.

8.6 SYSTEM CONFIGURATION AND DESIGN

A computing centre should be designed for service. Primarily availability
and response time is then understood. Normally response time receives
most attention when designing computer systems. The considerations relating to design for response time are already described in literature (see
for instance reference 1). In this section we will look at availability
and facilities as design criterions; noting that a full description of
modern capacity planning/system design would need another book.

8.6.1 Availability

AVAILABILITY is a measure of how much of the planned service time the service is usable to the user.

$$\text{AVAILABILITY} = (MTBF)/(MTBF+MTTR)$$

MTBF: MEAN TIME BETWEEN FAILURE
MTTR: MEAN TIME TO REPAIR

The following components influence availability:

- HARDWARE - and its interconnections

- SOFTWARE - applications, systems and combinations

- DESIGN - of the total computer system

- ENVIRONMENT - physical, society, attitudes

- DOCUMENTATION/PLANS - for installed systems and for the future

- PERSONNEL/FUNCTIONS/ORGANISATION

An EDP system can be described as a set of servers, each server carrying
out one or more tasks, for instance processing or data retrieval, see for
instance Figure 132 on page 218, where 4 interconnected servers are shown.

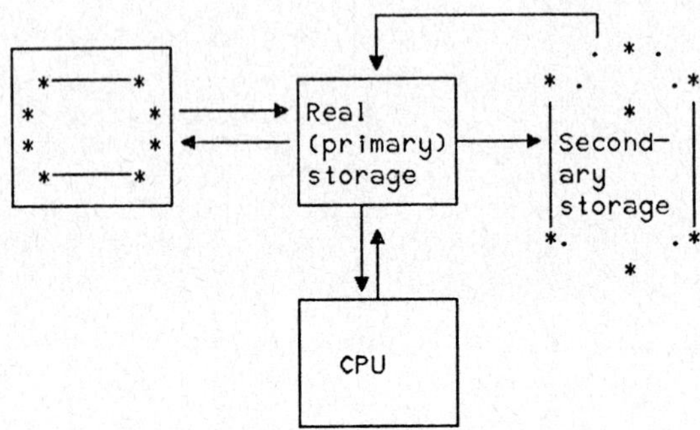

Figure 132.   Availability design - general considerations

Serial availability

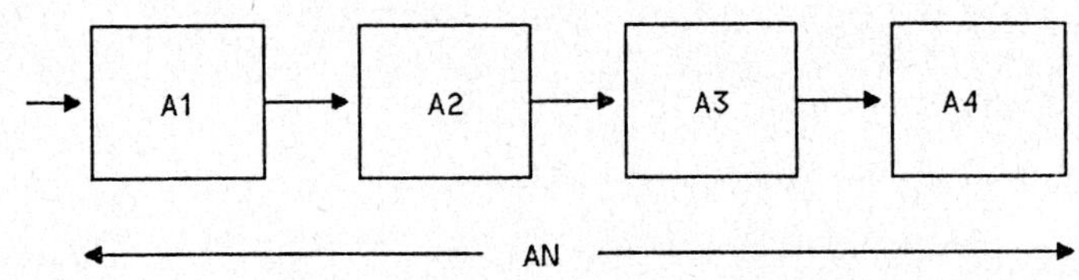

Figure 133.   Availability design - serial availability

Figure 133   shows 4 independent availability components.   The total availability of the complex will be:

AN = A1 * A2 * A3 * A4 (if A1 to A4 are independent)

Example:

A1 = A2 = A3 = A4 = 0.99 (99%)   => AN = 0.961 (96.1%)

Parallel availability (redundant system)

Figure 134 on page 219 shows how the transaction can choose either of many
paths,   for instance to paging or work disks.   The total availability will
then be better than for one component, and better if more components are
added:

AN = 1 - (1-A1)*(1-A2)*(1-A3)*(1-A4)

Note that for work and paging disks it is true that only when writing or allocating is a choice allowed; when a certain disk is chosen for page residence or for a certain work data set, then that disk must be used also when reading the data again.

Example with 4 components:

A1 = A2 = A3 = A4 = 0.90 (90%)   => AN = 0.9999 (99.99%)

Example with 2 components:

A1 = A2 = 0.90 (90%)   => AN = 0.99 (99%)

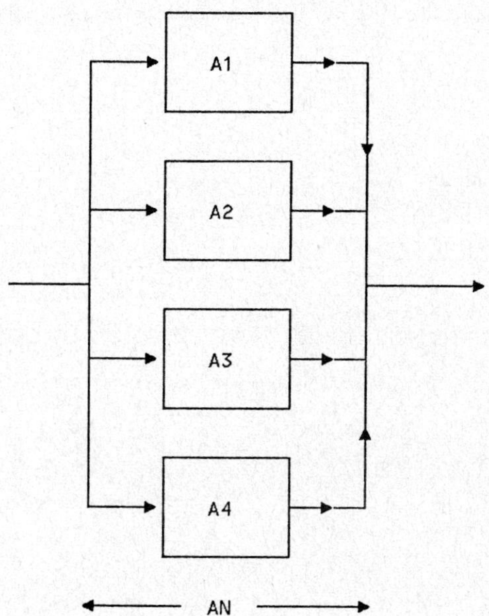

Figure 134.   Availability design - parallel availability

Combined example

With a serial I/O system, Figure 135 on page 220 depicts the dependencies:

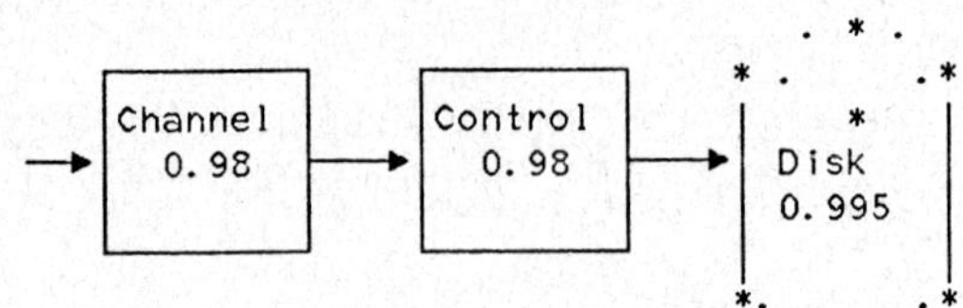

Figure 135.   Availability design - I/O example

AN = A1 * A2 * A3 = 0.956 (95.6%)

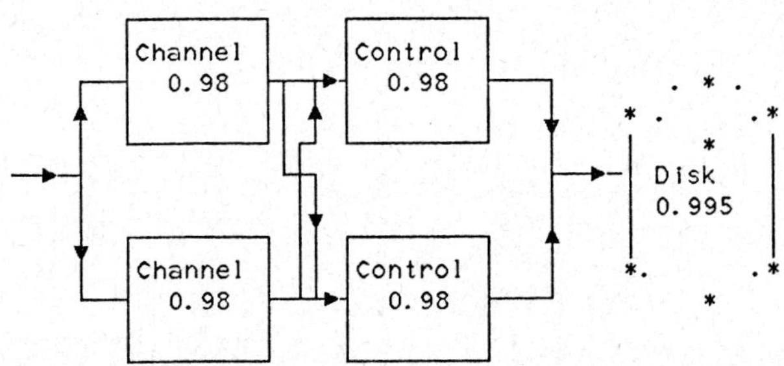

Figure 136.   Availability design - redundant I/O system

Adding some redundancies, i.e. alternate path and string switch, see Figure 136, gives the following availability:

AN = (1-(1-0.98)*(1-0.98))*(1-(1-0.98)*(1-0.98))*0.995

AN = 0.9996 * 0.9996 * 0.995 = 0.994 (99.4%)

Other components that can be duplicated are communications equipment and
processors.   With increased service requirements and decreasing hardware
prices, the cost/benefit of CPU backup is altered, and it may be worth
while considering if a backup CPU may be a good investment. This backup
CPU could be used for test or development when backup is not required.

The conclusion is that by adding redundant components, availability can in
many instances be improved, i.e. one can buy availability. The problem is
often that even single component availability is difficult to assess.

8.6.2 Facilities

The third service factor - facilities - may also be considered. All
facilities in the system should be accessible to all people having the

right to use them, whenever the service agreement states that this service
should be available.

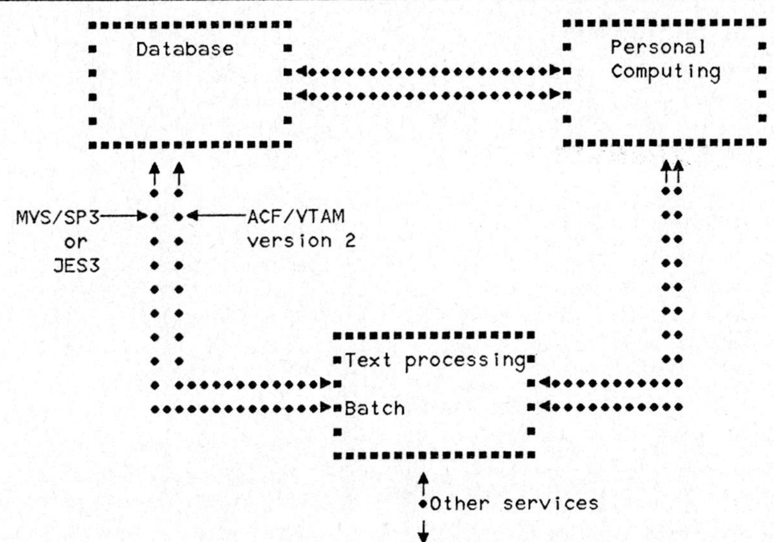

Figure 137.   Multi-processor system channel to channel adapter design

On Figure 137 three - possibly more - computers are joined by channel to
channel adapters, CTCs. A CTC joins one channel on one processor to one
channel on another, and can transfer data back and forth with channel
speed. The software products we deal with here cannot share CTC.

MVS/SP3 uses the CTC to keep global control on who uses what datasets in
the total MVS environment. Earlier JES2 based MVS systems did not care
what happened on another processor.

The same facility has been available for a long time with JES3.

In addition one could install ACF/VTAM release III that enables the users
to log on to any application in any of the systems, and to a certain
extent keep working even if one component in the total system fails.
That is, we move towards a fail soft environment. By adding
channel-to-channel adapters and ACF/VTAM version 2, any host can act as an
intermediate routing node, making us more independent of hardware and component availability.

The total environment is then more and more such that the users need not
care which system they run on, and how to access that system. Applications - for instance text processing and plot facilities - can then be
made accessible to all pertinent users.

In many instances/places this has already been achieved. The new releases
will bring an **added degree** of accessability and robustness. This must be
weighed against cost of installation, maintenance and complexity.

8.7 CAPACITY PLANNING

The control system provides one basis for capacity planning.

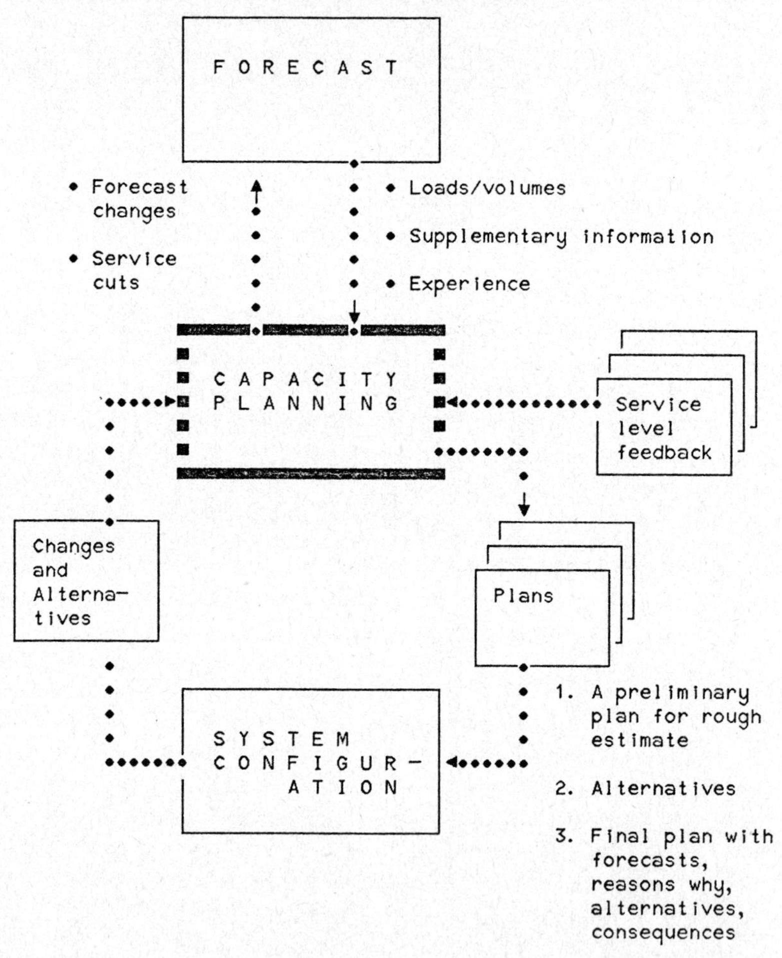

Figure 138.   Capacity planning cycle

Figure 138 indicates some of the concerns of capacity planning. Forecasting and capacity planning are closely linked. The input to capacity planning comes mostly from forecasting.   There is also a feedback cycle
involved.   When capacity planning realizes that certain targets cannot be
met or feels that certain forecasts are not adequate, there must be some
communication between forecasting and capacity planning.

Physically the two functions may be carried out by the same people, easing communications.   It should be noticed that the two functions are quite different: Capacity planning is a highly technical task; forecasting involves more coordination, communication, social awareness etc. It may be unwise to let one group perform such diverse tasks.   There needs to be a control even on the capacity planners, that also may be performance controllers.   The forecasters, i.e. the requestors of service, may be well suited for capacity planning control.

Note that capacity planning is supposed to be an iterative process. It is unlikely that the financial people will immediately take to their hearts capacity planning requirements to fulfill all user service requests. To ease the communication, a preliminary capacity plan is suggested as a starting point, perhaps containing only processor types and loadings.

Service levels are fundamental for capacity planning. If they are not considered, capacity planning is guesswork. The capacity planning people need deep understanding of service levels to evaluate the impact for instance of higher service levels, or a budget cut, or scattered highly active days.   The service level feedback is assumed closely connected with service agreements.   Backup and reduced service planning are parts of capacity planning.

System configuration comprises the technical processes of selecting components, configuring components for the total system, linking components and finding space both for the final configuration and intermediate configurations during installation.   All functions related to providing resources for centre services may be called system design - as in Central Systems Architecture.

System design is linked to economic evaluation and the decision process, perhaps providing several alternatives.

Short term capacity planning/system design and the control system are closely interrelated.   Capacity planning methods are applied to predict the result of changes.

The flow in Figure 139 on page 224 shows a possible capacity planning method based on performance control as presented in this book.

SMF records only 'problem program time'. To find total system time used by each service, the capture ratios suggested by 'Usage' (reference 13) can be employed. They are empirical measures of the ratio between problem program time and total system time for each service.

The capture ratios express how much overhead is incurred by one certain service.   The overhead could be task switching, performance control, paging etc.   These overhead factors apply to the total environment. If the environment is changed, most likely the capture ratios change too, to be a minimum in a dedicated, no paging environment. Remember, then, to adjust capture ratios to changing system designs.

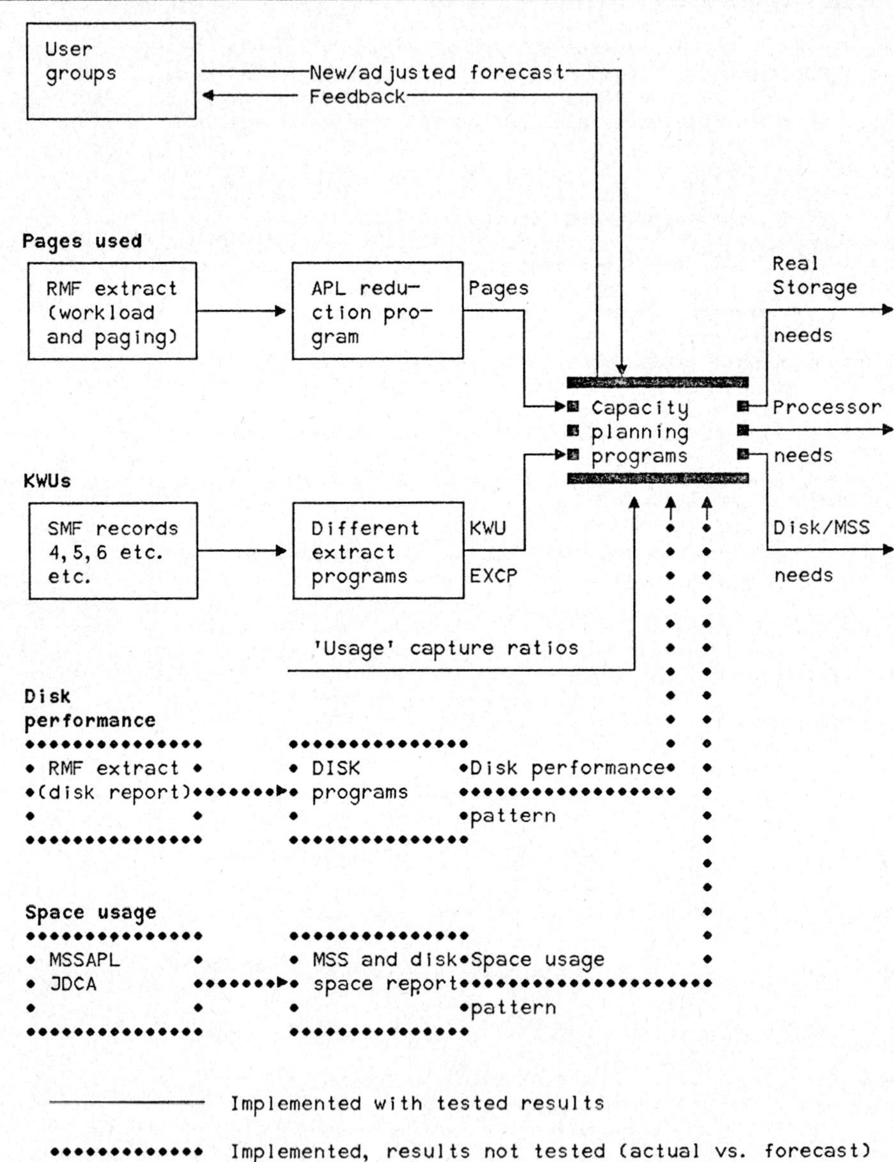

Figure 139. Forecasting and capacity planning implementation

For any combination of services on a particular machine, both real storage
and KWU capacity must be considered as both must·be accomodated. Other
important parameters are **virtual storage** where there are availability
risks, and **floor space** that is costly and scarce.

The DISK program complex was described in chapter 7. This program contains most of the data on disk performance and availability required for capacity planning. Combining this with forecast data required for KWU planning, should provide an adequate basis for disk planning, and also for balancing SIO rate between different machines.

Different data reduction programs for MSS were discussed in chapter 5. The MSS trace/SMF Correlation Aid program uses a SMF extract program, the Job Data Compression Aid that can be further used to analyze data set usage, placements etc. - in short: Space Management. Space management in addition receives input from different users on future space requirements - another important aspect of capacity planning.

The 'implemented' sections of the figure have been tried out in practice, with programs automatically converting control data to capacity requirements.

The dotted parts have been incorporated into a capacity planning structure, but results were estimated or hand calculated. As yet results from these components have not been verified by comparing forecasted resource usage and actual recordings.

8.8 CHALLENGES

Several key areas within EDP production planning and quality control are
poorly defined or lack established guidelines. The reason for this is
largely the rapid change from a dedicated batch environment to an environment offering multiple services especially to impatient terminal users.

8.8.1 Defining objectives

Defining service objectives have to be done individually in each firm.
Today's problem is that few guidelines and few consistent examples exist.
Also, a comprehensive description of what exactly the service objectives
should contain is missing. Reference 1 gives some guidance, though.

An obstruction to defining relevant and user oriented objectives, is the
lack of consistent and relevant measuring tools. SLR is currently providing some control system functions, but more is needed.

8.8.2 Weighing different aspects of service.

When the service objectives are vague, it is also difficult to take appropriate action on anomalies or user requests. Large computing centres
experience many and frequently conflicting requests for service. The
decision on what to run can be taken by managers, but then a very good
feel on the operating environment is needed.

Alternatively, the technical people can decide. However, they need guidelines on the political aspects. That ought to be included in the service
objectives/service agreement.

Response times, availability and facilities represent different user service aspects.   Sometimes availability is sacrificed to install new functions or to improve response times. The balance between different service
aspects is difficult to find.

8.8.3 Defining minimum measurements

Managers are often left with a vague picture as to how their centre is
running because key values for performance simply are not defined. Partly
this is because the definition of performance is still debated. Partly it
seems that a large set of numbers are needed to describe the workings of a
computing centre.

Difficulties arise because some people still look for **one** or a **few** magic
numbers.   Perhaps therefore, the search for a minimal set related to service objectives in a complex centre currently seems somewhat random.

Again, more powerful data reduction tools are needed. The weekly megabytes of performance trace data should be compressed to one page of
report. We still have work to do before this is possible.

8.8.4 Measuring, collecting and correlating

Short but telling reports are intended for managers. The professionals controlling the system also need condensed data, but not so much. The requirement is a total control system where data from different system components are collected, and service aspects - for instance response time - are correlated to load or problems in each component.

This constitutes one of the bases for capacity planning. If bottlenecks in the system are not clearly defined, capacity planning is guesswork.

8.8.5 Action on problems

Referring to the above discussion, today we do not know clearly what all problems are, and we do not know exactly what objectives will be achieved by solving the problems that we know. Consequently the correct action is difficult to determine, especially where human and equipment resources are scarce.

8.8.6 Relation to other computing centre tasks

The control system is intimately linked to most work within a computing centre. When the control system is missing or inadequate, all that dependent work suffer.

As pointed out earlier in this chapter, the control system is also dependant on other tasks, like problem and change management.

In addition software and hardware planning are closely linked, not to forget daily (nightly) operation and supervision.

These dependencies are as yet mostly established by individual effort, and seldom seem part of an overall strategy.

8.8.7 Lack of skills

A major reason for the lack of an integrated effort may be lack of skills. Few people are yet educated with respect to the environment they meet within modern EDP. In addition there seems to be an emphasis on **development** in most curricula. This is natural for Computing as a young science.

However, we are at least approaching the toddler stage, and the time seems overripe for more emphasis on **production.**

Until educationalists realise this, we have to live in an environment where most skills are learned by experiment. This slows growth.

However, the situation highlights the control system as a way to monitor the experiments and achieve higher standards.

CONCLUSION

The variety does not abrogate the unity - the souls are apart without
partition...　　They are no more hedged off by boundaries than are the
multiple items of knowledge in one mind.　The one Soul so exists as
to include all souls.

Plotinus
(after S. Spencer)

9.1.1 A philosophy - not a rule

The system described in this book is one of a multitude of ways to control
a complex EDP centre. However, it brings out the topics that characterize
any good performance control system. Few new components are presented
here, but well-known building stones from production engineering and management science are merged with the current state of computing science to
construct a feasible product. The product is not optimal, but has been
proved to work in a production environment.

9.1.2 Centre objectives

The objective of an EDP centre is to give service to its users, within the
framework, or ethos, of economy, technology and environment. This is analogous to the work of a building architect. For the systems architect,
the economical ethos is the cost and price of the services, and technology
the state-of-the-art of available computing science. Environmental ethos
reflects user interfaces, personnel skill levels or enthusiasm, societal
acceptance etc. etc.

The performance control system addresses two important aspects of the centre - or system architecture - objectives. A sensible performance control
system helps to establish feasible service objectives, and measures that
these are met.   Furthermore, the performance control system aids two other important aspects of architecture: Planning for continued acceptable
service and ensuring that even installation of new products do not disrupt
service.

9.1.3 Organisational placement

The main point about the control system is that one should be established.
The organisational implementation impacts its acceptance and use. Because
control like online supervision already is the concern of operators, the
performance control system may be made part of Production (Operations).

One concern is often raised: Production do seldom have the skills
required.

Firstly: The skill level of production people should be very high in a
complex environment.   If this is not true - and this is often the case
today - some skill upgrade ought to be planned. The performance control
system and its implementation can aid in upgrading skills.

Secondly: Establishment of the performance control system should be done
by skilled professionals - systems architects. After the performance control system is implemented, running, documented and understood, the system
architects may move to other tasks if desirable. Unfortunately, the category of people called 'systems architects' is not a defined group today.
The individuals that could qualify for the job may not be recognized and
their education is somewhat at random because the final objective of their
work is not stated - or it is felt to be of low importance.

The positive impact of systems architecture is considerable, on service to
users and financial savings.   A welcome side effect is the impact on work
conditions in the centre itself.   A performance control system is normally
well received by all involved parties, especially as work can then be
planned and the plan adhered to; an important prerequisite for everybody's
productivity.

In short: the Systems Architects should be recognized as a high skill,
useful group, and receive education and recognizion in accordance.

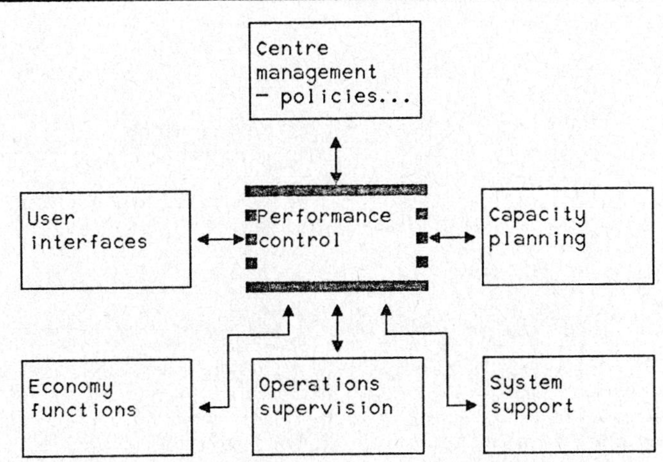

Figure 140.   Performance control - relation to other tasks

On Figure 140 performance control is visualized relative to other typical
centre tasks.

For instance, the control system depends on centre policies, but is
instrumental when new policies are established.   Such a new policy could
be to implement a new type of interactive services or to run batch only
during night shift.

User interfaces represent those functions within the centre dealing
directly with user service: delivering material, answering requests, following up errors, reporting on service.

Apart from the reporting function, the control system can help to establish reasonable objectives, and to change those objectives in a sensible
manner when the need occurs.   Capacity planning is thought to contain
hardware and software planning including system design and installation
scheduling.   Strong interdependencies with the control system are obvious.

Secondary dependencies exist relative to application programmers and user
groups.   In some cases these relations are direct, for instance when test-
ing new products for production.

9.1.4 Future

The control system should be interwoven with other work in the centre to
fulfill the same purpose as in other (non-EDP) production environments.
The flow of all work must be adequately planned, and problem reports immediately prepared when there are deviations from these plans. An action
plan should lead to either removal of the cause of the problem, or a
change in the performance control system; perhaps both.

Any changes must adhere to the same requirements for continued service as
existing work, and the accumulated effects automatically evaluated.

Users will receive continuous feedback on service and load; when applicable related to their forecasts. Slowly this will educate forecasters
towards a system where future requirements can be accurately assessed.
This affects cost and therefore pricing. Even if economy has been left
out of this document, the future control system will also encompass this
very important aspect.

9.1.5 Summary

In sum the control system should ensure that users receive adequate service at forecasted loads, and that service even in the future is acceptable.

CHAPTER 10

MANAGEMENT REPORT - case study (colour)

'After Ashur, Sin, Shamash, Adad, Bel, Nabu, Ishtar of Niniveh, queen
of Kidmuri, Ishtar of Arbela, Urta, Nergal and Nusku, had caused me
to take my seat joyfully upon the throne of my father who begot me,
Adad sent his rains, Ea opened his fountains, the grain grew five
cubits tall in the stalk, the ear was fivesixth of a cubit long -
heavy crops, and a plenteous yield made the fields continuously lux-
uriant, the orchards yielded a rich harvest, the cattle successfully
brought forth their young. In my reign there was fullness to over-
flowing, in my years there was plenteous abundance.'

Ashurbanipal
After: John Gray
Near Eastern Mythology

10.1 INTRODUCTION

10.1.1 Presentation techniques

The case study relates to the fictional Complex Computing Centre, CCC. It
provides examples of **Management type** reports, and indicates the usage of
colour (i.e. presentation techniques) in performance reporting. Colour
graphics facilities, built here on GDDM (see chapter 2) facilitates con-
cise and attractive reports. On the other hand, there is no high-speed
printer available with colour graphics (1981), and output from the graphics program cannot be integrated with other text processing facilities
even in black-and-white.

Some figures were prepared by using GDDM directly. Examples are
Figure 149 on page 248 and Figure 148 on page 248. GDDM can be menu driv-
en. This is quite helpful for the beginner or for someone not caring
about the advanced possibilities of colour graphing.

Other figures were prepared using the SLR PRINT CHART interface to GDDM.
This method starts out using online SLR, thus preparing a SLR report. The
PRINT CHART command moves the selected SLR data into a GDDM menu environment, and the rest is done using standard GDDM. Sometimes, for instance
when printing data for several months, it is necessary to edit the data
into appropriate columns as GDDM does not recognize that data for different months should be printed on different curves. Examples of graphs
produced with this approach are Figure 151 on page 249, Figure 154 on page
251 etc. etc.

APL Graphpak can be used for a non-interactive interface to GDDM facilities. Data already stored under APL can then relatively easy be displayed
and printed in colour. An example of this is Figure 153 on page 250.
This is a very attractive approach suited for APL databases that again are
suitable for performance control data storage.

The availability graph, Figure 147 on page 247 was produced using a PL/I
interface to GDDM facilities.

10.1.2 Key indicators

On the graphs in this chapter, **Key Indicators** for a complex computing centre are presented. The indicators may not be **all** that the centre want to
follow. For instance the number of tape mounts, the number of resolved
calls to the 'Help' desk or the development of text processing are alternative or perhaps additional indicators. The ones presented here are
included to give the flavour of a Key Indicator presentation.

The key indicators are the service and usage parameters that management
want to follow in order to assure that service is acceptable and resource
usage according to plan.

As indicated in the previous section, key indicators ought to be prepared
directly from base performance control data. A good example is the VSPC
report, Figure 153 on page 250. The base data are collected using the

VSPCRESP program described earlier in the book. This program can display
hourly VSPC data (Figure 33 on page 70), collect and display page usage
(Figure 62 on page 111), and finally present key indicators for both VSPC
and real storage usage.   A similar approach is chosen by SLR, and this
chapter shows examples of key indicator reports from SLR.

The data have been selected carefully to parallel user experience of the
system.   One **discarded** key indicator was average response to a VM benchmark program.   VM is normally so fast that most benchmark programs will
show impressive response times. However, one or two hours of disastrous
response times were hidden among the success stories.

Considering the IMS curve (Figure 150 on page 249), it is notable that
total transactions have been selected rather than primary transactions
recommended earlier in the book. The selection was made to be consistent
with earlier records, and we have in chapter 4 seen that primary transactions and total transactions are roughly proportional.

IMS response times (average RESPTIME1), are monthly based. This is a
rough estimate, but small variations in monthly response time seem to
indicate large variations in user satisfaction; i.e. when average response
time is low the users are (mostly) happy. Clearly, the key indicator does
not tell the whole story. It needs to be backed up with finer analysis,
perhaps even on a hourly basis.

However, the prime purpose of a key indicator is to give an impression of
the system: is it improving/deteriorating, are we soon running out of
resources, do users behave as forecasted?

10.1.3 Configuration

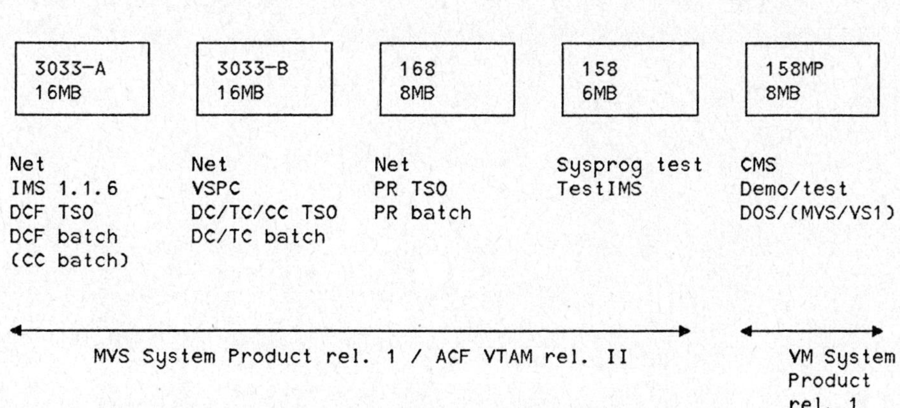

Figure 141.   CCC configuration December

The overall distribution of services in the Complex Computing Centre is as
shown on Figure 141, with system control programs as indicated.

The Data Centre(DC), TeChnical Services, PRogramming and the Computing Centre are different internal user groups.

The Data Centre provides EDP services to other firms: VSPC and batch main- ly. They can also provide systems programming assistance, for instance developing system control software for outside users. An EDP education centre is an important part of their service offerings.

The programming group develop or implement tools for administrative users, mainly in IMS.

The technical division is the major economical factor. They run a number of more or less ad hoc programs under CMS, use text and colour facilities heavily, want to utilize database extract techniques and are difficult to forecast because their development is fast, uneven and important.

3033-A is the primary residence for IMS, 3033-B for VSPC, 168 for TSO and 158MP for VM.

On the 3033-B the Education centre is an important user group, providing online facilities to industrious students.

DCF on 3033-A is a text management service to end users. Test IMS can not be run with production IMS due to dataset protection, and is difficult to fit in on the other production machines due to virtual storage require- ments. TestIMS is therefore run on a separate test machine (158), also used to develop and test new systems.

Some subsystems are run under VM to provide DOS/VS1 service to DC users. A larger VM machine is planned to accomodate more subsystems, especially MVS, and provide resources for instance to colour plots and database extracts.

10.2 REPORTS

10.2.1 Availability

The availability data are assembled by the operators and hand keyed into
GDDM. Weekly values are selected for feedback reasons; week seems to be a
natural unit for many feedback reports. The data represent 10 week moving
averages to reflect service agreement values.

Figure 147 on page 247 shows availability trends. VM availability has an
objective of 98% that has been exceeded almost the whole year.

TSO also has a 98% objective. Especially the last half year, TC TSO had
excellent availability. Programming TSO received availability under
objective 1Q81 and had even a very poor period in September.

VSPC availability objective is the same as for VM/TSO. VSPC availability
was only recorded from 3/81. 2Q81 numerous problems were encountered from
running close to resource limits, but the situation was stabilized by
several actions, for instance removing testIMS and limiting TSO.

For the IMS system, a 97% objective is in effect. This was clearly not
met during 1Q81. An availability project was established, leading to more
attention, stricter controls and even delays of possibly disturbing
installations. In addition online supervision of virtual storage was in
effect until IMS 1.1.6 was installed giving a virtual storage relief.

Several other ways of presenting availability are shown in chapter 4. One
important aspect of availability is attention; a graph like the one shown
in this chapter can draw attention to availability, and discourage people
from being the cause of one of the dips in the curve.

10.2.2 VM response times

The values on the VM service graph (Figure 149 on page 248) are obtained
from the VM Predictor. This means that more data is assembled than if for
instance VMAP is running alone, only providing systems utilizations.

The response values are taken monthly: a large amount of data is then necessary as a basis. These may be stored under APL on a daily basis and
computed per month like for instance VSPC.

This form of reporting needs more space for data storage than for instance
benchmarking as shown on Figure 44 on page 81, but contains values more
oriented towards user experiences.

From VMAP/SMART we obtain additional information. VM is utilizing a 158MP
nearly 200% for long periods during daytime. At the same time, paging is
high, often exceeding 150, and on 3340 disks that only have two thirds of
3350's transfer capacity. Still, VM delivers a reasonable service at most
times, unless when two or more subsystems (DOS, VS1 or MVS) are run, or
there is heavy, favored demo activity.

Number of users active or logged on are also fairly constant (40 active
i.e. using central resources, 100 logged on).

VS1 was removed as a subsystem between weeks 44 and 45. This influenced
response times in a positive way, see Figure 149 on page 248. The
response times are better at higher loads, apart from when VS1 is again
run.

After VS1 removal an increasing load is seen. The impression was that a
lot of work was not done earlier because resources were insufficient.
Especially this related to heavy demos(colour and database), and MVS under
VM. The planned 3033 is expected to fill up quite quickly. (See
Figure 131 on page 214).

10.2.3 MVS response times

IMS response times

Data to present for IMS service have been discussed earlier in this chapter.

Figure 150 on page 249 shows average response time (seconds) development
in 1981. Response time has decreased considerably after removing TSO service from the 3033A - after installing 3033B in October. At the same
time, M(illion) transactions per month (all transaction types) have
increased - nearly doubled when the non-typical January is discounted.

This somewhat contradicts development in the usage of problem program time
shown by Figure 148 on page 248. Perhaps resource usage per transaction
is less. More in line with observations is a suspicion that the many
breakdowns in 2H81 influenced accounting more than SLR that is the basis
for the curves on Figure 150 on page 249. SLR IMS accounting is done
based on the IMS logtape(s), and is therefore very accurate. SMF accounting is in the Complex Computing Centre done on tape, making it more
vulnerable. SMF accounting to Mass Storage is planned.

TSO response times

The 'average' TSO responses are derived from SLR. They are then averages
for weekends, all shifts and for months with different number of holidays.
Still the averages seem connected to user experience, and following TSO on
one system more closely, consistent responses over 2 seconds on a hourly
basis spelled bad user service. This means that average monthly response,
to indicate a good system, should be maximum 1.5 to 1.8 seconds.

The level of 4 seconds corresponds to the service level presented in chapter 3.

TSO response times suffered from lack of resources before 3033-B was
installed in October 1981. This is clearly seen from Figure 151 on page
249 showing very high response times in January through April.

Response time on the 168 has been poor in November. This is partly due to
many failures causing build-ups of work. Partly it is a result of unfore-
casted high TSO usage growth, especially many more simultaneously logged
on users, needing real storage even when inactive (swapped).

The number of logged on users has increased even more than problem program
time (Figure 148 on page 248). Figure 152 on page 250 shows maximum number of users on each machine. Because separate groups run on separate
machines, and because backup situations are edited out, the columns can be
added to find total number of logged on TSO users in any month. From a
level of 90, the number of users suddenly increased to 110-120 after the
B-machine (3033) was installed.

VSPC response times

VSPC values are only extracted for 1st shift and for days with valid measurements; i.e. excluding weekends, holidays and days with no measurements.
An average response of under 0.5 seconds indicates a well running system.
0.7 to 1 second and above should start an investigation, like on the curve
in August 1981.

Figure 153 on page 250 shows VSPC service development. Service problems
were encountered during the early part of the period and are shown by prolonged response times. Allocating more resources (real storage) to VSPC
gave the smooth running system indicated by the latter part of the curve.
There is a slight increase in the number of transactions run. The
increase is more pronounced on the hourly level, when transaction rates
can exceed 4 per second during peak periods.

The report includes some parts of 1982 to show the close correspondance
between the number of VSPC transactions and paging. Even if other services were run on the same machine, VSPC seems to determine the paging
rate in the shown example. In March 1982 occasional response time problems were encountered, indicating that the load ceiling were approached.

Batch service

The job elapse time is selected to represent batch responsitivity. It
only represents the time that the job executes in an initiator. However,
if we add other occurrences, we also add errors. Production jobs are normally submitted a long time before they are run and therefore will have
long input queue times. However, they are not really queuing, only waiting for other jobs to finish.

Test job output is often HELD by the originator to investigate the output
before the job is released (and only then marked ready by MVS). Finding
only one indicator of batch service is therefore quite difficult.

Figure 154 on page 251 shows development of batch service through 1981.
The number of jobs has increased. Despite an additional 3033, job elapse
times are only slightly better.   Partly this is due to a favouring of

interactive work, but also because MSS give problems that quickly add up to considerable amounts related to batch turnaround. A major service in the centre is printing. A 3800 was installed during first quarter of 1981 and has now been duplicated. The data centre that provides services to external customers, e.g. Payroll and Budgetting, accounts for a large part of the total print. The print load, with the data centre's share of the total, is shown on Figure 155 on page 251.

There are several considerations on printer data. First, not all data logically printed are physically printed. The data may be just displayed on a terminal and then deleted, or read into a dataset. External writer print data are not counted. 3800 prints pages only; it may be worth while to record print pages only. On the figure shown, million lines in reverence for tradition, and also because pre-3800 printers still exist.

10.2.4 MVS resources

Problem program time statistics

Figure 142 on page 241 and Figure 148 on page 248 show development of processor usage for some important MVS services. The unit is KWU - Kilo Work Units, an expression of problem program time used. Roughly 17 KWU fills a 158 - if it can be run 100% busy. 50-70% of the theoretical KWU level is feasible for interactive production with the jobmix considered. Installed gross KWU capacity is currently a little more than 200. This has left some, but not much, spare capacity for example to receive an expected influx of VSPC users.

Total systems usage during first shift is approximately as expected. However, Figure 148 on page 248 shows that VSPC is not growing as fast as expected, and the growth is instead on batch.

The forecasting units as received by the CCC are reflected on Figure 142 on page 241. The quality of each forecast is not good. However, November and December 1981 were not stable, and important measurement data were lost.

| 1981
1.shift | Recorded daily KWU | | | | | | | | Growth % | |
	JAN	FEB	MAR	APR	MAY	JUN		DEC	Forecast 12/81	Actual 12/81
Pr BATT	7.6	8.2	7.6	6.1	6.8	5.5		10.2	9	85
BATP	4.5	4.8	3.9	5.1	3.7	3.1		4.0	27	29
TSOT	9.5	10.3	9.4	7.7	9.4	8.9		9.7	9	9
TSOP	2.3	2.3	2.5	2.1	2.5	2.5		2.9	14	19
IMS	20.2	20.3	20.5	22.0	19.1	16.3		22.6	24	22
IMSB	.0	.0	.0	.0	5.2	4.7		2.3	24	10
IMST	.0	.0	.0	.0	.0	1.1		0.5	24	10
Net	5.7	5.2	5.5	5.8	6.1	8.0		7.6	30	20
GIS	5.1	2.8	1.7	1.4	1.6	1.7		2.8	15	65
DC BAT	3.8	3.2	3.2	3.5	3.2	3.2		4.1	84	28
TSO	1.3	1.1	1.5	1.3	2.0	1.7		2.3	0	35
VSPC	4.2	6.0	9.8	8.3	8.1	7.7		8.3	26	30
TC BAT	2.9	6.3	3.5	1.9	1.3	1.6		4.0	20	150
TSO	2.2	2.1	2.3	2.5	2.7	3.6		3.3	50	100
CC BAT	8.3	10.4	10.4	10.6	8.8	9.1		10.6	10	10
TSO	2.7	3.3	2.7	3.0	3.1	2.4		3.2	20	33
TOTAL	80.9	86.7	84.9	81.6	83.9	81.2		98.5		

The numbers express net (TCB) KWU per average working day.

TSOP: Users of programming services outside the programming group
IMSB: IMS BMPs - included as batch production till May 1981
IMST: IMS test - included as batch production till Jun 1981

Figure 142.   KWU usage MVS first shift 1981 (daily usage)

Measurement data lost due to failures cause misleading statistics. For the real storage measurements (Figure 157 on page 252), base data are 'doctored' and obvious measurement errors are ironed out.

With due precausions, the total year end status is close to forecast, with the following notes:

TSO is observed a lot above forecast during highly active weeks, giving paging problems, especially on the 168. There seems to be an interchange of work between TSO and (test) batch, and there are large fluctuations on weekly basis. Some weeks test batch is dominant for a single group, some weeks TSO is dominant. The resulting total is not far from the forecasted resource level, however.

Application test batch has been given good service to avoid resource heavy TSO commands. This is reflected in the growth for test batch, but December has been an exceptional month for test batch and for instance 28% higher than November.

VSPC is stable and below its estimate. However, there are no indications
that the long-range forecast for VSPC is not accurate, especially because
VSPC service is good.

The Usage method (reference 13) could be applied to convert the problem
program time on the figure, into total processing time, thus giving percent usage of each processor. This can be compared with the actual usage
to estimate the accuracy of the process, and also be used with capacity
planning to estimate future processor loads.

Processing power - total CPU statistics

The data presented on Figure 156 on page 252 are extracted for one hour:
1500 to 1600, expected to be the peak hour for most services.

A net 3033 was installed in October 1981 and processing power is now sufficient for most purposes in the centre. Figure 156 on page 252 shows
that the 168, used for TSO and batch is most busy; its work mix is well
suited for high processing power absorption. Currently the 168 is run
with 3340 disks for paging; with 3350 disks a higher processor utilization
would be feasible.

The 3033 A for IMS is sometimes quite CPU consuming. This is partly due
to batch running alongside IMS to absorb spare CPU power. However, IMS
itself + its share of network control, can use over 50% of the 3033 CPU
during peak hours. There is no immediate problem on the 3033 A, but when
it is used for TSO backup, IMS response suffers. Some TSO was moved to
this machine early in December, and more is requested. This must be carefully controlled.

The 3033 B is primarily used for VSPC, but also for high priority education centre work. Both have received satisfactory service on the 3033 B.
However, the number of TSO users on that machine has grown by one third
in November. Adding this to increased VSPC service can give problems early in 1982.

Real storage

Real storage is calculated from RMF data as shown in chapter 5. The real
storage thus found always (if no errors) add up to total real storage on
all machines. An allowable paging rate has been stipulated for each
machine in order to relate real storage used to forecast.

Figure 157 on page 252 shows that more real storage is used than forecasted. The YE81 column represents forecast. Some of the increase is
used for 'systems' comprising both direct MVS storage, and systems work
like 'writers' and HSM.

The systems areas have grown more than private storage. Only a proportional growth was forecasted. The total discrepancy is on the 168.

There is a distinct paging problem on the 168. Most of the TSO growth has occurred for the programming groups. This is partly because there are suddenly more users logged on. Another, very important, contribution comes from using 3340 as paging disks. These disks are slower, and thus requires more real storage for the same response time level. This also influences storage for the system areas.

MSS Performance

The most suitable performance index for MSS has been difficult to determine. Figure 80 on page 134 shows two performance indicators. Average time for a stage is directly reflected in user service, because the user - TSO or batch - is waiting for data to be staged. Average time for stage/destage has been added because many destages occur, and they affect staging time.

Figure 80 on page 134 shows the performance of the Mass Storage System (MSS). The load is measured by the total number of staged and destaged cylinders per minute, while the response time is measured in seconds per staged cylinder. The performance is measured on weekdays in the approximate period 1700 to 0100 hours, which by experience is the peak load period. The end-of-month situations at week 44 (October 26-30) and 49 (November 30 - December 4) may be noted.

Due to technical problems, only 3 out of 4 Data Recording Devices were operative up to week 45. From the beginning of week 49, staging space was increased by 50%.

10.3   CASE STUDY CONCLUSION

Some concerns of performance measurement and management in a complex environment are highlighted in this presentation. Performance data are seldom absolute and can be presented/interpreted in various ways. Distribution of workload is normally more important to performance than 'tuning' actions Accurate forecasting is difficult, but may be improved by user attention, perhaps helped by a report like this.

Centre performance parameters are expressed in a few graphs. More indicators could certainly be displayed, but it is difficult to see how radically **fewer** performance indicators could give a true picture of centre performance as defined in chapter 1.

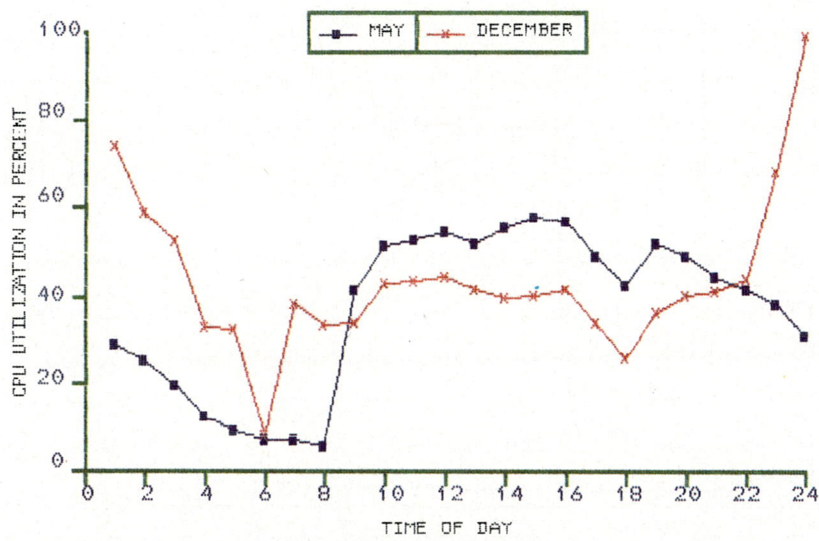

Figure 143. Percentage processor time usage by hour

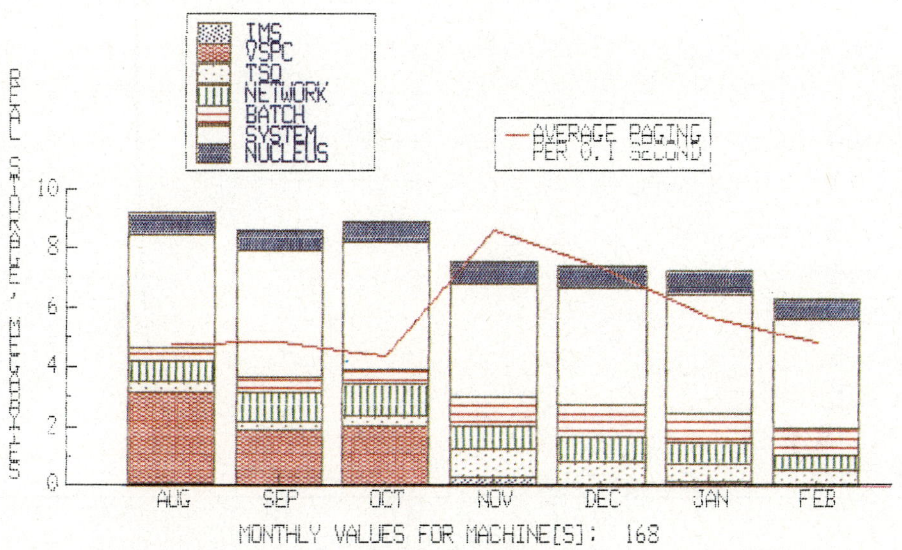

Figure 144. TRX - real storage monthly plot

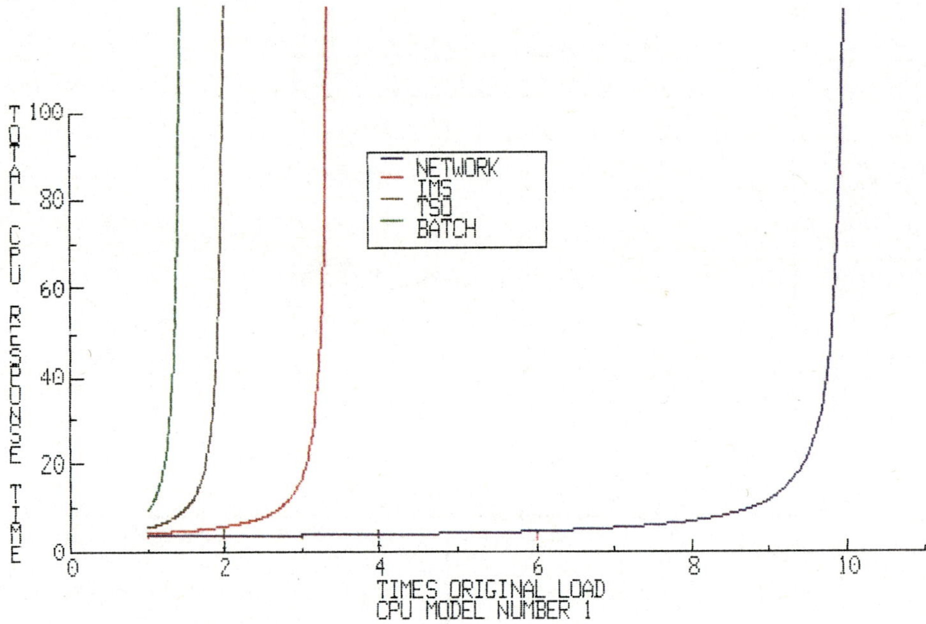

Figure 145. CPU simulation - increasing load

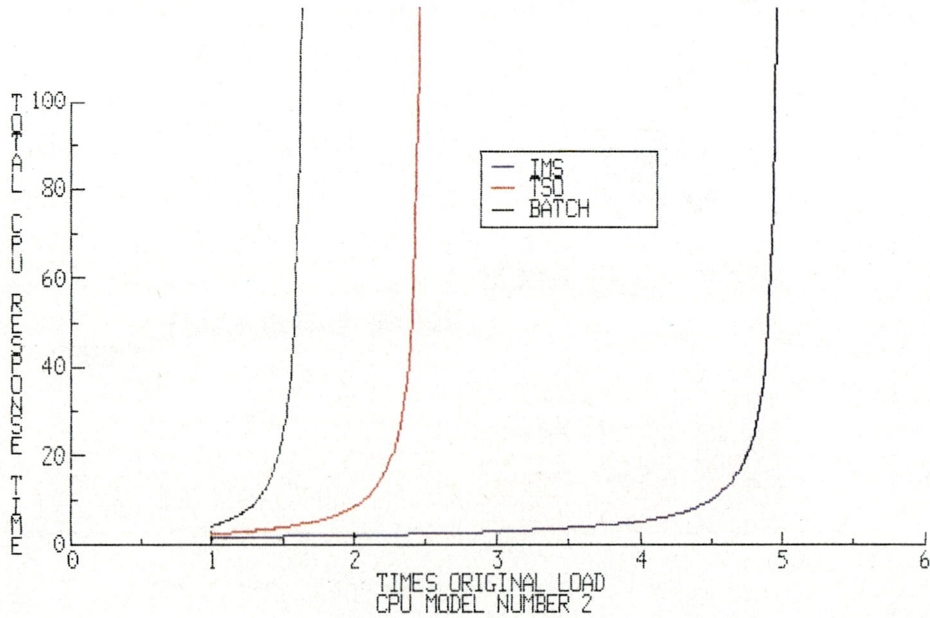

Figure 146. CPU simulation - removing one service

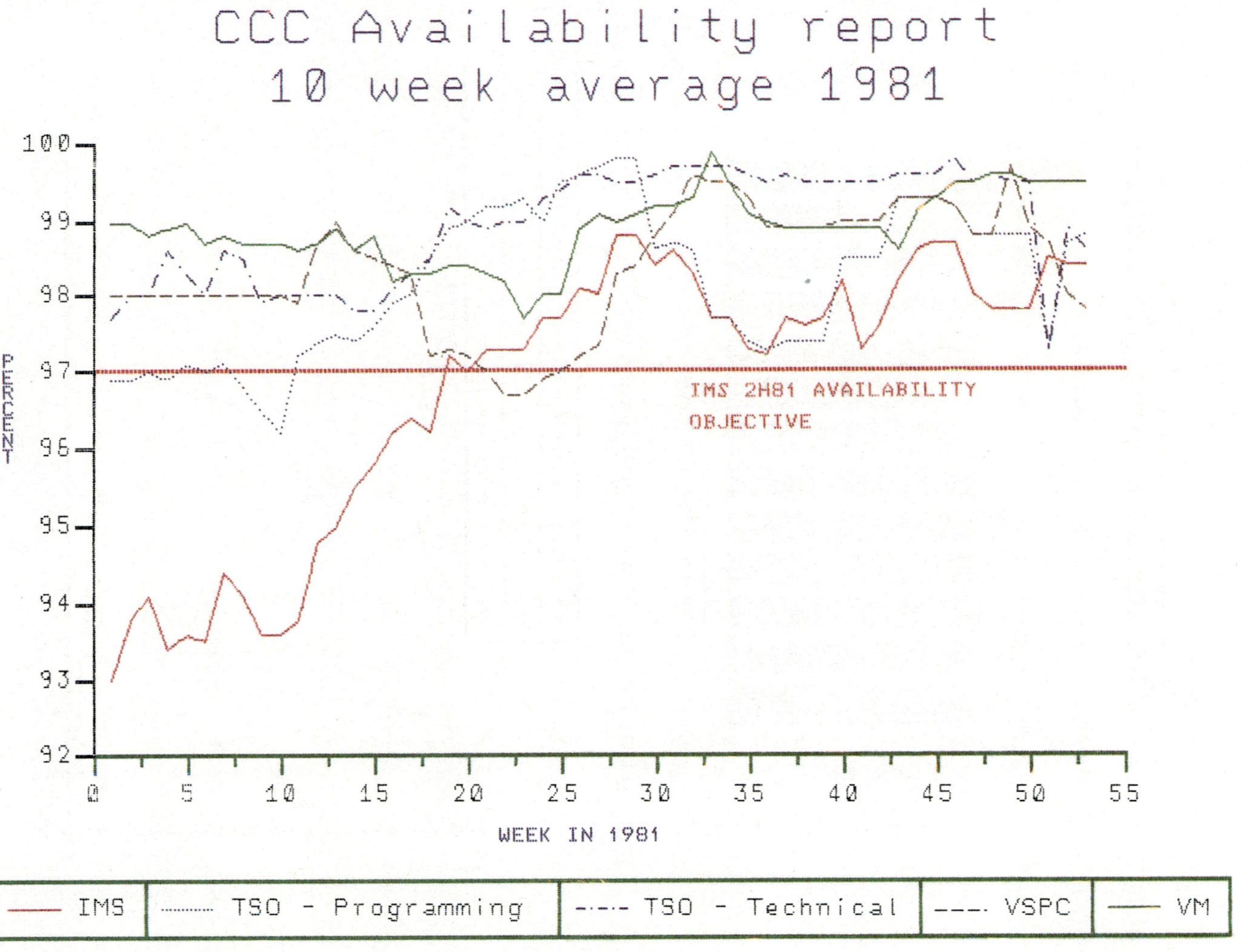

Figure 147. Availability statistics

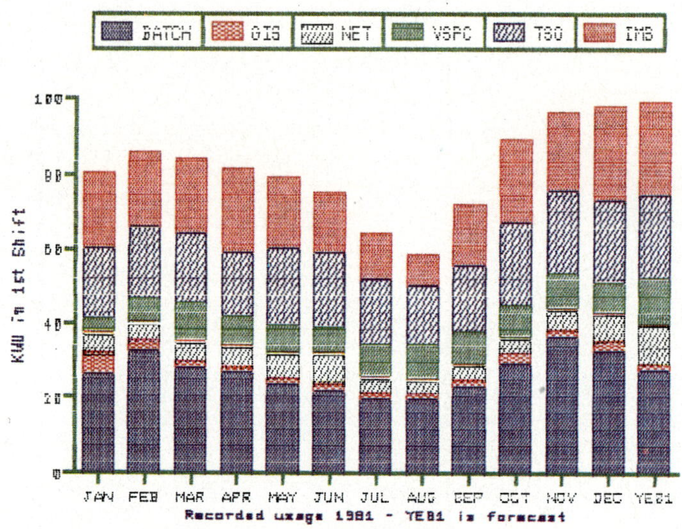

Figure 148. Key problem program usage indicators

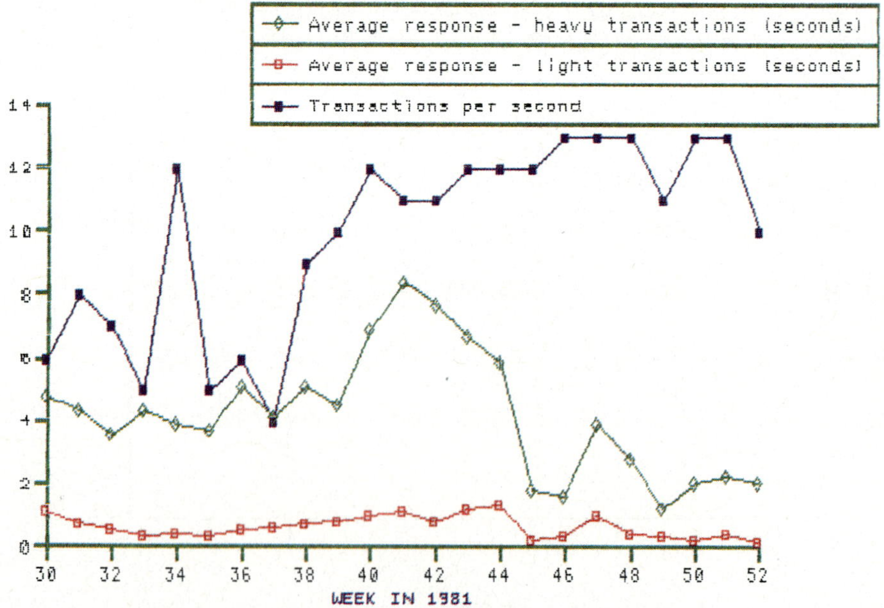

Figure 149. VM response time measurements

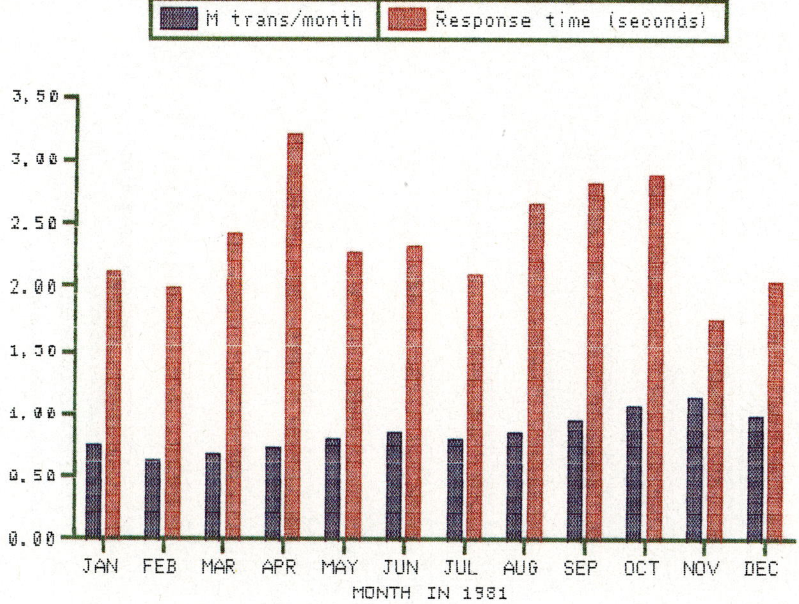

Figure 150. IMS load and response times

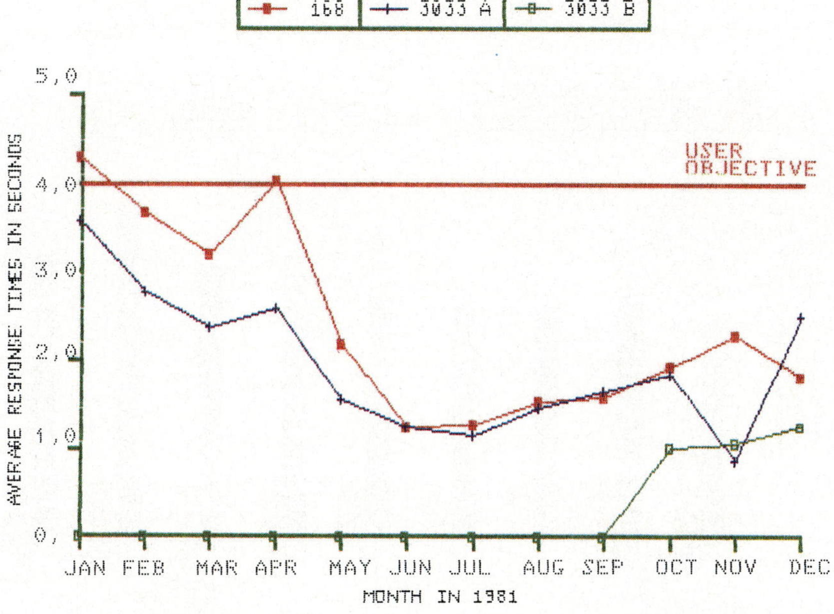

Figure 151. TSO response time development

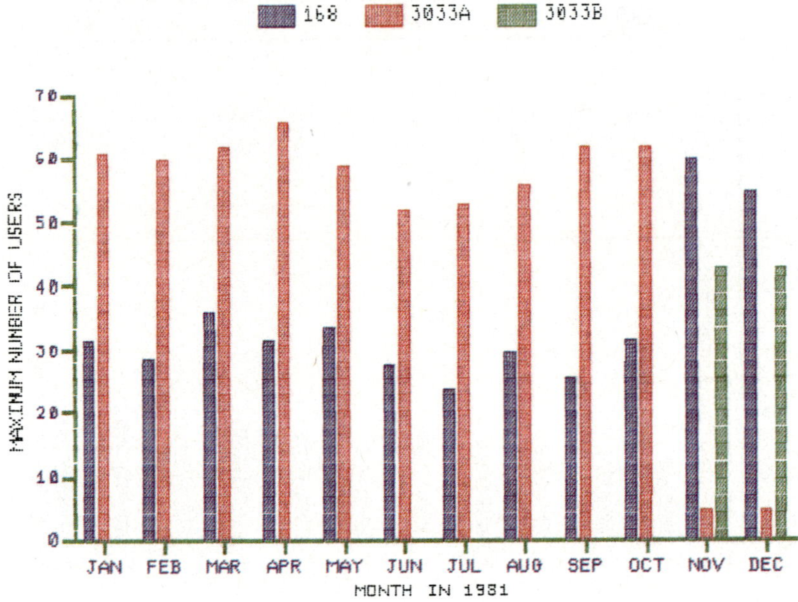

Figure 152. Maximum number of logged on TSO users

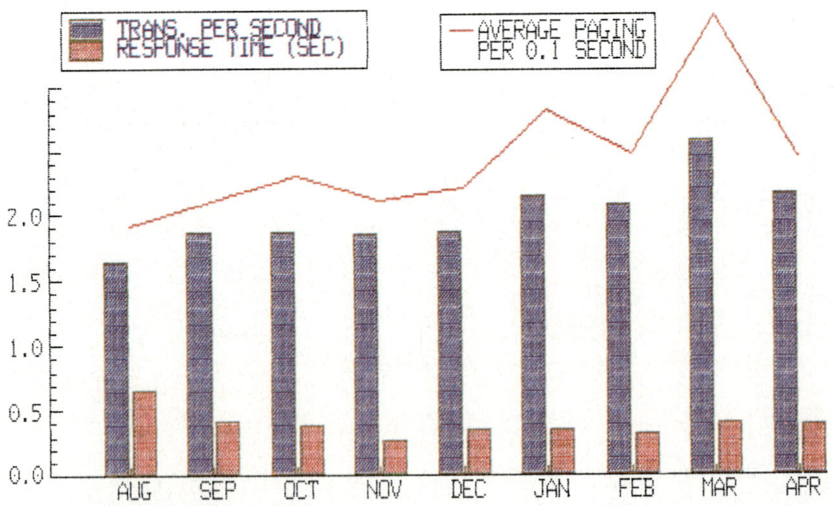

Figure 153. VSPC service

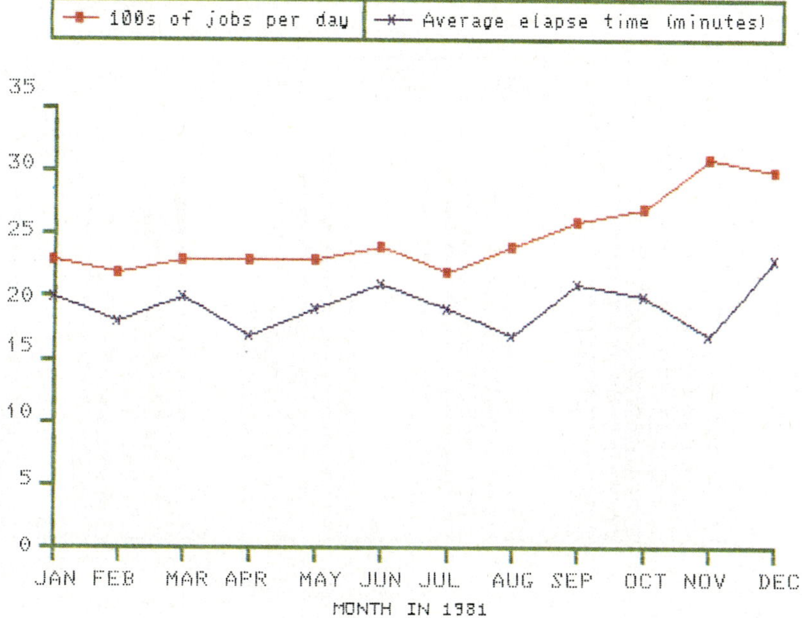

Figure 154. Batch service development

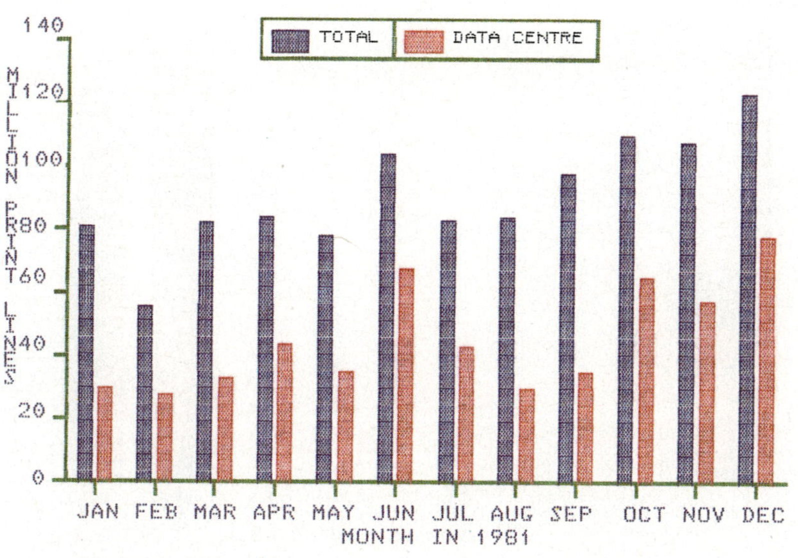

Figure 155. Print line development

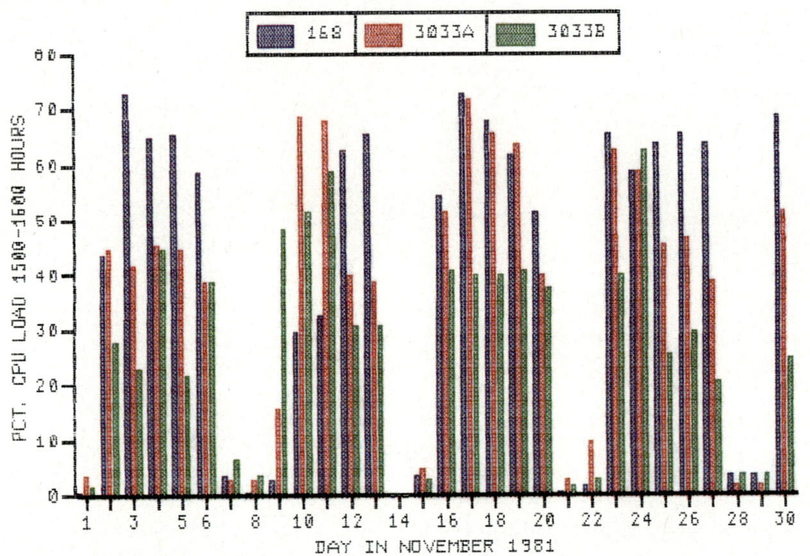

Figure 156. Peak hour total processor time usage November

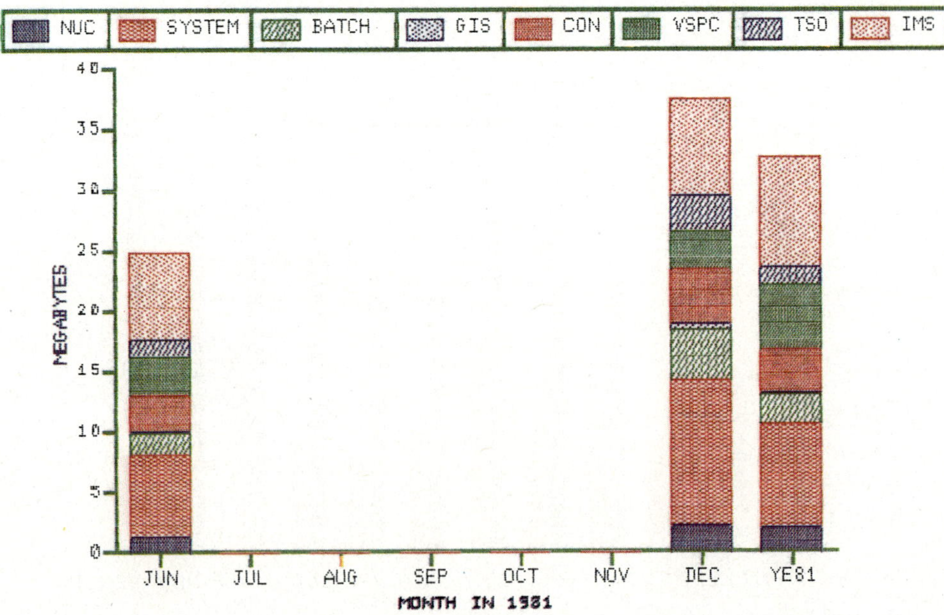

Figure 157. Real storage forecasts and measurements - first shift

Appendix I: REFERENCES

General cited and recommended references

1   Central Systems Architecture
        T. Høie
        North Holland Publishing Co, Amsterdam 1981.

2   Data Processing in 1980-85 -
        a study of potential limitations to progress
        SHARE study group
        Wiley & Sons, NY 1976

3   System Performance and User Behaviour
        W. Doherty
        SEAS Anniversary meeting 1981

4   Interactive Computing at IBM's Thomas J. Watson Research
        Centre
        W. Doherty
        GK20-1194

5   Software Psychology
        Ben Schneiderman
        Winthrop Publishers, 1980

6   Virtual Machine Facility/370
        C. Thiel (Editor)
        IBM Systems Journal, Volume 18, number 1, 1979

7   Audit and Control of Performance in Data Processing
        B.A. Stevens
        EDP Performance Review, Volume 6, number 1, 1978

8   Capacity planning: An introduction
        L. Bronner, 1977
        GG22 - 9001

9   Capacity Planning - Implementation
        L. Bronner, 1979
        GG22 - 9015

10   Computer Systems Performance Evaluation
        D. Ferrari
        Prentice-Hall, New Jersey 1978C

11   IBM Glossary
        GC20-1699

12   Psychology of Personal Computing
        G.W. Teule
        IBM European Systems Research Centre, 1974

13   USAGE: An Effective Capacity Planning Tool
        (IBM Internal)
        J.C. Cooper, C.K. Vickers, S.C. Hall
        ZZ05 - 0057

14   Introductory Guide to the Use of the Service Level Reporter
R. Vaswani
GG22-9215

15   A Guide to Communications Systems Management
(IBM Internal)
J. Boyce (Ed.), 1978
ZZ20 - 3897

16   Operations of Complex Systems
IATA Data Processing Sub-commitee
Geneva Switzerland 1979

17   Interactive user productivity
A. J. Thadani
IBM Systems Journal, volume 20 number 4, 1981

18   A capacity planning methodology
J. C. Cooper
IBM Systems Journal, volume 19 number 1, 1980

19   Overview of the capacity planning process for production
data processing
L. Bronner
IBM Systems Journal, volume 19 number 1, 1980

Description of tools and techniques

20   Service Level Reporter: General Information Manual
GH19-6169

21   Service Level Reporter: User's guide.
SH19-6149

22   Service Level Reporter: System programmer's guide
SH19-6150

23   RMF: General Information Manual
GC28-0921

24   RMF: Reference and user's guide
SC28-0922

25   Generalized Trace Facility Performance Analysis
Reporting System(GTFPARS).
SB21-2143

26   MSS trace/SMF correlation aid
Program description and operation manual
SH20-2045

27   IMS Primer
SH20-9145

28   IBM System/370. Tracking and Resolving
Problems and Coordinating Changes
IBM DP System Centre
GC22 - 9006

45   MVS Initialization and Tuning Guide
            GC28-0681

46   MVS Performance Notebook
            GC28-4755

47   Advanced Communications Function for VTAM (ACF/VTAM)
            Installation
            SC27-0468

48   Advanced Communications Function for VTAM (ACF/VTAM)
            Operation
            SC27-0466

49   SMF Job Data Compression Aid
            Program Description/operation Manual
            SH20-1882

50   The VM/370 Resource Limiter - Operations Manual (draft)
            D.M. Chess
            IBM, Yorktown Heights 1982

51   The VM/370 Resource Limiter
            D.M. Chess and G. Waldbaum
            IBM Systems Journal, volume 20 number 4, 1981

            Miscellaneous references

Processors

            A Guide to the IBM 3033 Processor Complex, Attached
            Processor Complex and Multiplexor Complex of System/370
            GC20-1859

            A Guide to the IBM System/370 Model 168
            GC20-1754

            IBM System/370 Model 168 Functional Characteristics
            GA22-7010

            A Guide to the IBM System/370 Model 158
            GC20-1754

Disks

            Introduction to 3350 Direct Access Storage
            GA26 - 1638

            Measurement, Modeling and Capacity Planning:
            The Secondary Storage Occupancy Issue
            H. Pat Artis
            ECOMA newsletter volume VI, March 1982

            Shared DASD design
            - A shared DASD Reconfiguration Story
            Paul Høltzl
            ECOMA newsletter volume VI, March 1982

What are the disks doing?
Ronald Paans
ECOMA newsletter volume VI, March 1982

Effective Use of DASD
B. Maxwell
IBM San Jose, California
SHARE XLVI, 1976

Operator's Guide for the Shared DASD
Data Set Integrity Feature
John D. Watson, 1979
SAS Internal Document

Mass Storage Subsystem

Introduction to the IBM 3850 Mass Storage System
GA32 - 0028

IBM 3850 Mass Storage System Principles of Operation
GA32 - 0020

Mass storage system activity and availability at
 Mountain Bell: A case study.
Carl Steidtmann
ECOMA newletter volume IV, March 1982

Installation Planning for MSS
William A. Hawkins, IBM
Presentation SHARE XLVI, 1976

OS/VS Mass Storage System Planning Guide
GC35 - 0011

Hierarchial Storage Manager (HSM)

OS/VS2 MVS Hierarchial Storage Manager
General Information
GH35 - 0007

OS/VS2 MVS Hierarchial Storage Manager Users Guide
SH35 - 0024

Printer (3800)

Printing Subsystem Characteristics
Al Sutra, IBM
Presentation SHARE XLVI, 1976

3800 performance - or pages per minute
A. Mitchell
ECOMA newsletter volume VI, March 1982

Computer Centre Management

Component Failure Impact Analysis
GC20 - 1865

Installation Management
B. Rockstroh
IBM Nachrichten, Heft 241, 1978

Change Management Tracking etc.
GH19 - 6028

The Network Control Centre
G226-3551

System Control Program

An Analysis of Time Shared Computing Systems
A.L. Sherr
MIT Press, Cambridge, 1967

IBM Virtual Machine Facility/370, Introduction
GC20 - 1800

VM/370 Features Supplement
GC20 - 1757

VTAM Concepts and Planning
GC27 - 6998

Introduction to Advanced Communications Function
GC20 - 3033

Performance

Performance Analysis of Virtual Memory
Time-sharing Systems
Yonathan Bard
IBM Systems Journal - G321 - 5022, 1975

Performance Criteria and Measurements
for a Timesharing System
Yonathan Bard
IBM Systems Journal 10 No. 3, 1977

Managing Performance in the Real World
L. Perkins
ECOMA 5 Conference Proceedings, 1978

Computer Performance Measurement and
Evaluation Methods: Analysis and Applications
L. Svobodova
Elsevier, NY, 1976

Complex Workload Performance Analysis - A Case Study
(IBM Internal)
D.C. Schiller
ZZ05 - 0034

Guidelines for the Measurement of Interactive
Computer Service Response Time and Turnaround
Time US Federal Information Processing Standard
Computer Communication Review, January 1979.

Performance Measurement Tools for VM/370
P.H. Callaway
IBM Systems Journal Vol. 14 No. 2
G321 - 5008

An Experimental Approach to System Tuning
Yonathan Bard
IBM Cambridge Scientific Centre Technical Report
GS20 - 2108, 1975

Experimental Evaluation of System Performance
Yonathan Bard
IBM Systems Journal 12, No. 3, 1973

Workload Management
R.F. Dunlavey
EDP Performance Review, May 1978

The Capacity of Computer Systems (Danish)
P.E. Husted
MS Thesis, The technical university of Denmark
1978

A Queuing Network of MVS
J.P. Buzen
ACM Computing Surveys, Volume 10, Number 3, 1978

SNAPSHOT version 7.1 User's Guide
IBM internal use
Raleigh Communication System Analysis Ctr.

Virtual Storage System Simulator
S. Rolich and J.N. Wheeler
Performance Practitioners' workshop
handout 16.11.77

Performance Model of MVS
W.W. Chiu and W.M. Chow
IBM Systems Journal, volume 17, no. 4, 1978

Memory can increase your capacity
C.C. Burns
GG22-9053 (July 1978)

Capacity analysis of the Mass Storage System
P. N. Misra
IBM Systems Journal, volume 20, no. 3, 1981

Central Systems Architecture
Tore Høie
ECOMA-8 Proceedings 1980

A control system
Tore Høie
ECOMA-9 Proceedings 1981

Appendix II: INDEX

A

B

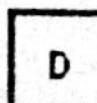

D

F

G

H

I

N

O

S

X

Y

3

Appendix III: LIST OF ILLUSTRATIONS

Box XII+1f

40 + 53 = 93

k - 28